ALSO BY RICHARD LINGEMAN

Sinclair Lewis: Rebel from Main Street
Theodore Dreiser: An American Journey, 1908–1945 (Vol. 2)
Theodore Dreiser: At the Gates of the City, 1871–1907 (Vol. 1)
Small Town America: A Narrative History, 1620–the Present
Don't You Know There's a War On? The American Home Front, 1941–1945
Drugs from A to Z: A Dictionary

DOUBLE LIVES

DOUBLE LIVES

American Writers' Friendships

RICHARD LINGEMAN

RANDOM HOUSE · NEW YORK

Published in the United States by Random House, an imprint of
The Random House Publishing Group, a division of
Random House, Inc., New York.

RANDOM HOUSE and colophon are
registered trademarks of Random House, Inc.

Library of Congress Cataloging-in-Publication Data

Lingeman, Richard R.
Double lives: American writers' friendships / Richard Lingeman—1st ed.
p.   cm.
Includes bibliographical references and index.
ISBN 1-4000-6045-1 (alk. paper)
1. Authors, American—Friends and associates. 2 Authors, American—Biography
3. Friendship—United States. I. Title.
PS129.L56 2006
810.9—dc22   [B]   2005046570

Printed in the United States of America on acid-free paper

www.atrandom.com

246897531

FIRST EDITION

Book design by Carole Lowenstein

CONTENTS

CHAPTER I

TWO SOLITUDES

3

CHAPTER 2

THE PURITAN AND THE PAGAN

Nathaniel Hawthorne and Herman Melville

20

CHAPTER 3

THE WESTERNERS

Mark Twain and William Dean Howells

52

CHAPTER 4

THE MASTER AND THE MILLIONAIRESS

Henry James and Edith Wharton

80

CHAPTER 5

FROM HEART TO HEART

Willa Cather and Sarah Orne Jewett

112

CHAPTER 6

THE BELIEVER AND THE SKEPTIC

Theodore Dreiser and H. L. Mencken

134

CHAPTER 7

POOR SCOTT, POOR ERNEST

F. Scott Fitzgerald and Ernest Hemingway

160

CHAPTER 8

THREE FOR THE ROAD

Jack Kerouac, Allen Ginsberg, and Neal Cassady

190

Notes

225

Index

243

DOUBLE LIVES

CHAPTER I

TWO SOLITUDES

Love consists in this: that two solitudes protect
and touch and greet each other.
—RILKE

CICERO in his classic essay on friendship paraphrases his friend*
Scipio to the effect that the most difficult thing in the world is
for a friendship to remain unimpaired to the end of life: "So many
things might intervene: conflicting interests; differences of opinion in
politics; frequent changes in character, owing sometimes to misfortunes, sometimes to advancing years."

Now jump across the centuries to our own time. In a broadcast on
National Public Radio in 2004, the noir-soul novelist Walter Mosley
ruminated about his many lost friendships. He remembered scoffing
when his father told him years before that he would be lucky if when he
was an old man he could count his friends on one hand. Now he realized how right his father was:

Amicus in Latin, derived from *amo*, to love.

I have lost almost every friend I've ever had. We argued, grew apart, moved away, changed psychologically, suddenly realized that we were using each other and not really concerned about the person on the other side of the relationship. Some of my friends found religion or a spouse that didn't like me. One of the fastest ways to lose friends is to become lovers with them. Love is deeper than friendship and far more fleeting. But as hard as love is on friendship, truth is the greatest test. Just tell someone what you really think, how you really feel. That will end almost any relationship within moments, even if you've been comrades for over 50 years.[1]

In Mosley's list of reasons why his friendships went sour, he touches on universal considerations affecting all friendships, not only writers'. But he speaks as a writer of superb gifts, and insofar as he is describing broken friendships with fellow writers, his testimony supports the popular belief that artists' friendships are more fragile than those of people in other callings. As the biographer and scholar Matthew J. Bruccoli writes in his book *Fitzgerald and Hemingway: A Dangerous Friendship,*

> The mortality rate of literary friendships is high. Writers tend to be bad risks as friends—probably for much the same reasons that they are bad matrimonial risks. They expend the best parts of themselves in their work. Moreover, literary ambition has a way of turning into literary competition; if fame is the spur, envy may be a concomitant.[2]

Not surprisingly, Professor Bruccoli's description fits the Fitzgerald-Hemingway model. Yet I see that case slightly differently; I see the glass fuller. At the minimum, even the up-and-down Hemingway-Fitzgerald friendship contributed something of lasting value to their lives and careers. It was a fragile tie indeed, torn by contradictory emotions—admiration, rivalry, envy, respect, vanity—yet the two men remained friends to the end. That is, there was never a final, complete break. Holding them were slender filaments of nostalgia trailing back to the good times in Paris when they were young and idealistic. Those memories had faded in the 1930s, yet Fitzgerald grimly hung on, while Hemingway modulated his public sniping at "Poor Scott" with occasional lapses into decency, even praising Fitzgerald's writing, though not when Scott most needed it. They caroused again a few times. After Scott died, though, Ernest launched a scorched-earth campaign against his reputation, denying the hand Fitzgerald had extended to him when he was an unknown young writer in Paris in 1927.

The Fitzgerald-Hemingway relationship is a case study in how rivalry can poison a friendship. In this instance Hemingway was the chief culprit. As he himself said to Fitzgerald in a rare reflective moment: "So why make comparisons and talk about superiority. . . . There can be no such thing between serious writers. They are all in the same boat."[3] Or, as one of his several cast-aside mentors, Sherwood Anderson, told him, "I thought it foolish that, while there was so much to be done in writing, we writers should devote our time to the attempt to kill each other off."[4] Hemingway was a serial killer of father figures.

One sees rivalry's destructive force in the friendship between two African American writers, Zora Neale Hurston and Langston Hughes. It started in the mid-1920s and might be considered a by-product of the Harlem Renaissance, in which both were leading figures. In her *Zora Neale Hurston: A Life in Letters,* Carla Kaplan writes that Hughes was Hurston's "closest friend in the twenties."[5] Almost his first reference to her in his letters to his friend Carl Van Vechten is: "Zora Neale Hurston is a clever girl, isn't she? I would like to know her. Is she still in New York?"[6] Their relationship, by all accounts, never bloomed into a love affair, usually a plus for friendship, as Mosley says. Hughes was homosexual or celibate, Hurston lustily heterosexual. In a busy life scarred by hardship, she had time for numerous love affairs and three short-lived marriages.

The bond between them was, rather, intellectual and artistic. They were fellow word-warriors with an interest in promoting African American culture in their writings. Hurston was an academically trained collector of Negro folklore, and Hughes a passionate amateur. In her letters Hurston frequently thanks him for his advice; she sends him material that suggested ideas for plays, novels, and poems. Both despised the minstrel-show negritude on display on Broadway stages and Harlem nightclubs (off limits to black persons except the hired help) in the twenties, as well as the many white ripoffs of black culture. "It makes me sick to see how these cheap white folks are grabbing our stuff and ruining it," Hurston typically complains to Hughes.[7] They devoted themselves to presenting authentic black culture in their writings. They dreamed of working together on a true Negro folk opera that would be an antidote to Broadway phoniness, but couldn't find the time.

In 1930, they collaborated on a play, *Mule Bone,* set in a rural all-black community, but later quarrelled over credit. Hughes was shocked to learn that Hurston had copyrighted the play under her own name. The upshot was that the play was never presented in their lifetimes (the first Broadway production was staged in the 1990s). Hurston came to regret her perverse behavior, which cooled the friendship. She called the quarrel "the cross of my life."[8] Rivalry over credit and money was the villain in this aborted friendship.

And yet, though they were never again as close as they had been in the twenties, Hughes later amicably turned over his rights in the dormant play to Hurston. The two continued to correspond sporadically and civilly. In 1948 Hurston asked Hughes to be a character witness in a legal matter—hardly a request to make of an enemy. Their earlier ethnic and cultural bonds still held.

In an analogous way, the friendship between Theodore Dreiser and H. L. Mencken was cemented in a fight against a common enemy—an Anglophile, puritanical literary culture that considered Dreiser's novels immoral. Theirs was an ideal collaboration between author and critic—Dreiser writing the novels that challenged the Old Order, Mencken trumpeting them critically. And even after cracks opened up between them in the 1910s and 1920s, shared memories of old wars remained strong enough to bring them back together. In the 1930s, they reminisced like old soldiers about bygone literary battles. "He was my captain in a war that will never end" was Mencken's final tribute to Dreiser after he died.

In contrast, the friendship of Mark Twain and William Dean Howells, joined when they were outsiders seeking acceptance from the Boston establishment, jogged across the years like Dobbin with rarely a serious quarrel over morals, politics, or personal differences. The ties between Willa Cather and Sarah Orne Jewett deepened in the short time that Miss Jewett had left, while the love between the apolitical Henry James and Edith Wharton strengthened during the older James's last years, when they pulled each other through grief and illness.

Nowadays, book review editors grill would-be reviewers on whether they are friends of the author. But why should the testimony of a friend automatically be ruled out as tainted? Friends see the best in us, while strangers may miss those qualities. Howells was Mark Twain's most perceptive contemporary critic. Conversely, a writer who would negatively review a friend's book is probably no friend of his; if he were, he would give his friend the gift of silence. (There are some authors who won't review contemporaries in order to avoid making an unnecessary enemy!) And then there is Norman Mailer, who in an *Esquire* article sparred with his contemporaries, scoring the "bouts" himself.

Negative criticism is a reef on which many a friendship has gone aground. Yet honest private opinion on a work in progress can be a lifeline to a floundering author, and there can be no helpful criticism that pulls its punches.

Mosley says that truth is the greatest test of friendship. How much honesty can a friendship stand? And if it can't stand very much, is it really a friendship? On the other hand, how much *flattery*—i.e., dishonesty—can a friendship take? Cicero grasps both horns of this dilemma:

> Compliance gets us friends, plain speaking hate. Plain speaking is a cause of trouble, if the result of it is resentment, which is poison of friendship; but compliance is really the cause of much more trouble, because by indulging his faults it lets a friend plunge into headlong ruin. But the man who is most to blame is he who resents plain speaking and allows flattery to egg him on to his ruin. On this point, then, from first to last there is need of deliberation and care. If we remonstrate, it should be without bitterness; if we reprove, there should be no word of insult.

When the truth is expressed in tactless or superior language, your friend will find the message difficult to accept. So literary friendships walk on eggshells. A friend writes a negative review at the friendship's peril. Dreiser took Mencken's critical blasts at his 1915 novel The *"Genius"* as personal insults, even though his friend's harsh words were honestly intended to save him from "headlong ruin" or the censor. Mencken always said what he meant in his reviews; the trouble was that he also said some things for effect. He believed that the first job of a reviewer is to entertain the reader. Satire and witty invective were two of his methods. Dreiser was a great admirer of Mencken's style—except when he was on the business end of it. How would *you* like being called an "Indiana peasant" in public? (Or does my being from Indiana make me extra sensitive to such a label?)

William Dean Howells, who was Mark Twain's most influential

critical booster, made it a rule never to review a Mark Twain book that he didn't like (he did not write about *Huckleberry Finn,* which he had edited and did very much like, only because he had no review outlet at the time). When asked, he gave a truthful opinion in private. And when he was editor of the *Atlantic Monthly,* he sometimes turned down a Mark Twain story, giving his honest reasons—usually that the piece wasn't worthy of its illustrious byline.

Literary friendships surely should avoid public scolding, but does that mean they include the duty of public praise? Generally, comity prescribes that one testify publicly for a friend—a blurb, a letter recommending a grant, a defense when the friend is attacked, even a review if you can sneak one past the guardians at the gates. Yet no true friend should expect a friend to lie for him on the record (expecting him to be kind is another matter). Cicero is on point here: The "first law of friendship," he says, is that "we should ask from friends, and do for friends, only what is good."

Edith Wharton extravagantly admired Henry James's earlier novels such as *The Portrait of a Lady,* but hated the labyrinthine psychologizing of his "Major Phase." But Wharton did not let her lack of admiration stand in the way of friendship; she worshipped the man more than his novels. Yet, out of affection, she arranged for the publication of a sympathetic critical appraisal of James's late novels by a mutual friend.

Early in her career, Wharton was often called a disciple of James's, and she resented it. Many writers of the first rank are touchy about ascriptions of "influences." Yet most at some point study an admired colleague as a model or even a mentor; this is part of one's apprenticeship, the process of finding one's own voice.

Sarah Orne Jewett's letters to Willa Cather contain some of the most eloquent advice ever bestowed by an older writer on a younger one. Cather, struggling to find her sexual and artistic identity, needed a woman mentor and role model, and in Jewett she found both. Their relationship showed signs of evolving into a friendship of equals, much as students become coevals of a beloved teacher in later life, but death cut it short.

William Dean Howells was a generous patron to many young writers, starting with his friend Henry James, spotting them in early career while editor of the *Atlantic Monthly*. When he was America's best-known literary critic in his *Harper's Monthly* column during the 1890s, his reviews could push an unknown into the limelight. He most encouraged younger writers who were practicing the kind of realism he advocated for American literature, such as Stephen Crane and Frank Norris. His essays on realism influenced writers like Sinclair Lewis and Theodore Dreiser when they were starting out.

Yet Howells did not admit Dreiser, who would become the greatest of his generation of writers, into his select band of protégés. Before Dreiser published his first novel, *Sister Carrie,* in 1900, he was keenly aware of Howells's power to launch a career and courted his pontifical blessing. He interviewed Howells, wrote a flattering article about him, and sent him letters detailing his esteem for him. In the end, though, Howells did nothing for *Sister Carrie.* "I did not like her," he blurted to Dreiser at a chance meeting. Always squeamish about sex, he was offended by Carrie's "immoral" career as a kept woman. Dreiser had taken realism farther than the Dean of American Letters deemed it should go. Realism was not a license to print filth.

Illustrative of the way a mentor can inspire a younger disciple is the relationship between Ralph Waldo Emerson and Walt Whitman. When Whitman first read Emerson's essays, he was an obscure Brooklyn carpenter and hack journalist. "Emerson," he said, "brought me to a boil." Mark Edmundson, a professor of English, writes, "Whitman had been reared to be modest and self-effacing. But Emerson offered him a new image of authority. He was, for a while, Whitman's second father."[9]

But in these quasi-parental relationships, the talented protégé regularly outgrows his parent. Whitman was a more barbaric bard than Emerson had bargained for when he so enthusiastically extolled the first edition of *Leaves of Grass* in a letter to the author. After the incorrigibly self-promoting Walt released this private missive to the press without the sender's permission, and before they had even met, Emerson's reservations about Whitman's poetry, especially its crude or indecent language, began to grow. And Whitman, for his part, decided Emerson was not the "Master" he had originally apostrophized; he cast him aside as a genteel philosopher who evaded life's meaner streets.

Nor do some mentor-protégé relationships survive the wear and tear of time. As we grow older we become more parsimonious in our affections. Youth is a spendthrift of love; in maturity we repent our promiscuity. People change, outgrow one another, shrink, regress, sail into different social spheres or away altogether. Recall Scipio's observation about the things that over time threaten a friendship, one of them being "frequent changes in character, owing sometimes to misfortunes, sometimes to advancing years."

Literary friendships are particularly vulnerable to altered states. Walter Mosley, in the radio essay quoted above, observes: "The best way to keep a friend is to stay the same because even if they change, your friends will look to you to be a familiar port in their storm of transformations. Keep the same job, the same spouse, the same address, the same tastes and appetites and sexual orientation."[10]

Inevitably there are fluctuations in fortune. A recurring pattern in literary friendships is one being up, the other down, and then the roles reversing. Envy tempts the loser, pride and ego the winner. Cicero claims that friendships are particularly difficult among politicians; his words could apply to authors as well: "Where can you find the man to prefer his friend's advancement to his own?" He warns against those who "betray their untrustworthiness and inconstancy, by looking down on friends when they are themselves prosperous, or deserting them in their distress." He proposes some remedies: "If any one of us have any advantage in personal character, intellect, or fortune, we should be ready to make our friends sharers and partners in it with ourselves. . . . Just as those who possess any superiority must put themselves on an equal footing with those who are less fortunate, so these latter must not be annoyed at being surpassed in genius, fortune, or rank." Sinclair Lewis, who had difficulty keeping friends after he became famous, was nevertheless generous in his public praise of his lesser-known contemporaries.

Hemingway and Fitzgerald rode the carousel of fortune. When they were young in Paris in the twenties and Fitzgerald better-known and a commercial success, they were linked by an idealistic commitment to art. "Ernest . . . was an equal and my kind of idealist," Scott said of his attraction to Hemingway, who in his writing for art's sake represented the integrity Scott envied. Each resolved to be the greatest writer of their time, but once Hemingway had reversed roles and become more successful and famous in the thirties, he acted self-important and superior, withholding a lifeline as Scott struggled against the riptides of fortune.

An entirely different reaction to success was that of Jack Kerouac, who was affected by the communal ethic characteristic of the Beat writers. The novelist Joyce Johnson, Kerouac's girlfriend at the time *On the Road* was published, notes, "Artists are nourished by each other more than by fame or by the public. To give one's words to the world is an experience of peculiar emptiness."[11] The Beats, whom she surely had in mind, were a collective generation, promoting one another, clearing the way for their new vision by helping one another. Then the Great American Publicity Machine ate them up and spat them out.

This happened to Kerouac. In the flush of early success he helped friends like Allen Ginsberg, but he himself wasn't genetically designed for fame. Sensitivity, easy hurt, and disillusionment doomed him; alcoholism drove him inward and in the 1960s made him lash out at the now more famous Ginsberg, who persisted in a near-saintly devotion to his old friend.

The broken friendship between the American critic Edmund Wilson and the Russian-born novelist Vladimir Nabokov seems to have been the result of changes in status over time, though other strains were at work. Wilson befriended the émigré genius not long after he arrived in this country in 1940 from Paris, where his family had fled the Bolshevik revolution. Nabokov's novels were well regarded in European intellectual circles, but in the United States he was an unknown just off the boat. Wilson helped him attain a foothold in myriad ways, correcting awkward idioms as he began writing in English, overcoming the prejudice of American editors against foreigners, finding him publishers and academic posts, opening doors for him at *The New Yorker,* where Wilson was resident book critic. Tensions between the two had their roots in clashing views of the Bolshevik revolution and in Wilson's tepid appreciation of Nabokov's novels. The breaking point came in 1965 when Wilson made a harsh attack on Nabokov's translation of *Eugene Onegin* in *The New York Review of Books.* This triggered a long, bitter exchange between author and reviewer, with other scholars taking sides. Wilson, in Nabokov's eyes, was continuing to treat him as an inferior, overlooking the international acclaim for his novel *Lolita* (which Wilson had told him he liked less than anything else he had written) and his new identity as a writer of brilliant English prose.

Another strain in the Wilson-Nabokov friendship was cultural. No matter how cosmopolitan both men were, their disparate backgrounds pulled them apart. Wilson came from old American stock but was a modern Marxist, while Nabokov was European in sensibility and fiercely anticommunist. Wilson loved Russian literature, but he was ignorant of the twentieth-century authors that had most influenced Nabokov. Nabokov venerated very few authors; Wilson was catholic in his appreciations. Nabokov loved America even as he satirized it with the émigré's cool detachment, but in Wilson's view he never really understood it, never overcame his alien strangeness. In the end, as Simon Karlinsky writes, Wilson the great critic never wrote a review in praise of Nabokov the great novelist. Instead, he "discovered, encouraged and shared with others the unique originality of Nabokov the man, thus enabling him to pursue and develop his second literary career, as an American writer."[12]

In contrast, the Euro-American mix was an attraction in the long friendship between the novelist Mary McCarthy and the philosopher Hannah Arendt. McCarthy had the reverence for contemporary European intellectuals common to her literary generation. According to biographer Carol Brightman, she found Arendt and another European friend a refreshing change from her New York circle of male political-radical intellectuals, who were single-mindedly ideological. Arendt relished the American woman's freedom and openness to experience. As Elizabeth Hardwick suggests, Arendt "saw Mary as a golden American friend, perhaps the best the country could produce, with a bit of our western states in her, a bit of the Roman Catholic, a Latin student, and a sort of New World, blue-stocking *salonnière*. . . ."[13] Their respective trades of novelist and philosopher were complementary: McCarthy sought Arendt's advice on her characters' moral dilemmas; Arendt relished McCarthy's acerbic wit and defended her against the "envy" of her male critics. They carried on a long correspondence in which they discussed great ideas and gossiped like sorority sisters. They had an almost physical yearning for each other when they were apart, like lovers (which they were not).

Another pitfall in literary friendships is faulty communication, which seems an odd impediment for masters of the Word. Yet Karlinsky says that Wilson and Nabokov's running quarrel about Russian poetry was "an instance of an argument in which the participants either talk past one another or talk about two different things."[14] Wilson thought Nabokov a fin de siècle aesthete who believed in art for art's sake, when actually Nabokov's early life had ingrained in him a revulsion at political extremism; his father was a classic liberal driven from his homeland by Bolshevik fanatics, then murdered in Berlin by right-wing assassins. Nabokov had even written a political fable, *Bend Sinister,* set in a totalitarian state. Wilson, who believed literature should carry a social message, also had fixed ideas about Russian verse that he refused to modify even in the face of Nabokov's greater knowledge and facility with the language.

The quarrels between Dreiser and Mencken were intensified by the wrongheaded ideas they formed about each other and clung to out of stubbornness. Mencken would never, for example, abandon his fixed idea that Dreiser was an impractical bohemian unfit for literary politics. And Dreiser would not give up his notion that Mencken disapproved of his flouting of the bourgeois proprieties. He traced Mencken's narrow-minded ideas of what was proper subject matter for a novel or play to the same source. Dreiser insisted on the right to follow his muse and libido wherever they took him. Mencken resented Dreiser's treatment of his mistress's sister; Dreiser resented Mencken's lectures. And so on.

Mencken had very exacting standards of friendship. The biographer Fred Hobson writes that Mencken "valued friendship even more highly than most people do, in part because he gave to friends the time and loyalty another man might have given to wife and children—and, even more, because he prized a camaraderie grounded in shared beliefs and prejudices, in an active interplay of ideas and, most of all, in good judgment."[15] Accordingly, if someone fell short in any of these areas, he would excommunicate them. "[When friends] begin to bore me," he wrote, "I get rid of them. . . . It is foolish to go with people who have ceased to be interesting, and become nuisances."[16] Ever the demanding critic—even in his personal life.

Literary friendships make literary history. Dreiser and Mencken were initially drawn together by a common cause, artistic freedom, and during World War I, by pro-German sympathies. A sense of fighting for literary freedom against the religious moralists also drew Herman Melville to Nathaniel Hawthorne, an older writer he admired. For the sixteen months they lived as neighbors in the Berkshires, Melville regarded them as a Conspiracy of Two against the contemporary breed of Puritans, the preachers and churchgoers of Massachusetts and New York, who were forces of respectability and conformity. Then Hawthorne gradually abandoned him—or so it seemed to Melville, as his career plummeted like a shot bird after *Moby-Dick*. He had believed in Hawthorne as a fellow Great Heart and Naysayer—a belief born in his own egoism. When in the end the older man abandoned him, Melville decided he was shallow, a pursuer of sham success. "All Fame is patronage," Melville told Hawthorne in the Berkshires. "Let me be infamous, there is no patronage in that." Hawthorne was unable to join Melville in his splendid isolation.

As the Melville-Hawthorne relationship suggests, nineteenth-century friendships were deeper, more passionate, more influential than those of today. Writers then were more isolated in their dealings with publishers and perhaps thus in greater need of editorial or business advice from trusted friends. Authors like Melville (and his lawyer brother) dealt with businessmen publishers, some of them crudely grasping like the Harper brothers.

Early American writers were also bereft of a tradition and of what might be called critical support. If they attempted something original that inevitably challenged the mindset of society's moral guardians, they were hard put to find critical defenders. Melville's sad fall into obscurity seems in part caused by his extreme isolation and the lack of support from his peers. Even his influential editor friend Evert Duyck-inck joined the pack of religious moralists castigating *Moby-Dick* for impiety. Hawthorne failed to speak out.

Dreiser was fortunate in having Mencken and other modernists to rally around his second novel, *Jennie Gerhardt,* with its controversial unwed-mother heroine. While Dreiser was still struggling to write that very novel, the British publisher Grant Richards told him sympathetically that what he was doing no one else in America had done so he had nothing to compare himself with.[17] Nineteenth-century writers had nothing to compare themselves with except the English from whom they were trying to declare independence.

But writing is a solitary act. No friend can do it for you. Sarah Orne Jewett told Willa Cather: "To work in silence and with all one's heart, that is the writer's lot; he is the only artist who must be solitary, and yet needs the widest outlook on the world."[18]

But note that "and yet." Jewett means that most writers do their work in privacy, but they must move in the world, physically and mentally, reading the classics and their peers, accumulating experiences and insights, formulating a philosophy of life and death. They—at least the great ones—must articulate the universal truths of the heart rather than the received wisdom of the moment.

Jewett accepted solitude as a necessary condition for doing the work itself. Most writers would kill for the solitude to do their work, because they know that is the only way they can find relief from the pain of ideas struggling to be born.

Even geniuses need social intercourse to fertilize their minds and reconnect with their public. That is why God invented coffeehouses, sidewalk cafés, salons, saloons, writers' colonies, and faculty lounges.

The danger of sociability, though, is that it can become an escape from that scary time when it will be just you and your writing instrument in a closed room. Some writers do all they can to escape this sentence.

Others cope with their blank-page anxiety with various mental stratagems. The old party Somerset Maugham proposed a useful technique: Always stop your day's writing in the middle of a paragraph, a sentence, or a thought. Then you'll have leftovers for your mind to feed on the next day.

Of course, still others happily go heigh-ho to work. These people experience most intensely in their sequestered study the pure joy of the work itself. This applies to any form of creative writing. The theater is deemed a collaborative enterprise, but someone must first withdraw and write the words. The late lyricist Fred Ebb (*Cabaret, Chicago*) once told me in an interview that his greatest joy came while sequestered with his partner, composer John Kander. Later, the necessary hard collective work of staging a musical—the revisions and the conflicts with others—replaced the pleasure of creation.

Screenwriting is the most collaborative art form (save, perhaps, television comedy writing). Often a chain gang of writers is hired to revise the previous revision. Cineastes still debate whether the author's role is a minor one and the director is the real auteur. At any rate, some screenwriters turn with relief to novel writing, or poetry, where only a sympathetic editor stands between them and the final result.

Solitude is a writer's natural element, the oxygen he breathes. Some writers joke about the desirability of a prison cell, where they'd have to work. Others settle for six months at Yaddo or MacDowell.

And yet, even the towering genius on his private Olympus, even the most self-absorbed, narcissistic writer bewails his loneliness, rattling the cage of his own making and seeking palliatives when he cannot have friendships. John O'Hara, in his drinking days, was famous for losing friends (and making enemies); in later years, he had friends, but when his biographer Geoffrey Wolff asked them what they talked about with O'Hara, none could remember, as though some void of affection existed between them. Dreiser always sought consolation for loneliness in the warmth of female flesh, and he loved the adventure and intrigue of infidelity. Sinclair Lewis, whose son spoke of his "vast loneliness," sought solace in the bottle, as did Kerouac, who ended up living with his mother and marrying the sister of his childhood friend, seeking to recover the boyhood security he had lost.

Lewis, in failing health and talent, spent the last year of his life wandering in Italy. At some point he compiled a list of all the friends he had lost over his lifetime through quarrels or neglect. It was a classic case of a great writer who had sacrificed everything—wives, children, and friends—and given the best of himself to his work. Was it worth it? He seems to say that it was: "Does any ambitious man have many [friends]?" He wrote of the "insatiable sick *disease* of friendship—like love—always demanding more, so always lonely."[19] Looking back, it seemed that friends were a distraction, though a welcome one at times; but in the summing-up only his work truly mattered.

The paradox is that authors like Lewis—difficult friends in life—give us books we love like friends. Writers work in the solitude of a lighthouse keeper, but the light they keep illuminates the way for distant lives.

CHAPTER 2

THE PURITAN AND THE PAGAN

Nathaniel Hawthorne and Herman Melville

When the big hearts strike together, the concussion is a little stunning.
—MELVILLE TO HAWTHORNE (1851)[1]
Melville, as he always does, began to reason of Providence and futurity.
—HAWTHORNE (1856)[2]

THE FRIENDSHIP of Nathaniel Hawthorne and Herman Melville is one of the most important in the nation's literary history. It came at a crucial time in both men's careers: Melville was writing *Moby-Dick,* and the success of Hawthorne's recently published *The Scarlet Letter* had won him a long-delayed emergence from obscurity. Their meeting in the Berkshires in western Massachusetts changed the nature of Melville's great novel, sending him diving to darker depths.

Scores of scholarly articles, including a book of essays and a special issue of a literary magazine, are devoted to the friendship. And as biographers and scholars have claimed broader latitude in writing about sexuality and art, the issue of a homoerotic attraction between the men has become a cause célèbre in the journals of academe.

Until Melville and Hawthorne published their great novels, there was no serious American literature. For years the Reverend Sydney Smith's taunt in the *Edinburgh Review*—"In the four quarters of the globe, who reads an American book?"[3]—summed up the young nation's standing in the English-speaking world. Though America had many scriveners, only James Fenimore Cooper and Washington Irving had achieved international respect as well as large readerships at home.

This growing acceptance of American authors in the mother country had the paradoxical effect of generating calls for a uniquely American literature, for writers still received their imprimatur from the London critics. Americans began rebelling, taking up pens against British cultural colonialism. Publications like *Yankee Doodle* and *Literary World* espoused a brand of literary nativism. The prominent New York publishing firm of Wiley & Putnam started a Library of American Books under the direction of the critic Evert Duyckinck, who was also editor of *Literary World*.

In the early 1850s, what is now called the American Renaissance began. The decade was marked by the publication of *The Scarlet Letter* and *Moby-Dick* (two of the three finest American novels of the century, the other being *Adventures of Huckleberry Finn*), Thoreau's *Walden*, and Whitman's *Leaves of Grass*.

The initial meeting of Nathaniel Hawthorne and Herman Melville took place on August 5, 1850, in Stockbridge, Massachusetts, a village set in the green Berkshire Mountain country. The occasion was an outing of a group of writers who were summering in the area. A contemporary article in *Literary World* described the event. The anonymous author coyly identifies the better-known participants with noms de plume, assuming his readers will immediately recognize the people. Hawthorne, for example, is Mr. Noble Melancholy ("the charming sketcher of New England mystic life"), and Melville is New Neptune ("the sea-dog of our Berkshire homestead").[4] The account and the occasion conjure up an allegorical painting of native poets and writers disporting themselves at the springs of American Literature on the civilized greensward with untamed Wilderness looming in the background.

The host of the gathering was David Dudley Field, a book-loving New York lawyer and local historian, who had a home and family connections in Stockbridge. He had planned the event on the train coming up from New York with two fellow travelers—slender, blond Evert Duyckinck and plump Cornelius Mathews, a poet, satirist, and editor of *Yankee Doodle,* who was the anonymous author of the *Literary World* article. Mathews had a bloated sense of his importance as a novelist, and his friend Duyckinck encouraged him, touting him as the great American author the country needed. The two of them were central figures in the "Young America" movement promoting native writing. Melville was a vocal fellow traveler.

Duyckinck had praised Hawthorne in his magazine, and as editor of the Library of American Books had published Melville's first novel, *Typee.* The exotic sensuousness of this South Seas romance appealed to the repressed sexuality of early Victorian America, and it became a popular success. Less popular with religious reviewers were the author's gibes at missionaries who tried to expunge the native customs and religions. Melville's publisher would not bring out a second edition until Duyckinck persuaded the author to delete blasphemous matter.

The two remained friends, and Melville had invited him and Mathews, whose magazine he had written for (it was indeed a small literary world), to spend a summer weekend on his cousin Robert Melvill's farm, one mile south of Pittsfield, Massachusetts. (The place had originally belonged to Herman's grandfather, old Major Melvill, a Revolutionary War hero. Herman's branch of the family added the "e.") The Melville family was already in summer residence: Herman, wife Elizabeth (Lizzie), son Malcolm, mother Maria Gansevoort Melville, and two sisters. With that crowd and Robert's family on the premises, Duyckinck and Mathews would end up sleeping in the haymow. Evert described the main house, Broadhall, as "quite a piece of mouldering rural grandeur. The family has gone down & this is their last season."[5]

Weary of eking out a bare living at farming and taking summer boarders, Robert Melvill had recently sold the farm. This news had come as an unwelcome surprise to Herman, who had loved the rambling old place since summering there as a boy. Fortunately, the purchasers were in no rush to move in. They were a wealthy New York couple named Robert and Sarah Morewood, who had joined the growing ranks of prosperous city people escaping to the unspoiled Berkshires. There was a small but growing writers' colony in the area, including the novelist Catharine Sedgwick; G.P.R. James, a visiting best-selling British author; and Oliver Wendell Holmes, the poet and essayist, who spent summers at an ancestral farm near the Melvill place. The August 31 *National Intelligencer* reported that J. T. Headley, "one of the few of our writers who has made money out of literature may be seen at the Stockbridge Inn."[6]

Nathaniel Hawthorne, who had finally made money out of literature from *The Scarlet Letter,* had recently arrived. As the Boston *Transcript* reported in April, he had "taken up his residence in Lenox, and added another celebrity to that genial atmosphere of talent and genius." With his wife, Sophia, son Julian, and daughter Una, he had rented the handyman's cottage on a larger estate about six miles from the Melvill farm.

Hawthorne had come to work on his new novel, not for a vacation. He was jealous of his privacy, and Sophia fiercely protected it. He had always been a solitary soul. After graduating from Bowdoin in 1825, determined to become a writer, he immured himself for twelve years in his boyhood room in Salem, learning his trade by turning out anonymous hack work, lightweight essays and allegorical tales of Puritan saints and sinners inspired by local legends and his own family history (his great-grandfather was a judge at the Salem witch trials). Until the publication in 1837 of *Twice-Told Tales,* he had been, he confessed, "the obscurest man of letters in America."[7] That same year, he wrote to his more famous Bowdoin classmate, Henry Wadsworth Longfellow, "I have made a captive of myself, and put me into a dungeon, and now I cannot find the key to let myself out—and if the door were open, I should be almost afraid to come out."[8]

Hawthorne's shyness reinforced his natural reticence. He was a strikingly handsome man, much yearned over by his wife (and other women), with raven-black hair, depthless gray-green eyes, and (in some of his pictures) a faint, quizzical smile. His love for Sophia was his only warm, flesh-and-blood contact with the world, he once said, though he had a few close male friends, including his Bowdoin classmates Franklin Pierce and Horace Bridge.

In the Berkshires his solitary ways won him a reputation for being standoffish. His nonattendance of church scandalized the pious locals, who still remembered that the fiery Puritan divine Jonathan Edwards had thundered from a local pulpit. A contemporary history mentions disapprovingly Hawthorne's "aversion to social intercourse" and the "hatred of traits of the Puritan character" apparent in his stories. The historian notes that "the shadow of the occupant of the house of the two gables seldom, if ever, darkens a church door."[9] When he met a local person on a path in the woods, he would scurry off into the brush.

For all his aloofness, Hawthorne was no hermit, and he must have been hungry for intelligent, cultivated companionship, which would explain his acceptance of the invitation to the Monument Mountain excursion. Although Sophia stayed home with the children, he brought along his luxuriantly bearded publisher, James T. Fields, who had come down from Boston in a splendid carriage with his young wife. His visit was probably prompted in part by his interest in Hawthorne's progress on his next novel, *The House of the Seven Gables.* In his elegant town attire—dandyish suit, silk cravat, and patent leather shoes—Fields added an effete note to the rustic excursion.

Lawyer Dudley Field's plan called first for an excursion up Monument Mountain, a gentle prominence near the town. The picnickers would assemble in Stockbridge and proceed in wagons to the foot of the mountain. After debarking, they would hike to the summit. Upon their return, they would enjoy a gala luncheon at Field's home.

The host had succeeded in snaring a dozen excursionists and their wives. The most famous guest was Dr. Oliver Wendell Holmes, the waspish Boston poet/essayist ("Mr. Town Wit" in Mathews's nomenclature) and founding Brahmin. As they started trudging onward and upward, all were in good spirits despite the lowering sky. Duyckinck chatted with Hawthorne, a literary hero. About halfway up, a sudden shower sent them scrambling for shelter under a nearby ledge. Holmes extracted a bottle of champagne and a silver cup from his handy medical bag and they took sips until the rain stopped. The champagne brightened Melville's spirits; Mathews reports that he "bestrode a peaked rock which ran out like a bowsprit, and pulled and hauled imaginary ropes."[10]

After the former mariner was lured off his rock, the party straggled to the summit, where they rested and Mathews declaimed William Cullen Bryant's ode to Monument Mountain. This offered a pretext for more champagne to toast Bryant and any other poets who had Berkshire connections.

Flushed with wine and patriotism, the troop returned to the mountain's base where waiting wagons conveyed them to Field's home. There followed a lengthy, vinous luncheon, at which Holmes launched into a tongue-in-cheek declamation on the superiority of British men to Americans in physical prowess and literary genius. Melville, sensing the voice of Anglophiliac Boston, fired back for the American side. Hawthorne, smiling his enigmatic smile, occasionally interjected words of support for Melville.

After lunch, the party hiked to Icy Glen, a formation of massive glacial rocks that harbored oozing dark crevices so cool that ice formed year-round. Most of the guests were tipsy. Hawthorne had become positively voluble, and amid the echoing rock walls he shouted mock warnings of eternal doom.

During the long, roistering day, he and Melville had talked and discovered much in common. Hawthorne insisted they get together again—an unprecedented gesture of sociability for him. It was not entirely the wine talking, according to James C. Wilson, to whose scholarly study of the Hawthorne-Melville friendship I am indebted; he later told a friend, "I met Melville the other day and like him so much that I have asked him to spend a few days with me before leaving these parts."[11]

Until they met that August day in 1850, Hawthorne and Melville had pursued their careers with little awareness of each other. Melville had lost his father at an early age, terminating the family's comfortable lifestyle and forcing him to go to work at age thirteen. After a few years of drudgery he ran away to sea, and in 1844 he shipped out on a whaler bound for the Pacific. Three and a half years later, after going through a mutiny, captivity by friendly cannibals, and dalliances with Polynesian maidens, he returned on a U.S. Navy ship, his brain stocked with enough material for several books, which he proceeded to write, with diminishing success.

Hawthorne grew up in Salem, then a thriving port; his father was a ship's captain who died in Surinam of the yellowjack when he was still a boy. Hawthorne often listened to the old salts' yarns of their seafaring days and hankered to test his manhood before the mast. Instead he ended up as one of those landlubbers who "have no variety in our lives."[12]

He had a limited acquaintance with Melville's work, mainly his popular South Sea adventure *Typee*. Indeed, Hawthorne had reviewed that novel for the Salem *Advertiser*. As a writer who questioned religion in his own stories and novels, he sympathized with Melville's ideas and defended his right to hold them:

> [The author] has that freedom of view—it would be too harsh to call it laxity of principle—which renders him tolerant of codes of morals that may be little in accord with our own; a spirit proper enough to a young and adventurous sailor, and which makes his books the more wholesome to our staid landsman.[13]

The attacks on his antireligious views seem to have stiffened Melville's back. He attended church only when dragged there by his mother, which increased suspicion of him in Lenox, as did his irreligious opinions. Sarah Morewood, who became friendly with the Melvilles, observed, "It is a pity that Mr. Melville so often in conversation uses irreverent language—he will not be popular in society here on that very account—but this will not trouble him—I think he cares very little as to what others may think of him or his books so long as they sell well. . . ."[14] Townspeople knew him only as a frowning, black-bearded man who galloped his wagon into town daily to pick up his mail. The local bookseller was once asked about Herman Melville. "Oh, he's the fellow who bought the Brewster place," the man said. He had no idea that this was Herman Melville the author, whose books he occasionally sold.

Turning out five books in almost as many years, whose sales fell in direct proportion to their seriousness, had made Melville a semirecluse like Hawthorne. Yet he hungered for *literary* companionship—a soul mate. And he invested in Hawthorne, fifteen years older, his thwarted filial need for his own dead father.

With a growing family dependent on him, Melville despaired of the chances for a serious writer to make a decent living in America. He expressed his gloomy conclusions in a letter to his British publisher, Richard Bentley: "The majority of Americans cared nothing about literature. This country is at present engaged in furnishing material for future authors; not in encouraging its living ones."[15]

After making his debut with a best-seller, Melville had become more and more determined to write, as he put it, what came from the heart (the uncalculating truth, like the allegorical *Mardi*) rather than from the head (calculated to make money, like his second South Seas adventure, *Omoo*).

Hawthorne had always made a threadbare living, and even the success of *The Scarlet Letter* did not ease his financial insecurity. He was counting on *The House of the Seven Gables,* now under way, to build on the popularity that *The Scarlet Letter* had won him.

Three days after the picnic, Melville showed up at Hawthorne's door accompanied by his houseguests, Duyckinck and Mathews. Their host uncorked a couple of bottles of champagne from a case presented to him by an admirer. After consuming them, the men strolled down to the nearby lake known as Stockbridge Bowl.

Following this visit, Duyckinck, who had been nagging Melville to contribute to his magazine, suggested he write an essay on Hawthorne. Melville, who abhorred writing book reviews or otherwise bylining his personal views, was so taken by Hawthorne that he agreed. But the only book by Hawthorne he owned was *Mosses from an Old Manse,* an 1846 collection of stories that his aunt Mary had recently given him. He hadn't even read it, but after leafing through it he allowed he could find something to praise. He had to get to it immediately so Duyckinck could wedge his essay into the next issue. The editor postponed his return to the city in order to take Melville's manuscript with him.

Melville wrote a sincerely flattering piece, but he also used the occasion to broadcast his own political-literary heresies. He enlisted Hawthorne in the Young America movement's project to overthrow the English domination of American literature and in his war on organized religion. He hid his opinions behind the persona of "a Virginian spending July in Vermont."

He started out by claiming that he had been given Hawthorne's book by a young cousin named Cherry (so much for old Aunt Mary), who recommended it over his current reading matter—the Reverend Timothy Dwight's *Travels in New England and New York,* a long, pious, and dull work.

He contrasts Hawthorne's writing: "the rich and rare distillment of a spicy and slowly oozing heart." Most people think of Hawthorne as "a sequestered, harmless man from whom any deep and weighty thing [can] hardly be anticipated—a man who means no meanings." But Melville explains that he only *seems* to be a writer who "means no meanings." In reality he possesses "a deep intellect which drops down into the universe like a plummet." The "hither side of Hawthorne's soul . . . like the dark half of the physical sphere—is shrouded in blackness, ten times black." Melville, in effect, dismisses Hawthorne's essays like "Rills from the Town Pump" (apparently one of the few things by Hawthorne he had previously read), which were the most popular products of his pen. In Jonathan Edwards country, he finds more interesting Hawthorne's "Calvinistic sense of Innate Depravity and Original sin, from whose visitations, in some shape or other, no deeply thinking mind is always and wholly free."

Among the stories he singles out is "Young Goodman Brown," a tale set in early Salem days. The hero attends a witches' sabbath at which he is distressed to see all the pillars of the town. It is gradually revealed that he and perhaps his wife, Faith, are about to sign a pact with the Devil. "Evil is the nature of mankind," a dark presiding figure tells him. "Evil must be your only happiness." All this may have been a dream, Hawthorne suggests, but young Brown's contemplation of earthly evil (presumably the sexual orgies that allegedly took place at these events), even drawing in his sweet, innocent Faith, haunts him for the rest of his life. Religion is hollow; "the anthem of sin" drowns out the hymns of the godly. This view fit Melville's Manichean world-view; he calls the story "deep as Dante."

All great artists, Melville contends, seek to please the masses while concealing their vision of darker truth. The prime example is Shakespeare, a crowd-pleasing dramatist playing to the rabble at the Globe Theatre who created tortured figures like Hamlet, Lear, Timon, and Iago to express his dark belief in a universe where evil reigns. Like all great artists, he must hide such ideas because "in the world of lies, Truth is forced to fly like a sacred white doe in the woodlands; and only by cunning glimpses will she reveal herself. . . ."

Though Hawthorne may not be another Shakespeare, Melville says, he comes close. His insights match the "short quick probings at the axis of reality" in the greatest of Shakespeare's plays. Hawthorne possesses "the largest brain with the biggest heart" in American literature; he is a "Shiloh" (Redeemer) who will lead it to true greatness. At this point the modern reader begins to suspect that this is as much Melville describing himself as it is Melville describing Hawthorne.

He anticipates that readers will object to the comparison of a humble native writer with the immortal Bard. But as a literary patriot who believes in democratic equality, he does not think it so far-fetched. "Believe me, my friends, Shakespeares are this day being born on the banks of the Ohio," he declares. The Bard "is sure to be surpassed by an American born or yet to be born."

Melville calls on Americans to honor their own rather than patronize foreigners. If ever there is to be a truly American literature, native writers must stop aping the English. He deprecates Washington Irving, without naming him, as "that very popular and amiable writer" who "owes his chief reputation to the self-acknowledged imitation of a foreign model, and the sturdiest avoidance of all topics but smooth ones." In short, a commercial hack who means no meanings.

"Let us boldly contemn all imitation . . . and foster all originality," Melville says, "though at first it be as crabbed and ugly as our own pine nuts." "We want no American Goldsmiths," he brags, "nay we want no American Miltons." He swipes at Boston: "Let us away with this Bostonian literary flunkeyism toward England." Better to praise a mediocre American author than a brilliant English one.

To be sure, choosing the harder path of originality poses a greater risk of failure. So be it. "Failure," proclaims Melville, "is the true test of greatness." A proud boast his career would unfortunately exemplify.

Only a few of the illuminati will comprehend Hawthorne's dark vision, Melville continues (or, he might have added, Herman Melville's). "For genius, all over the world, stands hand in hand, and one shock of recognition runs the whole circle round." He envisioned a small band of writers, diverting the public and concealing their own gloomy views of the power of evil.

Behind Melville's words lay a perception of the dilemma faced (he believed) by American writers, who must (if they aspire to the greatness of Shakespeare) be tellers of unpopular truths, but who, in order to make a living, must write books that sell, that please the public. Examples of the latter included Washington Irving, one of the few American authors who earned a living from his books (supplemented by a private income).

Melville used his review to put down sunny writers like Irving and celebrate Hawthorne's metaphysical blackness—the coloration he intended to infuse into his own work. Then he peeks out from behind his mask to proclaim his oneness with Hawthorne in sexually charged language that has resonated down to the present: "Already I feel that this

Hawthorne has dropped germinous seeds into my soul. He expands and deepens down the more I contemplate him and further, and further, shoots his strong New England roots into the hot soil of my Southern soul."[16]

Psychoanalytical critics and the more recent school of "queer theorists" blazon this passage as evidence that Melville had a homosexual crush on Hawthorne. Indeed, in an issue of the *Emerson Society Quarterly* devoted entirely to the Hawthorne-Melville friendship, Robert K. Martin and Leland S. Person, not ones to mince words, say that "the image is one of anal penetration."[17] The biographer Edwin Miller, among the first to "out" Melville's and Hawthorne's alleged sexuality in a scholarly study, calls Melville's review a "love letter," in which he takes the passive feminine role. Later, Miller theorizes, Melville became the real-life aggressor and made a sexual advance that put Hawthorne in panicked flight from the Berkshires.

Nearly thirty years earlier, Newton Arvin, who was a closeted homosexual, wrote a study of Melville. Perhaps sensitive to the vibrations of homosexual attraction (or projecting his own desires), he noted that the *Mosses* review revealed Melville in "a state of quite special responsiveness." It was "in such an atmosphere of warmth and appreciation that Melville composed his greatest book."[18]

Hawthorne did not see the article in *Literary World* until his old Bowdoin friend Longfellow sent him a copy with a note: "I have rarely seen a more appreciating and sympathizing critic."[19] He showed it to Sophia, who exulted, "At last some one dares to say what in my secret mind I have often thought—that he is only to be mentioned with the Swan of Avon."[20]

Without revealing to Hawthorne who had written the article, Duyckinck shipped him copies of all of Melville's books. Hawthorne read through them in August "with a progressive appreciation of the author," he wrote Duyckinck. "No writer ever put the reality before his reader more unflinchingly." Showing how perfectly he was on Melville's wavelength, he singled out for praise the allegorical *Mardi,* a novel that had been much criticized, calling it a "rich book, with depths here and there that compel a man to swim for his life."

Oblivious to any connection, he mentions the article in *Literary World* and says the author (whoever he may be) must have a "generous heart." He is happy that such a superior man would praise him more than he deserved.[21]

That September, Melville appeared at the door of the Hawthorne cottage and confessed that it was he who had written the review. Hawthorne's reaction is not recorded, but his gratitude to his unknown benefactor was already on record in the letter to Duyckinck. Sophia found new virtues in the man who had coupled her Nathaniel with Shakespeare. In a letter to her sister she calls him "a man with a true warm heart & a soul & an intellect . . . sincere & reverent, very tender & *modest*—And I am not sure that he is not a very great man. . . ."[22]

That September, Melville purchased a farm adjoining the old Melvill place. Hawthorne's presence in the area undoubtedly influenced his decision. He would be living six miles away from the man with "the largest brain with the largest heart" in American literature. Socially and spiritually isolated in godly Jonathan Edwards country, he had found in Hawthorne the soul mate he was seeking.

His new place comprised 160 acres of land, mostly woodland but some under cultivation; there was a large old house, a barn, and out-buildings. He named it Arrowhead for the Indian relics his plow turned over. He intended to live in it year-round, farm it, and make expensive renovations. These included a piazza on the northern part of the house, which offered an awe-inspiring view of Mt. Greylock, the tallest mountain in Massachusetts, sometimes called Saddleback because of its shape.

In his book about Melville, Newton Arvin writes that "the sense of Hawthorne's sympathetic and understanding nearness" in the Berkshires was "vital" to Melville's completing *Moby-Dick*.[23] Arvin contends that Melville drastically revised his novel to make it more pessimistic and tragic.

The bare facts available about the composition of *Moby-Dick* tend to confirm that he changed course midway through. We know that on May 1, Melville reported that he was half finished to Richard Henry Dana, a New York lawyer friend and the author of *Two Years Before the Mast,* the most popular sailor's tale of the time. Dana had urged Melville to write a whaling yarn, presumably a straightforward adventure tale. In his letter, Melville told Dana that his new novel had become a "strange sort of book."[24] In June, Melville described the work in progress as "a romance of adventure, founded upon certain wild legends in the Southern Sperm whale fisheries" and personal experience.[25] He predicted to his British publisher, Richard Bentley, in June, that the book would be completed by late autumn 1850.

In August he met Hawthorne and embraced him as a kindred spirit. Hawthorne was not the only literary influence on him at this time; he had also been reading Shakespeare and Carlyle. But neither of them lived six miles away.

This we know: Melville's novel was not in fact completed until July 1851. Authors' predictions are notoriously inaccurate, but Melville was a prolific artisan who had delivered five novels. The reason for his taking eight months longer than he originally said he would was surely not indolence. Rather, it reflected some profound change in the design of his novel. Perhaps he scrapped what he had done so far and rewrote it; perhaps he added symbolic baggage to his existing narrative.

There is another inspiration Hawthorne may have provided, this one materialistic. The success Hawthorne was having with his "hell-fired novel" (as he called *The Scarlet Letter*) encouraged Melville to believe that his own venture into heavier seas in *Moby-Dick*, leaving behind the safe harbor of exotic tales that had earned him money, would be similarly rewarded.

The final irony is that Hawthorne had just gone through the worst year of his life. Psychological blows, debts, financial insecurity, and deteriorating health had cast a shadow over the belated success of *The Scarlet Letter*.[26] After the psychological stress attending its publication—including wild rumors that the novel's central character, the adulterous minister Dimmesdale, was based on himself—he distanced himself from it, assuring his publisher that he would inject more "sunshine" into *The House of Seven Gables*. Finally, he was increasingly haunted by the fear that he was losing his powers, that he had "reached that point in an author's life, when he ceases to effervesce."[27]

During the sixteen months that they were neighbors in the Berkshires, Hawthorne and Melville exchanged at least half a dozen confirmed visits and probably many more that were not recorded. Melville promised his friend: "I mean to continue visiting you until you tell me that my visits are both supererogatory and superfluous."[28] Mainly the contacts were between the two men; their wives and children came along infrequently. In January 1851, Sophia declined an invitation from Melville to bring Nathaniel and the children. Melville told her to ask Hawthorne to come anyway: "We will have mulled wine with wisdom, & buttered toast with story-telling & crack jokes & bottles from morning till night."

Hawthorne's son, Julian, grew fond of Melville, who let him ride in the driver's seat of his wagon or swept him up on the saddle of his horse. After one such treat, he told his father that he loved Mr. Melville "as well as me, and as mamma, and as Una," his sister.[29] As a grown man, Julian still remembered Melville arriving on a snowy day accompanied by a large, bounding Newfoundland, "shaggy like himself, good natured and simple."[30] Once while Hawthorne was walking with Julian, a "cavalier on horseback" rode up and saluted them in Spanish. It was the costumed Melville. Both father and son were delighted.

Melville enjoyed masquerades and pranks. He was a fount of stories, acting them out as he went along. Telling the Hawthornes a South Seas anecdote, he described a fight between two Polynesian bravos, swinging about vigorously with an imaginary club, which the next day they both swore had been real.

Since the Hawthornes had no vehicles, Melville volunteered his farm wagon for light hauling. He rode into Pittsfield daily to pick up his mail, after a morning of writing, breaking off for lunch at two. Hawthorne once asked him to collect a box coming from Boston, and while he was at it, would Melville buy him a kitchen clock? He had in mind a good Connecticut-made wooden one costing $1.50. Sophia added a P.S. saying she doubts he can find a clock for less than $2. And, oh yes, would Mr. Melville relay a message from her to the cabinet-maker who was making a bed for them?[31] Melville cheerfully complied.

But the heart of the relationship was the long talks they held into the night over a bottle of port or brandy and cigars, discussing "time and eternity, things of this world and of the next, and books, and publishers, and all possible and impossible matters," Hawthorne recalled.[32] Melville did most of the talking, while Hawthorne listened in silence like a psychoanalyst. Sophia described the more passionate Melville in eruption: "Nothing pleases me better than to sit & hear this growing man dash his tumultuous waves of thought up against Mr. Hawthorne's great, genial comprehending silences . . . such a love & reverence & admiration for Mr. Hawthorne . . . is really beautiful to witness."[33]

Generally, Melville was a welcome guest. One night he dropped by and was entertained royally with Champagne Foam, a concoction of beaten eggs, sugar, and champagne. He invited Hawthorne and family to come for an extended visit the next day.

Sophia declined, but Hawthorne brought Una and a thoughtful bread-and-butter present, a four-volume tome from his library with a long-winded title: *The Mariner's Chronicle: Being a Collection of the Most Interesting Narratives of Shipwrecks, Fires, Famines, and Other Calamities Incident to a Life of Maritime Enterprise. . . .* [34] It was a rich trove of seafaring anecdotes (including tales of whales attacking vessels sent out to kill them), which he knew Melville could use in his work in progress.

Surely they discussed Melville's novel. Hawthorne recalled talking to his host in his study beside a table littered with manuscript pages. Mount Greylock was visible through the window. Hawthorne would write in his children's *Wonder-Book* the following year: "On the hither side of Pittsfield sits Herman Melville, shaping out the gigantic conception of his white whale, while the gigantic shape of Greylock looms upon him from his study window." [35]

On another occasion Hawthorne thanked Melville for his hospitality by giving him a copy of *Twice-Told Tales.* After the impassioned language of his essay, Melville's opinion of this collection comes as a surprise. He liked these earlier stories better than the ones he had praised so extravagantly in *Mosses from an Old Manse.* But he found something lacking in Hawthorne: "He doesn't patronise the butcher—he needs roast-beef, done rare."* In other words, his characters are bloodless and passionless. Nevertheless, he writes to Duyckinck, "I regard Hawthorne (in his books) as evincing a quality of genius, immensely loftier, & more profound, too, than any other American has shown hitherto in the printed form. [Washington] Irving is a grasshopper to him—putting the souls of the two men together, I mean. . . ." [36]

---

*One is reminded of Edgar Allan Poe's assertion that Hawthorne should break with the Boston-Concord axis and their erudite journals: "Get a bottle of visible ink, come out from the Old Manse, cut Mr. Alcott, hang (if possible) the editor of *The Dial,* and throw out of the window to the pigs all his odd numbers of the *North American Review.*" [1]

Between visits they exchanged letters. Melville later destroyed Hawthorne's, but his to Hawthorne survive, rich with talk of literary and philosophical matters and personal concerns. The sardonically humorous tone shelters a deeply feeling man.

In April 1851, a few days after Hawthorne presented him with one of the first copies of *The House of the Seven Gables,* Melville delivered his opinion. He compares the novel to "a fine old chamber, abundantly but still judiciously furnished, with precisely that sort of furniture best fitted to furnish it." This metaphor evokes the tame Hawthorne who means no meanings. But Melville claimed also to see the Hawthorne he had praised in his essay. He explains, "The grand truth about Hawthorne is this: He says NO! in thunder, but the Devil himself cannot make him say *yes.* For all men who say *yes,* lie."[37] But "NO! in thunder" is Melville on Melville rather than on the Hawthorne of *The House of the Seven Gables.* He blackens Hawthorne to induct him into his own tribe.

Then, he reverts to the country neighbor who feels "great exhilaration and exultation" at the thought "that the architect of the Gables resides only six miles off, and not three thousand miles away, in England."[38]

As summer neared, Melville sent occasional progress reports on his novel and bemoaned his growing weight of debt. In June he writes that he must soon go to New York, shut himself in a garret, and write the ending of his "Whale," even as the printer is setting the earlier parts. He is unsettled, pulled this way and that by circumstances. "The calm, the coolness, the silent grass-growing mood in which a man *ought* always to compose,—that, I fear, can seldom be mine. Dollars damn me; and the malicious Devil is forever grinning in upon me, holding the door ajar." Not Satan, but the printer's apprentice demanding copy. But he is snared in a dilemma: What he really wants to write won't sell, but when he writes what will sell the result is "a final hash."

An honest novelist who tries to make a living by telling the Truth will end up at the soup kitchen, because "Truth is ridiculous to men." He is determined to finish the "Whale," but what's the use? There's nothing "so short-lived as a modern book. Though I wrote the Gospels in this century, I should die in the gutter."

He abandons pessimism long enough to tell Hawthorne he has seen many flattering allusions to *The House of the Seven Gables;* also, the announcement of an upcoming volume from his pen. Hawthorne's star is in the ascendant, but that cheers him very little: "All Fame is patronage." He boasts that he'd rather be "infamous: there is no patronage in *that.*" His own reputation is "horrible." He'll go down in history as the "man who lived among the cannibals!"[39]

On June 29, Melville reports he has herded half of his novel through the press. After it is done he will "treat myself to a ride and a visit to you. Have ready a bottle of brandy, because I always feel like drinking that heroic drink when we talk ontological heroics together." He asked if he should send Hawthorne "a fin of the *Whale*"; the whole book has been "broiled" in "hell-fire." He confides his book's secret motto: "Ego non baptiso te in nomine—"[40]

Ego non baptiso te in nomine Patris, sed in nomine Diaboli. (I do not baptize thee in the name of the Father but in the name of the Devil.) This blasphemous benison by Satan-serving priests Melville had found in a history of medieval witch hunts by Francis Palgrave. Hawthorne should appreciate the allusion, but his critics in the religious press will not. They will broil him in hell-fire.

The last novel Melville published in his lifetime, *The Confidence-Man,* he dedicated to the "victims of the auto-da-fé."[41]

Melville completed his hell-fired book and then did his spring plowing and other farm chores. On August 1, his birthday, he treated himself to a ride to Hawthorne's place, and they talked half the night of time and eternity and ontological heroics. Sophia being away on a visit to her sister, they boldly smoked cigars in "the forbidden sitting room."[42]

Then in September Hawthorne quarreled with his landlord. Sophia had picked apples on the property, and the owner remonstrated with her as though she were a thief. Hawthorne was fed up with the Berkshires anyhow. He told a friend, "I find that I do not feel at home among these hills. . . . I hate Berkshire with my whole soul, and would joyfully see its mountains laid flat."[43] He needed to be near the salt sea. Meanwhile, his brother-in-law, Horace Mann, who had been elected to Congress, offered him the rental of his home in West Newton, Massachusetts. After some procrastination he agreed.

They did not leave until mid-November, by which time Melville's great book was published. Melville celebrated his publication day with Hawthorne at the Little Red Inn in Lenox. The two of them kept the dining room open long after the lunch hour had ended, talking over brandy and cigars, according to Melville's biographer Hershel Parker. The book carried a printed dedication: "In Token of My Admiration for His Genius, This Book is Inscribed to Nathaniel Hawthorne."

As Parker reconstructs events, Hawthorne spent the next few days frantically reading *Moby-Dick, or the Whale,* so he could pen an appropriate comment before they departed. His letter reached Melville when he was on his way to a party at the Morewoods', and he devoured it later that evening. The letter does not survive; all we know about what Hawthorne thought of *Moby-Dick* is found in Melville's brief reference to it in a letter he later wrote to Sophia.

She had sent Melville a long, belated letter of approval. In his reply Melville says he was impressed with her imaginative interpretation of the book's symbolic meanings, which he, perhaps disingenuously, claims he had not intended. He insists it was only "after reading Mr. Hawthorne's letter, which, without citing any particular examples, yet intimated the part-&-parcel allegoricalness of the whole" that he realized that certain parts had deeper interpretations.[44] In her letter, Sophia singled out the chapter entitled "The Spirit-Spout" as an example of "allegoricalness." This is the place where a water jet appears and reappears ahead of the ship. Ahab's crew imagines it to be the spouting of the White Whale, and it lures them on to a fateful rendezvous.

This shows that Hawthorne had perceived *Moby-Dick*'s "allegoricalness," that is, its latent meanings. His letter had surely conveyed the understanding that Melville so desperately wanted. In his reply, Melville tells his friend: "A sense of unspeakable security is in me this moment, on account of your having understood the book." He feels a transcendent oneness with Hawthorne: "Whence come you, Hawthorne? By what right do you drink from my flagon of life? And when I put it to my lips—lo, they are yours & not mine. I feel that the godhead is broken up like the bread at the Supper, and that we are the pieces."

Hawthorne had offered to write a review of *Moby-Dick*. Melville discourages him: "Don't write a word about the book. . . . I am heartily sorry I ever wrote anything about you—it was paltry."[45]

He signs the letter "Herman"— the only letter not to a family member that he ever signed with his first name.

That passionate language about lips meeting on flagons has been seized on by some scholars as further evidence of Melville's homosexual desire for Hawthorne. But it seems more plausible that the flowery rhetoric, typical of the times, was meant as effusive thanks for Hawthorne's gift of understanding, so deep and complete that Melville considered them to be separate hearts beating in a single body.

The readers who take Melville's words as a protestation of physical desire further speculate that he later declared his love in person and that this confession so repelled or frightened Hawthorne that he decided to move his family away from the Berkshires.

Now possibly there were unrecognized homoerotic feelings on Melville's part; perhaps, in a passive sense, on Hawthorne's too. Melville was familiar with the belowdecks homosexuality of men at sea and probably had a more pantheistic attitude toward such love than the more sheltered Hawthorne did. But there is not the tiniest crumb of evidence that he "came on" to Hawthorne in an amorous way. The impassioned declarations surviving in his letters can more plausibly be interpreted in the context of the times when men routinely shared a bed in a boardinghouse or with brothers—that is, as normal, if fulsome, expressions of affection or respect with no sexual connotations. The extravagance of Melville's metaphors is a hallmark of his style, everywhere evident in *Moby-Dick* and other novels. In his nature he was an overbearingly passionate and extravagantly emotional man, imprisoned in a household of good women.

An example of Melville's nineteenth-century language being misread in our time is provided by the scene in *Moby-Dick* when Ishmael and the Polynesian harpoonist Queequeg share a bed in a Nantucket boardinghouse. Ishmael, who had been leery of the savage, gets to know him and they become friends. Melville describes their bonding in hymeneal language: "Thus, then, in our hearts' honeymoon, lay I and Queequeg—a cozy loving pair." In the 1940s, for example, the critic Leslie Fiedler interprets this scene as a description of a homoerotic passion between white man and colored man. Readers in the 1840s would not have taken the situation as interracial or erotic, but as a jocularly described quasi-domestic tableau.

As we have seen, Hawthorne had several reasons for leaving Lenox, none of which involved a quarrel with Melville. About all that can be said for sure is that, as Hawthorne biographer Brenda Wineapple puts it, "Hawthorne cared for Melville and Melville loved Hawthorne, of this there can be no doubt. . . . But Hawthorne did not love Melville, not the way—whatever it was—that Melville needed love."[46] To which one might add: Whatever love Melville needed, it was not homosexual love in our sense; more probably it referred to a spiritual communion embodied in Hawthorne's perfect understanding of his masterpiece—two "big hearts" striking together.

Early on November 21, "in a storm of snow and sleet," the Hawthornes took a carriage to Lenox, where they boarded a train to Pittsfield. There they met another train that carried them to their new home in West Newton, arriving that same evening. The Berkshire chapter was closed.

The earliest review of *Moby-Dick* to appear on these shores was from the London *Athenaeum,* reprinted in the *Boston Post.* The reviewer called *Moby-Dick* "an ill-compounded mixture of romance and matter-of-fact. . . ." He attacked Melville: "The style of his tale is in places disfigured by mad (rather than bad) English. . . ." It belonged "to the worst school of Bedlam literature. . . ."[47] This would not be the last Melville review to question the author's sanity. The *Boston Post,* which had campaigned against Melville's pagan books, added some snide digs of its own. After that, the condemnation proliferated like a virus.

Positive reviews eventually began to trickle out, but the bad drove out the good. A review by a writer as famous as Hawthorne might have turned the tide, but he remained on the sidelines, with one exception.

Duyckinck wrote a lukewarm two-part notice in *Literary World.* He singled out for reproach Melville's irreverence, his "piratical running down of creeds and opinions. . . ."[48] Melville was hurt and canceled his subscription to *Literary World;* he would caricature Duyckinck in his next novel. Hawthorne sent the critic a mild protest: "What a book Melville has written! It gives me an idea of much greater power than his preceding ones. It hardly seemed to me that the review of it, in the Literary World, did justice to its best points."[49] That private, muted protest was not much assistance to Melville's beleaguered book. Might not Melville have regretted telling him not to review the novel? Might Hawthorne have reviewed it anyway—perhaps in *Literary World*? Did the critical mob's howls of "irreverence" dissuade this somewhat timid man from raising a public row?

Duyckinck's only response to Hawthorne's letter was to reprint the review in another magazine he edited.

That Christmas, Sarah Morewood invited the Melvilles to Christmas dinner to make up for her recent neglect of them. Her description—as quoted in Jay Leyda's invaluable *Melville Log*—provides a snapshot of the author of *Moby-Dick:* "I hear that he is now engaged in a new work [*Pierre*] as frequently not to leave his room till quite dark in the evening. . . . I laughed at him somewhat and told him that the recluse life he was leading made his city friends think that he was slightly insane—he replied that long ago he came to the same conclusion. . . ."[50]

Hawthorne invited his friend to visit him in Concord, where he and his family had landed after further peregrinations. Melville declined. He wrote, in July 1852, that he had been touring Nantucket and nearby islands and needed time at home. He mentions that Hawthorne's name was on everyone's lips. And when he arrived home, imagine his surprise to see on the table with his mail a copy of his friend's latest book, *The Blithedale Romance*! This is a satire of Brook Farm, the Transcendentalist utopian colony where Hawthorne had once uneasily sojourned.[51]

The character of bearish, bearded Hollingsworth in the novel was clearly based on Melville. "There was something of the woman moulded into the great stalwart frame of Hollingsworth," Hawthorne writes, "nor was he ashamed of it, as men often are of what is best in them." The character of Coverdale, a cold, bloodless man, is Hawthorne's unsparing judgment on his own nature. In one scene Hollingsworth tries to enlist Coverdale in an idealistic cause, but the latter clings to his icy detachment. Finally, Hollingsworth makes an impassioned plea—"Coverdale, there is not the man in this wide world whom I can love as I could you. Do not forsake me!"—but Coverdale refuses. "As I look back upon this scene," he says, "there is still a sensation as if Hollingsworth had caught hold of my heart, and were pulling it towards him with an almost irresistible force. It is a mystery to me how I withstood it." If not literally autobiographical, the words may express symbolically Hawthorne's sense of a psychological rupture—and his guilt over his own failure to give Melville something the other had desperately wanted. Love, affirmation, his soul, perhaps.

Melville's only comment on the novel was that he has read just far enough in it "to see that you have most admirably employed materials which are richer than I had fancied them. Especially at this day, the volume is welcome, as an antidote to the mooniness of some dreamers—who are merely dreamers—Yet who the devel [*sic*] ain't a dreamer?"[52] The last sentence can be read as a gentle protest in light of Melville's next novel, *Pierre,* about a maladjusted idealist. Melville was a dreamer too.

In the fall of 1852 Melville visited Hawthorne in Concord. They discussed a true story Melville had heard from a New Bedford lawyer he met in Nantucket. He had sent along some documents the man provided and suggested Hawthorne convert them into a novel. The narrative is reminiscent of a short story of Hawthorne's, "Wakefield," about a man who walks out on his wife and lives for many years unrecognized in the next street. Melville's tale concerns a Nantucket woman who rescued a shipwrecked man washed up in a storm, nursed him back to health, and then married him. But the man leaves one day and never returns. Unknown to her, he marries another woman bigamously. As Melville saw it, every day for years the real wife faithfully trudges to the post box, expecting a letter from him, until the box rots away.

Hawthorne had no real interest in the material (Melville later wrote the story). His creative juices were all but dried up. In the recent election, his Bowdoin friend Franklin Pierce, for whom he had written an unctuously flattering campaign biography, was elected president of the United States. Pierce owed Hawthorne a debt of gratitude and rewarded him with a consulship in Liverpool, England. He and his family sailed in July 1853. Weary of the financial insecurities of authorship, he wanted to build a nest egg. He would not write another novel for seven years. As biographer Wineapple writes, "Hawthorne needed the consulship as much as he needed to write."[53]

Melville would bring Hawthorne into his next novel, *Pierre, or The Ambiguities,* published in 1852. Robert Milder theorizes that "his feeling of bereftness at Hawthorne's departure made him aware that in some fashion . . . he had been 'in love' with another man," and in his next novel he sought to "excavate the foundations of his attachment to Hawthorne."[54] Others theorize that he found in Hawthorne an understanding father who abandoned him, as his own father had, leaving him angry and bitter.

In the novel, there is a character, Plinlimmon, who resembles Hawthorne in his cold aloofness. He symbolizes the practical thinker opposed to Pierre, the sincere but naive idealist. Pierre's incestuous love for his half sister, Isabel, has been taken by some critics as Melville's disguised reference to his forbidden love for Hawthorne. Dark-haired like Hawthorne, she lives in a little red farmhouse like his in the Berkshires. She is a rival of Pierre's blond wife, just as Hawthorne was a rival of Melville's wife. Hershel Parker interprets Isabel more artistically: She is Pierre's tragic muse, leading him to darker truths, as Hawthorne did for Melville when he was writing *Moby-Dick.* Indeed, another of Hawthorne's influences is Melville's psychological analysis of his characters.

Melville sold *Pierre* to the Harper brothers on ruinously unfavorable terms. The hostile reviews of his last novel had badly weakened his bargaining position. As Parker shows, an angry Melville, just before the book went to press, added 160 pages to *Pierre* describing the title character's career as an author, a profession not previously ascribed to him in the book. He flays publishers and critics—particularly Evert Duyckinck, whose review calling *Moby-Dick* irreligious was the coup de grâce to their friendship.

The book was thunderously damned by the same critics, including Duyckinck, because of the incest theme. Reviewers again consigned Melville to a mental ward. The debacle all but finished his ability to make a living from novels. With stubborn, quiet courage, he turned to writing short stories. Some of them ("Bartleby the Scrivener," "The Encantadas," "The Two Temples," and "Benito Cereno," for example) were among the finest products of his pen.

His family, worried about his psychological state, urged him to stop writing and seek a consulship as Hawthorne had done. He wearily agreed. His mother pleaded to a relative with political connections that her son needed a change: "This constant working of the brain, & excitement of the imagination, is wearing Herman out."[55] Hawthorne himself interceded with his friend President Pierce. Hopes rose that Melville would be appointed to Honolulu; but the posting never came through.

In 1856, with his writing career in drydock, Melville embarked on a trip to the Middle East, financed by his supportive father-in-law, Massachusetts chief justice Lemuel Shaw. Along the way he stopped in Liverpool. Hawthorne thought he looked "a little paler, and perhaps a little sadder," with the same "gravity and reserve of manner." He was relieved that Melville bore him no ill will over the failed consular appointment. Instead, he writes, "we soon found ourselves on pretty much our former terms of sociability and confidence." (So much for the stories of a sudden break in the friendship in Lenox.)

Melville confessed he had not been well. Hawthorne comments, "His writings, for a long while past, have indicated a morbid state of mind." He stayed a few days and Hawthorne took note of the minimal clothing he had brought: "He is a person of very gentlemanly instincts in every respect, save that he is a little heterodox in the matter of clean linen."[56] (Actually, there is evidence that Melville sent his undergarments to the laundry.)

The two took a long walk in the sand dunes, smoking cigars and talking of philosophical matters as they had in other days. Hawthorne remembered that Melville "informed me that he had 'pretty much made up his mind to be annihilated' " (meaning he did not believe in an afterlife). "He can neither believe, nor be comfortable in his unbelief; and he is too honest and courageous not to try to do one or the other."[57]

Hawthorne was concerned about Melville's mental state: "The spirit of adventure is gone out of him. He is certainly much overshadowed since I saw him last; but I hope he will brighten as he goes onward."[58] (Earlier that same year, Hawthorne had inscribed in his own journal: "Really, I have no pleasure in anything. A weight is always upon me. Nothing gives me any joy. . . . Life seems so purposeless as not to be worth the trouble of carrying it on any further.")[59]

The next day Melville sailed. He checked his trunk with Hawthorne, taking only a carpetbag to the Middle East. He explained: "This is the next best thing to going naked; and as he wears his beard and moustache, and so needs no dressing-case—nothing but a toothbrush—I do not know a more independent personage. . . . Yet we seldom see men of less criticizable manners than he."[60]

One is reminded of words Melville had written in the Berkshires. After praising Hawthorne as one of the few who say "NO! in thunder," he continues that such men "cross the frontiers into eternity with

nothing but a carpet-bag—that is to say, the Ego." The "*yes*-gentry,"
however, are overloaded and "will never get through the Customs
House."[61]

On his return voyage, Melville stopped in Liverpool to pick up his
trunk. Hawthorne does not mention the visit in his journal. Years later
his son, Julian, recalled that Melville "seemed depressed and aimless.
He said good-bye and wandered away."[62]

That was the last time Hawthorne and Melville met. In 1864
Hawthorne died. Soon after, Melville wrote a poem called "Monody."
The first stanza utters a piercing cry of unbearable grief over a double
loss—in life, in death.

> *To have known him, to have loved him*
> *After loneness long;*
> *And then to be estranged in life,*
> *And neither in the wrong;*
> *And now for death to set his seal—*
> *Ease me, a little ease, my song.*

Hawthorne's death stimulated a revival of interest in him, and he was
hailed across the land as a great American writer. Exploiting the moment, Sophia issued his journals in an edited version, as well as some
inferior romances with which he had struggled in his last years. In the
wave of tributes, Melville could discern posterity's verdict on his own
ruined career. If he was mentioned at all in the obituaries and articles,
it was as a minor writer of sea tales—"a man who lived among the cannibals," as he had predicted to Hawthorne.

In 1883, when Julian Hawthorne visited Melville seeking informa-
tion for a biography of his father, Melville told him that "some secret in
my father's life accounted for the gloomy passages in his books," and

that this same secret explained why the two of them had become estranged after the last meeting in Liverpool. What the secret was, Melville could not say. Could it be that there was *no* secret? Possibly the reticent Hawthorne had recoiled from Melville's passionate intensity, his "morbid state of mind," his Ahab-like hatred of humanity expressed in his last novels, his voracious hunger for the Absolute. Yet the older man was never estranged. His affection and respect for Melville remained undimmed at their last meeting. One suspects that it was Melville, the great Isolato, who, out of his vast egoism, became estranged—or rather envious and embittered because Hawthorne's dark sun seemed permanently to have eclipsed his reputation.

Hawthorne had always been luckier. Unable to write novels since *The Confidence-Man* in 1856, Melville had not kept silent; he turned to writing short stories, and then haunting poems during the Civil War. Beginning in 1870, when he drudged obscurely as a New York customs inspector, he composed a long narrative poem, *Clarel,* a meditation on his journey to the Holy Land. In it the protagonist is strongly drawn to, and then rebuffed by, a character named Vine, who is based on Hawthorne and is portrayed as handsome, charming, vain, and shallow. Through the poem Vine deteriorates mentally. When he rejects Clarel's overtures, Clarel says, "The negatives of flesh should prove / Analogies of non-cordialness / In spirit."[63] He has already admonished himself that he has a wife; his obsession with Vine—which might be read as male friendship though not homosexuality—is foolish. In *Clarel,* Melville probes his long obsession with Hawthorne and tries to lay it to rest. Perhaps he later regretted his harshness.

At some point after Hawthorne's death, Melville added a second stanza to "Monody" suggesting that he had come to terms with his loss:

> *By wintry hills his hermit-mound*
> *The sheeted snow-drifts drape,*
> *And houseless there the snow-bird flits*

Beneath the fir-trees' crape;
Glazed now with ice the cloistral vine
That hid the shyest grape.[64]

The imagery conjures up a lonely, snow-sheeted grave, presumably Hawthorne's. The "cloistral vine" refers to the Hawthorne character in *Clarel,* a shy, withholding man, a man with ice over his heart. Yet beneath the glaze was "the shyest grape," the sweetness Hawthorne withheld—or was unable to give.

CHAPTER 3

THE WESTERNERS
Mark Twain and
William Dean Howells

You are really my only author; I am restricted to you;
I wouldn't give a damn for the rest.
—TWAIN TO HOWELLS (1885)[1]
You have pervaded your century almost more than any other man of letters.
—HOWELLS TO TWAIN (1898)[2]

THE FRIENDSHIP between Samuel Clemens and William Dean Howells is a model of such relationships between two authors. It ran for forty years with some bumps but without serious breakdowns.

When they met, Clemens was beginning to win popular acclaim as a humorist. Howells was assistant editor of the *Atlantic Monthly,* the most prestigious literary magazine in the country. Both were young, ambitious Westerners from small towns. Clemens, thirty-three, grew up in Hannibal, Missouri; Howells, thirty-two, spent his early years in Jefferson, Ohio.

Both had worked for newspapers. Clemens started as a printer's devil in Missouri. Howells learned the printing trade working for his father's paper in Ohio. He moved on to a larger paper in Columbus, but the violent and sordid scenes he witnessed on the police beat lacerated his sensitive nerves, and he switched to literary criticism.

Both had escaped the dullness and drabness of village life. Clemens drew on his memories of Hannibal to paint the stagnant river towns in *Huckleberry Finn;* Howells resented the "meanness and hollowness of that wretched village life."3 Clemens escaped to the West—the "territories" Huck Finn would "light out" for—Howells to the East, to literary Boston.

While working for the paper in Columbus, Ohio, William Dean Howells began submitting poems to the *Atlantic Monthly* in Boston. Several were accepted, and the editor, James Russell Lowell, the eminent poet and satirical essayist, was so encouraging that in 1860 Howells visited Lowell in his Cambridge home. The editor provided him with introductions to Boston's triple-named literary elite—Ralph Waldo Emerson, Henry David Thoreau, and Oliver Wendell Holmes—along with Nathaniel Hawthorne in Concord.

Most useful in his career was an introduction to James T. Fields, main partner in the publishing house of Ticknor & Fields, which owned the *Atlantic,* and his intelligent, charming young wife, Annie. Howells would encounter Fields again later in the decade.

Lowell took Howells to dinner at the Parker House with Dr. Holmes, who was impressed by the young man and compared the occasion to a "laying on of hands," unaware of how prophetic he was. When Hawthorne's name came up, the doctor delivered one of his witty, cutting observations: "He is like a dim room with a little taper of personality burning on the corner of the mantel."4 But Howells found Hawthorne friendly and generous-minded, lacking the chilly condescension he sensed in Holmes and others of the Brahmin caste.

Howells returned to Ohio reality, his head spinning with dreams of making his literary mark in the "Hub of the Universe." His chance came when he was commissioned to write a campaign biography of the obscure Illinois politician Abraham Lincoln, whom the new Republican Party had anointed its presidential candidate. Too shy then to interview Honest Abe, he would never meet him, but he did a superb job of introducing the American public to the unknown Lincoln. He was rewarded upon Lincoln's election in 1860 with a consulship in Venice.

As biographer Kenneth S. Lynn remarks, this sojourn was Howells's Yale and Harvard. His duties were light and he had plenty of leisure to read, rummage through libraries and museums, and write articles that were later collected into a book. While abroad he married Elinor Mead, a brainy, loquacious, neurasthenic Columbus girl.

After returning from Venice in 1865, Howells landed an editorial job with *The Nation* in New York. By chance he encountered James T. Fields, who had succeeded Lowell as editor of the *Atlantic*. Fields had rejected Howells's poetry, seemingly ending his relationship with the magazine, but now he needed an assistant editor, not a poet. Lowell had already recommended him, and so he was hired. Howells claimed that his new boss was mainly interested in his composing-room experience because he needed a drudge to see the magazine through the printer's. But the elderly Fields groomed him as a possible successor.

Fields sensed that the magazine needed new, Western blood. In 1868, *Atlantic* contributor James Parton told him that the magazine should publish "more articles connected with life than literature." He also opined that "it would be possible to make the 'Atlantic Monthly' far more popular if a writer named Mark Twain be engaged."[5] The second piece of advice was not unrelated to the first.

In the December 1869 issue, Howells (who was the house book reviewer) made an overture on the magazine's behalf: He wrote a review of Clemens's first book, *The Innocents Abroad*. Howells's notice was one of the few the book received. Its publisher, the American Publishing Company, was a subscription house, whose titles were peddled door-to-door to rural folk. Prestigious magazines like the *North American Review, Harper's,* or the *Atlantic,* which were owned by publishing houses that sold their books in stores, snubbed the wares of the subscription houses.

Aside from misspelling the author's real name as "Clements," the review glowed with praise, though Howells was a trifle defensive. As though Western humor were per se crude, he gingerly wrote that Twain's style was "always good-humored . . . even in its impudence"; that the satire was never "indulged at the cost of the weak"; and that the author avoided being "insolent." More boldly (and prophetically), Howells celebrated Mark Twain as more than a mere comic writer: "There is an amount of pure human nature in the book that rarely gets into literature."[6] Thus was Mark Twain awarded the *Atlantic*'s seal of approval, certified Safe for Boston Parlors.

Actually, Oliver Wendell Holmes himself had praised *The Innocents Abroad,* but he confined his approval to a private letter and instructed Clemens not to let his publisher quote from it "for the rascals always print everything to puff their books. . . ."[7] Thus did Clemens lose a blurb from the famed Autocrat of the Breakfast-Table.

Clemens's first meeting with Howells took place at the *Atlantic*'s office above the Old Corner Bookstore in Boston, also owned by Ticknor & Fields. James Fields was present, Howells recalled, and was not visibly shocked by the Westerner's flamboyant sealskin coat worn fur side out, or indeed his "crest of dense red hair" and "flaming moustache."[8]

Thereafter, whenever Clemens came to town for one of his readings, he would lunch with Howells, Fields, the writer Thomas Bailey Aldrich (who would succeed Howells as *Atlantic* editor), and other local literati. Over beefsteaks and soufflés at Ober's French restaurant they yarned away the afternoon. "Those were the gay years," Howells later recalled, "and bless god, we *knew* they were at the time."

But he also noticed that Clemens "seemed not to hit the favor of our community of scribes and scholars."[9] At one of these sessions, the California humorist Bret Harte, who had been Clemens's mentor, was at the table. He sarcastically commented: "Why fellows, this"—meaning the lunch with the Boston literati—"is the dream of Mark's life."[10] And it may well have been.

Harte was there as a result of Howells and Fields's effort to bring in more Western writers. Originally from Albany, New York, Harte had settled in California and issued a popular collection of mining-country yarns, *The Luck of Roaring Camp and Other Stories.* In 1868, when Harte was at the peak of his fame, Howells recommended that the magazine offer him a contract paying an unheard-of ten thousand dollars for twelve stories in a year.

Harte accepted and came to Boston, staying for a time with the Howellses, who were smitten by his smooth charm. But his literary goods were becoming shopworn. He later moved to the society playground of Newport, Rhode Island, where he ran up hefty bills at the shops and borrowed from friends, neglecting to pay either back. One of the victims was Samuel Clemens. This and their ill-starred collaboration on a play, in which Harte's arrogance and swollen ego made working with him a nightmare, poisoned their friendship for good. The play failed miserably.

Howells, a man with few enemies, remained friendly with Harte and helped him in various ways—most notably using his wife's Ohio family ties with President Rutherford B. Hayes to win him a consular appointment to Germany in 1878. Knowing Clemens's violent dislike of Harte, Howells never told him what he had done, thus preserving their friendship.

Howells grasped the wheel of the *Atlantic* in July 1871, still determined to bring in more Westerners. Initially, he moved cautiously. There was a historical as well as a tactical basis for his prudence. When he had been acting editor while Fields was in London, the magazine published an article by an esteemed but imperious contributor, Harriet Beecher Stowe, defending her friend the late Lady Byron. The article, which Fields had approved, contained a brief allusion to the poet's affair with his half sister. Even a hint of incest was shocking to the magazine's readers; fifteen thousand of them canceled their subscriptions.

With that touchiness in mind, Howells procrastinated over the seemingly simple question of whether to review Edward Eggleston's *The Hoosier Schoolmaster.* The novel was set in frontier Indiana and larded with realistic frontier slang that Bostonians might find offensive. But his literary conscience won out, as it nearly always did, and in the March 1872 issue, he praised the book's fidelity to Hoosier life "between the days of pioneering and before the days of civilization. . . ."[11]

No one took offense, but Howells would always be a cautious editor, wary of a backlash from conservative Boston readers (he would never publish Walt Whitman because of his bohemian reputation, for example). But the Westernization campaign continued. As the *Atlantic* historian Ellery Sedgwick writes, Howells's strategy was to attract readers beyond the Alleghenies by featuring more Western writers and Western subjects.

He also sought to attract a younger audience by publishing the new generation of writers. One was a young man in Cambridge named Henry James. He had met James during his very first trip to Boston in 1860, and they became friends. Before James moved to Europe in 1876, they held impassioned discussions of the need for social and psychological realism in the novel. As assistant editor, Howells had defended James's stories against objections that they were too pessimistic. As editor in the 1870s, he serialized many James novels, including *The American, The Ambassadors,* and *The Portrait of a Lady.* James would always be grateful, writing Howells in 1912, "You held out an open editorial hand to me . . . with a frankness and sweetness of hospitality that was the making of me. . . . You showed me the way and opened me the door."[12]

In backing James, Howells was allying himself with the future of the American novel. He projected a national, multicultural vision, encouraging, among others, a Norwegian American, H. H. Boyesen; a Southerner, John W. DeForest; and a Maine woman, Sarah Orne Jewett. Before the century was out he would befriend and champion just about every important American author of his time.

But in 1871 the author whose byline he most coveted in the *Atlantic,* Mark Twain, was preoccupied with other matters. In 1870 he married petite, cameo-pretty Olivia Langdon (whom everyone called "Livy"), daughter of a rich Elmira, New York, coal merchant. It was quite a dizzying ascent for the former printer, riverboat pilot, Civil War deserter, failed prospector, and San Francisco bohemian.

Livy's doting father bought Clemens a financial interest in a newspaper in Buffalo and also a magnificent home. Clemens worked as co-editor of the paper, but grew bored with office routine and devoted more time to his own writing. The result was *Roughing It,* a shaggy chronicle of Clemens's dire and comical adventures in the Nevada Territory, Virginia City, and points west in the 1860s.

The book was an immediate hit, and its popularity encouraged him to quit the newspaper trade. The couple moved to Hartford, where the American Publishing Company was located and where he intended to live by his pen. As money began sluicing in from his books, he reveled in the joys of conspicuous consumption, building an ornate twelve-room house in the wealthy suburban enclave called Nook Farm at a cost of over fifty thousand dollars, part of which he borrowed from his wife's fortune.

He was certainly moving up. As he had done with *The Innocents Abroad,* Howells praised *Roughing It* in the June 1872 *Atlantic.* That review Clemens accepted as a further validation of his respectability. He wrote Howells that he felt "as uplifted and reassured . . . as a mother who has given birth to a white baby when she was awfully afraid it was going to be a mulatto."[13]

Intensifying Clemens's relief was the fact that Livy had been particularly pleased by Howells's reference to his "growing seriousness of
meaning." He told Howells that "what gravels her" is that he was often
dismissed as a "mere buffoon."[14] The term was commonly applied to
humorists, who were ranked a peg or two above performing seals and
actors. Indeed, the diplomat-author John Hay, who would become a
friend to both Howells and Clemens, had dismissed *The Innocents Abroad*
as buffoonery. Now Howells, whom Clemens would always consider
"the recognized critical Court of Last Resort in this country," had testi-
fied that his work not only was literature but carried a serious moral
message.

Clemens was now saluting "Friend Howells" in his letters, and
Howells reciprocated. His critical praise of Mark's humor flowed from
a firsthand delight in the man's talk. Clemens took to injecting tomfoolery into his letters as well. For example, he said he had noticed
Howells's picture on the cover of a recent issue of the ladies' magazine
Hearth & Home and urgently requested a copy to put up in his parlor
alongside his portraits of Holmes and Bret Harte. This trinity would
bring many more "souls to earnest reflection" on their sinful deeds.[15]

The wives and children were introduced and family visits exchanged. The women were complementary in personality and background, both tending to brains, frail health, and nervous temperaments.
The Howellses had three children, the Clemenses four. The families
soon bonded. After one stay by the Clemenses, Howells wrote a host's
bread-and-butter letter extolling the visit as "a perfect ovation" for
them. Although the smoke from Clemens's strong cigars, the hot
Scotches he loved, and the talking into the night almost killed them,
after the Clemenses left, the Howellses would look at each other and,
Howells wrote, say "what a glorious time it was, and air the library, and
begin sleeping and dieting, and longing to have you back again."[16]

From the beginning, Howells separated Samuel Clemens from

Mark Twain. He never called him "Mark," as many did, because, he said, the name "seemed always somehow to mask him from my personal sense."[17] They were always "Clemens" and "Howells" to each other, the standard nineteenth-century form of address between close male friends. Down the years they made quite a pair: Howells, only five feet four inches tall and plumper every year, walrus-mustached, with weary, kindly eyes, favoring obscure dark suits with spats; Twain, over six feet, deadpan droll, jumpy, eccentric, a font of stories, with a tousled mane of red hair that eventually turned snowy white, given to clothes that emphatically announced him, like the sealskin coat or the white suits he wore in later years.

Early in Howells's editorship, the firm of Hurd and Houghton purchased the *Atlantic.* Houghton was a square-dealing businessman (he was said to be the model for Howells's best-known character, Silas Lapham). He regarded the money-losing magazine as a prestigious loss leader for his publishing house. He shared Howells's belief "that Mark Twain was literature" and said Twain belonged in the magazine for that reason alone—not merely to raise circulation. He was willing to pay Twain "a sum we could ill afford" to write for the *Atlantic,* Howells marveled.[18]

With his lavish lifestyle, however, Clemens needed to write best-selling books, not articles for the *Atlantic,* even at its top rate of twenty dollars a page. So he did not get around to answering Howells's standing invitation until 1874 when, out of the blue, he submitted two stories. He apologized that one of them wasn't funny; that was the one Howells chose. Called "A True Story," it was narrated by an old black woman, a former slave. Clemens rendered the Negro dialogue pitch-perfectly, yet this was no minstrel show turn, for he infused his tale with an undercurrent of moral condemnation of slavery. His use of first-person narrative and local dialect anticipated *Huckleberry Finn.*

His next project for Howells was a series about his riverboat-pilot days on the Mississippi. The idea came to him, he told Howells, while reminiscing with the Reverend Joe Twichell, his closest Hartford friend, about life on the river. Twichell suddenly interjected: "What a virgin subject to hurl into a magazine!"[19]

The seven-part series ran as "Old Times on the Mississippi." Clemens would later publish the serial (with added material) as a book titled *Life on the Mississippi*. Clearly, at this juncture in his career, Howells provided the sympathetic editorial encouragement Clemens needed to break the mold of vernacular humorist and grow into historical chronicler and, ultimately, novelist. Upon reading the first chapter, Howells exulted at the descriptive realism: "It almost made the water in our ice-pitcher muddy as I read it. . . ."[20] Fearing that Clemens might choke up at the thought of writing for a Bostonian audience, he offered some valuable advice about future episodes. He told him to "stick to actual fact and character"and "give things in *detail*." Steamboat life on the river was so much in the past that it will seem novel to a modern audience. He urges Clemens not to try to write for a highbrow *Atlantic* audience but to "yarn it off as if into my sympathetic ear." He should not "be afraid of rests or pieces of dead color"[21]—not hurry or stick grimly to the point. His advice freed Clemens to be leisurely, expansive, anecdotal, and digressive—all hallmarks of his mature style.

On the other hand, he could not turn Clemens completely loose. If the material was too racy for conservative *Atlantic* readers, he would face the dilemma of either publishing it and putting his job at risk, or rejecting it and putting their friendship at risk. In the event, Clemens crossed the line only once—when he served up riverboat pilots' talk peppered with "damns" and "hells." Rather than directly challenge Clemens, Howells told him that Elinor disliked the "profane words" and thought it better to let "the sagacious reader" infer the epithets such rugged types would use.[22]

Howells's letter unleashed a petite tornado in the form of Livy, who had intercepted it. Clemens reported the ensuing storm, in uppercase headlines: "SHE LIT INTO THE STUDY WITH DANGER IN HER EYE" demanding to know "WHERE IS THE PROFANITY MR. HOWELLS SPEAKS OF?" Clemens confessed that he had omitted it when he read her the manuscript, as was his custom. Only "inspired lying" got him off the hook.[23]

Howells probably meant to get to Clemens through Elinor—giving *her* view rather than his own, women being more authoritative in matters of profanity. Both men used their wives as surrogates to avoid personalizing editorial disputes. Howells knew that Mrs. Clemens read everything Clemens wrote. He once complained that she made him rewrite a chapter of "Old Times on the Mississippi" three times.[24]

Howells was under business pressure not to offend the *Atlantic's* readers, but his personal taste was involved as well. He was a very squeamish man, viscerally shocked by violence, strong language, and sexual subjects. Even while calling for more realism in novels, he drew a bright red line when it came to "obscenity." He believed that the American novel should contain nothing unsuitable for young women.

Clemens respected Howells's judgment of what was fit to print in the *Atlantic,* but he could never be hobbled without bucking. Once, when Howells cut some profanity from a piece, he insisted that blank spaces be inserted where the words had been so that the reader would know that he had "sustained a precious loss which can never be made good to him."[25]

Ribbing his friend's timidity, he sent him bawdy articles as mock submissions. Once he told Howells he had written a complaining letter to the editor of *The New York Times* littered with "goddams" and signed Howells's name because it would have more effect.[26]

Clemens's *Atlantic* contributions enabled him to vent his serious political concerns, which he sometimes clothed in humor but often presented unadorned. He said that the magazine's readers were "the only audience that I sit down before in perfect serenity for the simple reason that it don't require a 'humorist' to paint himself stripéd & stand on his head every fifteen minutes."[27] He added that "the awful respectability of the magazine" made up for the low pay.[28]

Despite his popularity with *Atlantic* readers, Clemens remained ill at ease in the more genteel precincts of New England. In *Mr. Clemens and Mark Twain,* Justin Kaplan writes that "between Mark Twain and certain aspects of literary Boston there existed, and would always exist, something less than perfect harmony."[29] Howells biographer Kenneth Lynn suggests that "at the secret heart of Twain's hatred of New England was a self-hatred for having himself sought the region's recognition and approval."[30]

This held for Howells as well. Out of his insecurity about his position came a kind of compulsion to certify Clemens's moral suitability for Boston readers—as he had in his review of *The Innocents Abroad.* Clemens seems to have noticed this tic. When Howells came to Hartford to deliver a lecture in December 1877, Clemens slyly vouched for his friend's "moral character," even though, as editor of the *Atlantic Monthly,* his literary reputation was impeccable.[31] On his home ground, *he* was the one certifying the outsider's moral suitability.

Clemens's ambivalence about Boston was behind perhaps the greatest misstep of his public career—his speech at the dinner honoring James Greenleaf Whittier in December 1877. Present were fifty-eight distinguished *Atlantic* contributors, including Whittier, Longfellow, Emerson, and Holmes, and intellectuals like Charles Eliot Norton, editor of the high-domed *North American Review,* and Francis Parkman, the historian. A notable absentee was James Russell Lowell, who was serving as ambassador to Spain—a political plum Howells had plucked for him through his influence with cousin Rutherford in the White House, thus paying back Lowell for his earlier help.

Howells, serving as master of ceremonies, introduced Mark Twain with his usual disclaimer: Here was "a humorist who never makes you blush to have enjoyed his joke; whose generous wit has no meanness in it, whose fun is never at the cost of anything honestly high or good";[32] but this time his assurances were in vain.

Twain held forth with one of his tall tales. While tramping through the California gold country, he alleged, he had stopped at a miner's lonely cabin. He introduced himself as Mark Twain to the morose-looking man who answered the door, expecting recognition of his literary celebrity. But his revelation seemed to depress the fellow even more. He complained that Clemens was the "fourth littery man" who had knocked on his door that day. The others were Longfellow, Emerson, and Oliver Wendell Holmes—"dad fetch the lot!"

The sagacious Emerson he described as "a seedy little bit of a chap—red-headed." The diminutive Dr. Holmes was "fat as a balloon" with "double chins all the way down to his stomach," and handsome, dignified Longfellow was "built like a prizefighter." All were drunk and yammering poetry. Twain wove quotes from famous poems by each of the scribes into his tale. When "Holmes" is admitted to the miner's dilapidated, grimy hovel, he comments: "Build thee more stately mansions, O my soul!"

Finally, Twain protests to the miner that these surely weren't the poets revered by all Americans. They must have been impostors. To which the miner replies with what Mark intended as his "snapper," or punch line: "Ah—impostors, were they? Are *you*?!"[33]

Usually the "snapper" saved him, bursting the uneasy tension he had built up with a string of irreverent jokes that skirted the insulting. But this time Twain felt his story had fallen as flat as a miner's skillet bread. He later recalled that his listeners' faces had "turned to a sort of black frost." He struggled on, hoping someone would laugh and break the ice, but the audience "seemed turned to stone with horror."[34] He sank into his chair, scarcely hearing the next two speakers.

Howells sat through the performance mortified, staring down at his plate rather than watch his friend's public meltdown. At one point he peeked at the objects of Mark's sallies. Longfellow seemed to be "regarding the humorist with an air of pensive puzzle," Holmes busily scrawled notes on his menu, and Emerson sat obliviously smiling.[35]

Such were Clemens's and Howells's recorded memories. Howells later described the occasion as "the amazing mistake, the bewildering blunder, the cruel catastrophe."[36] He surely agonized over the effect it would have on his own standing in Boston. But he was overreacting. Henry Nash Smith collected reviews of the speech in the press and found that all four Boston newspapers reported that it had drawn gales of laughter and that everyone, including the victims, appeared to be having a good time.

But that was little consolation to the perpetrator. "All *right*, you poor soul!"[37] Howells soothed his guilt-wallowing friend. But Clemens was unconsolable. "My sense of disgrace does not abate," he moaned to Howells. This was another in a long list of sins, "which keep on persecuting me regardless of my repentencies."[38]

Their mutual exaggeration of the impact of the speech was a sign of both men's insecurity. Clemens's chronic guilt complex was never more evident. He once told Annie Fields that his life was a continual apology. Howells, his friend, might have at least said that the speech was funny. By not doing so he tacitly confirmed Clemens's gaffe. Livy suggested that out of consideration for Mr. Howells's position, Clemens withdraw a story the *Atlantic* had accepted because his disgrace would hurt the magazine.[39]

But Howells assured his friend that he had no intention of banning him from the *Atlantic*. He suggested apologizing to the three ancients. Clemens had been thinking the same thing but feared he would embarrass Howells. He quickly penned a groveling letter, rife with phrases like "I am only heedlessly a savage, not premeditatedly."[40]

In the aftermath, the *Transcript,* the superego of Back Bay, decided, on second blush, that the speech had been "in bad taste and entirely out of place."[41] But the other papers remained unfluttered by Clemens's gaffe.

Indeed, it was the *out-of-town* press that was most outraged. Their reactions ranged from grumbling about Mark Twain's bad manners to a snide editorial in the Worcester *Gazette* that speculated that the "of-fence" could cost Mark Twain his place "among the contributors to the Atlantic Monthly, where indeed his appearance was in the beginning considered an innovation."[42] A journal in Cincinnati exposed its West-ern inferiority complex when it said the whole travesty illustrated the mistake of bringing eminent poets of a refined society into "intimate relations with whisky, cards, bowie-knives and larceny."[43] Other corre-spondents protested the lèse-majesté of mentioning these august au-thors in the same breath as Western mining camps. Clemens's speech, one journal said, was subversive of good morals and manners. If Amer-ica lost its reverence for its great poets, than it was reverting to savagery.

As for Clemens, the quintessential new Western writer, his pro-fessed reverence for the three luminaries may have been a bit hypocriti-cal. Subconsciously, his speech was an act of aggression against them; his devil made him do it. As Justin Kaplan writes, "It was possible for him to entertain a demon and not suspect it."[44] He had an untamed hostil-ity toward authority; subversive anger propelled his best humor, open-ing him to the morning-after guilt of transgression.

Yet the old prospector in his story had it right: *He* was the impostor—and his friend Howells as well.

For all the anguish it caused the two Westerners, the Whittier din-ner speech was quickly forgotten by its supposed victims. Holmes said he had not been irritated by the performance. Longfellow told Howells that as far as he was concerned the thing was "most pathetic."[45] As for Emerson, he smiled sweetly.

The canker of guilt, however, continued to gnaw at Clemens. Five years later he still felt like an "unforgiven criminal."[46] He periodically reread the speech until finally, in later years, guilt gave way to professional pride and he decided it was funny after all.

Howells continued to publish his friend as often as possible. Under Mark Twain's byline appeared such much-discussed stories as "A Literary Nightmare." In 1878, when Clemens and family were living in Europe, Howells begged him for some sharp satires on European culture in the spirit of *The Innocents Abroad.* Clemens replied he was too angry to write good satire. He hated everything about being a tourist in Europe—Culture, the Old Masters, the Grand Opera. He wanted to "stand up before it & *curse* it," rather than spoof it.[47]

Howells was never so hungry for material that he wouldn't reject something by Clemens he considered unworthy or that crossed the line into libel or bad taste. Once, returning an anecdote about real people that Clemens had been reluctant to sign, he reproved him: "This sketch, as it stands, is not good enough to go without your name, and your name is too good for it."[48]

Clemens turned the tables. In a letter he narrated in such exciting detail a real-life family misadventure that Howells begged him to turn it into a piece for the magazine. Clemens refused because he couldn't use the real names. "Delicacy," he sighed, "—a sad false delicacy—robs literature of the two best things among its belongings: family-circle narratives & obscene stories."[49]

Despite his sensitive deference and tact, Howells couldn't completely avoid being snared in a conflict between professional obligations and friendship. When Clemens first informed Howells that he was composing *The Adventures of Tom Sawyer,* Howells urged him to make it an *Atlantic* serial. When Clemens said he was unsure whether to carry forward Tom's life into young manhood, Howells replied: "I really feel very much interested in your making that your chief work; you won't have such another chance; don't waste it on a *boy*, and don't hurt the writing for the sake of making a book. Take your time and deliberately advertise it by Atlantic publication."[50]

Now Howells's advice was honest (though he hadn't seen the manuscript), but it was tailored more to his interest than to Clemens's, particularly the notion that he write up the thing as a serial rather than a novel and not make it a boy's book. And of course he must "advertise it" in the *Atlantic.*

In his genial way Clemens made mincemeat of that self-serving scenario, reminding Howells that he could earn more money selling it as a subscription book. And if he first serialized it in the magazine, the Canadian papers would pirate it before the book came out (because American authors had no foreign copyright protection). That had happened to "Old Times on the Mississippi."

At this point, as Henry Nash Smith points out, Clemens had been uncertain about whether he was writing a story for young people, or a novel *about* young people for adults. If the latter, he might have let Tom grow into manhood. But in the letter of July 5, 1875, in which he tells Howells he won't publish it in the *Atlantic,* he says decisively that he will not follow Tom into manhood. If he did, Tom would be just another fictional character, nothing special, "& the reader would conceive a hearty contempt for him." But he also insisted that this was a book adults would read. He asked Howells to scan the manuscript and decide if he was right. Howells called it the "best boy's story I ever read." He strongly advised Clemens not to serialize it.[51]

That letter confirmed Clemens's instinct. In September, he turned over the manuscript to Howells for editing, and the latter blue-penciled it with a juvenile audience in mind. Assured by Clemens that all the obscenities had already been "tamed," Howells questioned only a few things. For example, the reference to a dog that sat on a pinching bug in church and ran howling up the aisle, "with his tail shut down like a hasp." Howells thought the tail reference scatological; Clemens cut it without demur.

After Howells returned the edited script, Clemens, who hated editing his own stuff, wrote, "There [never] was a man in the world so grateful to another as I was to you day before yesterday, when I sat down . . . to the dreary & hateful task of making final revision of Tom Sawyer, & discovered, upon opening the package of MS that your pencil marks were scattered all along. This was splendid, & swept away all labor."[52] He gleefully announced that on a final read he had found an obscenity his scrupulous editors had missed! Huck complains that the servants "comb me all to hell."[53] Howells confessed he had missed it because "hell" was just what Huck would say, but agreed that it was over the line in a book for young people.

Howells served as Clemens's personal critic, his court of last resort (with Livy having the final veto). He advised on whether an idea was worth pursuing. For example, on January 18, 1886, Howells wrote him to praise his idea of a "Hartford man waking up in King Arthur's time." By then, Howells had left the *Atlantic,* and he regretted that he had no magazine "to prod you with, and keep you up to all those good literary intentions."[54]

A Connecticut Yankee in King Arthur's Court was never serialized in the *Atlantic* or anywhere else, but Howells did edit it. Moreover, Howells's earlier publication of "Old Times on the Mississippi" had led Clemens to expand the material into a classic work, *Life on the Mississippi.* And writing a history of steamboat life had turned his thoughts back to his Hannibal boyhood, unlocking a flood of memories which drove the writing of *The Adventures of Tom Sawyer.* Huck Finn appears as a character in that novel, and the author was so taken by him that he immediately started "Huck Finn's Autobiography." After writing fifteen chapters he became stuck and put it aside. He would not finish *Adventures of Huckleberry Finn* until 1885.[55]

Their interchange was a two-way street. Both these books inspired Howells to write his own boyhood memoir, *A Boy's Town.*

As for Clemens, he was deeply grateful for Howells's editing. He felt like a country lad who is taught the printing art by an experienced city job printer. He hated editing his own writings. "Nothing that has passed under your eye needs any revision before going into a volume, while all my other stuff does require so much."[56]

He did not perform similar services on Howells's many novels, however. He avidly read each one when it came out, often aloud to his family, and sent Howells extravagant praise. On Howells's *Indian Summer,* about an autumnal romance, he wrote: "a beautiful story, & makes a body laugh all the time, & cry inside." Howells was the only novelist he could read—George Eliot, Hawthorne, Henry James (to name his recent tries) had bored and exasperated him.[57]

Professional disagreements were extremely rare. They flared up only during the two men's occasional comical attempts at literary collaborations. Clemens was the chief instigator of these farragoes. Once, he proposed writing a skeleton plot on which a motley crew of authors— ranging from Henry James to Bret Harte—would each hang a chapter. This project never came off, but Clemens actually wrote his story (he called it "A Murder, a Mystery, and a Marriage").

Clemens was serious about collaborating on a play, however. He always needed money; his household expenses alone were horrendous. That made him an incorrigible prospector for the big Broadway strike. Compounding the potential for folly, his first foray into the theater, the 1875 dramatization of his satirical novel *The Gilded Age,* had been a great success, mainly because John T. Raymond, the actor who played the main character, the rapscallion Colonel Sellers, was popular with audiences. He had casually boasted to Howells about opening a letter containing a royalty check for $1,616.16 from the play's first week in Philadelphia.

Howells liked to live well, and there were times when he needed money too. And he did have experience writing for the stage—one-act Christmas masques. After seeing one of them, *A Counterfeit Presentment,* Clemens wrote his friend a congratulatory note and mentioned that he had found in his drawer an unproduced play about a detective. He proposed that Howells write a new version around Clemens's central character. That particular collaboration didn't pan out, but it set the pattern for future ventures. Clemens would create a central character and write comic dialogue; Howells would construct the play.

Next, Clemens badgered Howells to write a play based on the life of his hapless older brother Orion, involving a sad procession of lost jobs, bizarre religious conversions, and boneheaded business ventures. Clemens sounded the bugle call to action: "This immortal hopefulness, fortified by its immortal and unteachable stupidity is the immortal feature of this character, for a play; and we will write that play."[58] In 1879, Clemens stepped up the heat. Angry with Orion for cadging a loan, he exhorted Howells to put him into a novel or a play at once—he might die tomorrow and "your very greatest work would be lost to the world."[59] A few months later, he was back, imagining an Orion character on stage, as befuddled and foolish as the original, bursting with religious nonsense and crackpot schemes to change the world, "always inventing something & losing a limb by a new kind of explosion at the end of each act."[60] But the squeamish Howells recoiled from the violence of his friend's vision. He tactfully explained that he would handle Orion with "an alien hand and might inflict an incurable hurt to his tender heart."[61]

Eventually, the Orion character with his outlandish schemes and inventions mutated into the fictional Colonel Sellers, who had a proven popularity with the theater-going public. In 1886, Howells drafted a play with Sellers as the central character and Clemens filled in the dialogue. Because the hero was his invention, he requested a larger share of the potential royalties. Howells deferred to him, as he generally did when they had a potential clash of interests.

The work, a comedy in three acts, was titled *Colonel Sellers as Scientist*. It employed many special effects related to the title character's inventions, which had a tendency to self-destruct. The famed inventor Thomas A. Edison was engaged to supply gadgets for the play's "museum of inventions," including a phonograph that would "do its own talking & singing, & to the satisfaction of the audience too," Clemens, who loved gadgets, crowed.[62]

Just as he was putting the machinery in motion, however, the neurotic Howells got cold feet. He was seized by visions of failure with himself the laughingstock of Broadway. He panicked and sent off alarums to Clemens: The Sellers character was a lunatic! Three acts of him would drive the audience into the street! He pleaded for a chance to go over the script and tone down the madness. A day later, he telegraphed Clemens in New York: Withdraw the play immediately for more work.

But Clemens had negotiated contracts with a producer and with Daniel Frohman, the theater owner. He had already reserved the theater for two weeks. Now he had to tell them the play was off. Only a promise to pay Frohman a thousand-dollar penalty got the authors off the hook. Howells's relief was palpable. He wrote Clemens that he deserved equal blame for the folly and magnanimously offered to pay half the penalty.

Clemens retorted that he would not allow Howells to assume his "share" of the blame. Oh, no, he was going to lay "every ounce of it" on Howells. He adds a P.S.: Livy has just read his letter and ordered him not to send it because the harsh language "might make Mr. Howells feel bad." Said Clemens: "*Might* make him feel bad! Have I in sweat & travail wrought 12 carefully contrived pages to make him feel bad, & now there's a bloody *doubt* flung at it?"[63]

Howells sent back a meek mea culpa, adding that the nervous strain of the past week had almost killed him. He enclosed a check for $500 and begged Clemens not to tell Elinor about their escapade.

The 1880s were glory years for both men. Howells became such a prominent critic, writing the "Editor's Study" column for *Harper's Monthly,* that when he moved from Boston to New York in 1888 the press proclaimed that the nation's literary capital had moved with him; which it had, as most publishers were now in Manhattan.

In the latter part of a decade rocked by labor unrest, both men became sympathetic to radical ideas. Howells converted to Tolstoy's doctrines of nonviolence and complicity in the sufferings of the poor. Clemens seethed with hatred for hereditary monarchs and nobility, especially the British variety (an animus vented in *A Connecticut Yankee*). He praised the French Revolution as one of the noblest uprisings in the history of humankind.[64]

In 1886 Howells, the plump, dapper literary gentleman who confessed to Henry James, "I wear a fur-lined overcoat and live in all the luxury my money can buy," publicly supported eight alleged anarchists who had been randomly detained after a bomb was set off at a labor rally in Chicago.[65] Based on no evidence other than their unpopular political opinions, they were convicted of the murder of a policeman, and several were sentenced to be hanged. Howells was sickened by this lynch-law justice and in his finest hour raised a lonely protest; he wrote his father, "This free Republic has killed five men for their opinions."[66] Later, he told Henry James: "After fifty years of optimistic content with 'civilization' and its ability to come out all right in the end, I now abhor it, and feel that it is coming out all wrong in the end unless it bases itself anew on a real equality."[67] In this climate Howells wrote his strongest social novel, *A Hazard of New Fortunes,* which mobilized a diverse cast of New Yorkers to dramatize in fictional form the central problem of the age: the widening gulf between labor and capital.

Clemens agreed with his friend about labor but went on pouring money into various risky projects, notably the Paige typesetting machine, which he believed would make him a wealthy capitalist. Yet technology appalled even as it fascinated him; he wrote *A Connecticut Yankee* in part as a satire of the sinister side of technological "progress." In 1889, Clemens cajoled Howells to read proofs of the novel, saying Livy was incapacitated by pinkeye and feared he would leave in "coarsenesses which ought be rooted out & blasts of opinion which are so strongly worded as to repel instead of persuade."[68]

Friend Howells fell to and pronounced it "a mighty great book."[69] Seeing he felt that way, Clemens urged him to review it in "The Editor's Study." Howells called it a "delicious satire."[70] But the pessimistic view of the Gilded Age underlying the satire matched his own.

He warned his friend that religious folk might choke on his irreverent remarks about the Church of England. Not that Howells was offended; as an agnostic and Christian socialist he followed Jesus' social gospel, but he made no brief for the pomp and pageantry of organized religion. With Clemens he took care never to quarrel over the subject. The farthest he would go was equably to suggest that religion did much good whenever it followed Christ's original teachings.[71] Clemens replied that the next time they met he would explain why his yankee "could not honestly say any pleasant word for the church."[72]

Clemens told him his main regret was that he had left out of the novel his most incendiary indictments of society, but they would require "a pen warmed up in hell."[73] This book was intended to be his swan song to literature. He assumed that his Paige typesetter would make him a millionaire and free him from living by his pen.

Instead, the infernal machine became a money eater; Paige always needed just five or ten thousand dollars more to perfect it. By the time he finally had the sleek contraption up and running, his chief competitor, the Mergenthaler linotype, had been proved simpler to use and less prone to breakdowns. The cantankerous Paige continued to tinker with his invention and erected legal barriers that delayed its manufacture. All told, Clemens dropped nearly $200,000 (perhaps $4–8 million in current dollars) on this venture.

The great depression of 1893 was ravaging the country. The publishing company Clemens founded went bankrupt; he had skimmed the revenues from General Grant's hugely successful autobiography to pay for the typesetter. It was only with the legal help and financial advice of an admirer, the Standard Oil executive Henry H. Rogers, that he was able to avoid the disgrace of bankruptcy, the prospect of which had horrified Livy. Rogers told Clemens his greatest asset was his good name. Therefore, he should spurn the many offers of bailout money from various wealthy admirers and pay back every cent himself.

With Rogers shrewdly investing his money and organizing his accounts, Clemens and his family spent most of the nineties in Europe, where living was cheaper. He told Howells only that they were going for Livy's health, an unusual reticence in their long friendship. Howells knew about Clemens's financial troubles but avoided mentioning them in the letters he wrote during Clemens's expatriation. Clemens embarked on a round-the-world lecture tour to earn money, and in 1899 he bragged to Howells that the money was rolling in, including "a quite unexpected $10,000."[74]

But his financial setbacks had driven him to the brink of despair and caused the delicate Livy nervous strain that probably shortened her life. Adding to this anxiety, in 1896, their daughter Susy, whom he had adored with a love that bordered on the Oedipal, died of meningitis at their home in Hartford. He and Livy were in England when the news reached them. He told Howells, "It is one of the mysteries of our nature, that a man, all unprepared, can receive a thunder-struck like that and live."[75] He flagellated himself mercilessly with his failures as a father. After some months he was able to return to work on a new humorous travel book, confiding to Howells, "It puzzles me to know what is in me that writes and that has comedy fancies and finds pleasures in phrasing."[76]

When he heard about Susy's death, Howells wrote Clemens that he and Elinor suffered with the Clemenses. Seven years earlier, they had lost their older daughter, Winnie. Her death was doubly painful because the Howellses lacerated themselves for approving what had turned out to be the wrong treatment. In May 1889, Howells wrote Clemens that he had thrown himself on Winnie's grave "and experienced what anguish a man can live through."[77]

He recalled Clemens's kindness. "You came in one day when we were bleeding from the death of Winnie, and said to me, 'Oh did I *wake* you?' because I suppose my heavy heart had got into my eyes, and I looked sleep-broken. I have never forgotten just how you said it, and the tender intelligence you put into your words. . . ."

There was not much more he could say. He added some conventional assurances that the Clemenses would meet Susy again in a better place.[78] Clemens replied that of all their friends, only Howells and Elinor could appreciate the pain of his and Livy's grief. As for a heavenly reunion, oh yes, there would surely be one, he said bitterly, "if it can furnish opportunity to break our hearts again."[79]

Neither wife ever recovered from the death of her child. Livy had spells of poor health marked by asthma attacks and heart trouble. Elinor became deeply depressed, and experienced a complete nervous collapse in 1898, after a winter in Italy.

Howells wrote Clemens in Europe that after seeing a picture of Susy in *Harper's Monthly,* accompanied by an elegy by her father, he dreamed that he met his friend in Vienna, and "I put my arms round you." Then they cried like "two sad old children."[80] Clemens replied that if they met again, "I think we could cry down each other's necks, as in your dream. For we *are* a pair of old derelicts drifting around now, with some of our passengers gone & the sunniness of the others in eclipse."[81]

His venerable enemy the Almighty had prepared another shock for Clemens. From Florence, where they had traveled for Livy's health in the spring of 1904, he wrote Howells that he had gone to her room to say good night, only to discover that she was dead.

"I am tired & old," he said. "I wish I were with Livy." He sent his love—and Livy's—to Howells and Elinor.[82]

At the turn of the century, both men were living in New York City and they saw each other frequently. Howells told his sister Aurelia that he and Clemens "have high good times denouncing everything. We agree perfectly about the Boer war and the Filipine war, and war generally."[83] America's imperialistic adventures in Cuba and the Philippines incensed both of them. Mark Twain wrote a scorching satire of colonialism in his story "To the Person Sitting in Darkness."

That was published, but much of the black, bitter stuff that he wrote toward the end of his life was not—by his own choice. As he explained to Howells in 1899, now that he no longer had to write for money, he was working on "a book without reserves" in which he could speak his heart's bleak truth.[84]

This was probably *The Mysterious Stranger,* one of his most irreligious works, starring Satan and published posthumously. Howells understood his feelings, even if he disagreed with him on religion. The farthest he would go in arguing, however, was to advise Clemens to read Alfred Russell Wallace's *Man's Place in the Universe,* and then perhaps he "would not swear so much at your own species."[85]

Clemens was having none of that. In New York, he founded the Damned Human Race Club, which met regularly for lunch. The members were himself, Howells, the humorist Finley Peter Dunne (creator of Mr. Dooley), and George Harvey, the flamboyant head of Harper's, now also Clemens's publisher. Harvey would produce a grand literary banquet honoring Clemens's seventieth birthday. It drew New York's most glittering literary and cultural names. Howells served as toastmaster, as he had at the Whittier dinner, but this time Clemens delivered a graceful, elegiac speech.

Howells was stoically confronting the indignities of old age. He confessed to Clemens that he feared death but not getting old. Age would have many advantages "if old men were not so ridiculous and ugly." As for death, more and more he wondered how people could stand the idea. He had trouble believing he would someday die.[86] His father had thought it all through—the fear of death—and achieved a kind of resignation. He hoped he could do the same.

Clemens sent his friend some condolence letters that Howells had written him and Livy during the "black times." He couldn't bear to look at them, but Howells was stronger and might take comfort in experiencing his grief, for grief "is all we have left of them."[87]

All of Clemens's children had died young except Clara, who became an opera singer. He had been a doting, moody, tyrannical father to them. Once he wrote Howells in sheer horror that he had discovered his children were *afraid* of him! The revelation (typically exaggerated) plunged him into a new cycle of guilt and self-abasement.

For all his own neurotic tics, Howells was a more temperate parent. His son, John, would become an architect and build Clemens's last home, Stormfield, in Connecticut.

In January 1910, he and Howells had a final encounter in New York. They reminisced about Clemens's beloved butler George Griffin and discussed economic issues, agreeing that labor unions were the "sole present help of the weak against the strong." When Howells departed, he told Twain's biographer Albert Bigelow Paine, who had escorted him to the door, "There was never anybody like him; there never will be."[88]

Suffering cruelly from angina pains, Clemens sailed to Bermuda, where his health declined precipitously. In April he hurried home so that he might die at Stormfield.

Howells had always understood the eternal boy in Clemens. In a posthumous tribute, he recalled a time that he had visited him at Stormfield. Every morning Clemens would get out of bed early and pace the hall. When Howells looked out, "there he was in his long nightgown swaying up and down the corridor, and wagging his great white head like a boy that leaves his bed and comes out in the hope of a frolic with some one."[89]

Recalling that Livy's pet name for her husband was "Youth," he writes, "He was a youth to the end of his days. The heart of a boy with the head of a sage; the heart of a good boy, or a bad boy, but always a wilful boy, and the wilfulest to show himself out at every time for just the boy he was." He was, Howells said, "the Lincoln of our literature."[90]

Howells lived another ten years, dying at eighty-three. He had survived to become a living symbol of the Victorian values the writers of the 1920s were overturning. As he wrote to a friend: "I am comparatively a dead cult with my statues cut down and the grass grown over them in the pale moonlight."[91]

CHAPTER 4

THE MASTER AND THE MILLIONAIRESS

Henry James and Edith Wharton

*It was as if we always had been friends and were to go on being
(as he wrote to me in February 1910) "more and more never apart."*
—EDITH WHARTON [1]

THE FORMER Edith Jones was a very rich woman of impeccable
Old New York pedigree. Her family tree groaned with Rhine-
landers, Cadwaladers, Van Rensselaers, Schermerhorns, and Astors
(the reigning Mrs. Astor, queen of the "400," was her first cousin).

In 1885, a plain, shy twenty-four-year-old, she had married a Boston
gentleman, Edward Wharton, known as Teddy. Thirteen years older
than she, he was a comfortable bachelor who had been voted hand-
somest in his class at Harvard. His stint in Cambridge was otherwise
unremarkable. An amiable man, Teddy was chiefly interested in dogs,
hunting, fishing, golf, tennis, travel, and the pleasures of New York society with its perpetual round of calls, teas, dinners, opera boxes, and
cotillions. He had an allowance from his mother of two thousand dollars a year and no occupation beyond managing his wife's trust fund.

It was a considerable one. Even before she started producing best-
sellers and publishing a stream of magazine stories, she drew an annual

income from the trust fund variously estimated at from twenty to fifty thousand dollars (more than a million in today's dollars). This enabled her after her marriage to maintain a regal lifestyle—a Park Avenue home; a summer château, the Mount, near Lenox, Massachusetts, in the Berkshires; an apartment in the Faubourg St.-Germain in Paris—and still have ample income left over for travel and walking-around money for Teddy.

After her marriage, Edith soon rebelled against being a decorative young wife. She started writing poems again and placed three with *Scribner's Magazine,* which also began publishing her first short stories. Scribners, the publishing house, collected these in a book, *The Greater Inclination,* released in 1899 to excellent reviews.

Teddy thought "Puss" awfully clever to write poetry and stories, but he had scant interest in the literary matters that now consumed her. Going in to dinner, Teddy once commented to a friend: "Look at that waist! No one would ever guess she had written a line of poetry in her life."[2] Inviting the venerable scholar and Brahmin Charles Eliot Norton to visit their summer mansion in the Berkshires, he said: "I should like you to see 'the Mount,' to prove that Puss is good at other things besides her to me rather clever writing."[3] As a woman in society it behooved Edith to speak of her scribbling as a hobby, rather like embroidery. She wryly recalled her family's attitude toward writers: "Authorship was still regarded as something between a black art and a form of manual labor."[4]

Her parents seemed to consider the authors who wrote the novels they read as on a level with the tradesmen who brought coal and groceries to the servants' entrance. When her stories began appearing, family members did not mention them, as though to be published were slightly scandalous.

Reviewers assumed that writing about the wealthy made her trivial. To her editor at Scribners, William Crary Brownell, she protested:

"The assumption that the people I write about are not 'real' because they are not navvies & charwomen, makes me feel rather hopeless. I write about what I see, what I happen to be nearest to."[5] In the face of such attitudes, Wharton sought validation for her literary career from her peers. The writer whose name meant the most to her was Henry James, America's most honored novelist, if one whose recent work was largely unread by his compatriots. Early in her career she set her cap for him—literally her *hat* on one occasion. In the late 1880s, on two occasions, first in London and then Venice, she attended dinner parties at which James was regaled, and her only thought, she later confessed, was making herself pretty so he would notice her. First she tried a tea rose–pink gown, and the next time a flowery châpeau. But James was too enveloped in his own celebrity to notice the former Miss Jones.

Eventually Wharton swam into his lofty ken; after all, they moved in concentric social circles. Her sister-in-law Mary Cadwalader Jones (known as Minnie) was an old friend of his. He had also heard about her from another old friend, the French novelist Paul Bourget, who met her in Newport circa 1893 and vouched for her talent while noting her inordinate craving to meet titled foreigners.

In the rare moments when James thought of her at all, he considered her a promising writer who was reputed to be his disciple. He called her an "almost too susceptible *élève* [pupil]."[6] She was, after all, to the Jamesian manner (and subject matter) born. She moved in a similar upper-class milieu. James wrote about a rarefied international upper-class world of an earlier day, while she focused on her own sphere of parochial New York society.

In truth, Wharton admired only the novels of James's early and middle periods—*Daisy Miller* and *The Portrait of a Lady*. She found unreadable the recent convoluted, intellectual works like *The Sacred Fount* (1900), *The Wings of the Dove* (1902), *The Ambassadors* (1903), and *The Golden Bowl* (1904).

In this opinion she received enthusiastic backing from her editor, Brownell, a reclusive, scholarly man; he had written two studies of nineteenth-century American and English novelists. Though sympathetic to American writers, he was unsympathetic to the poorly selling late novels of Henry James. When the manuscript of *The Sacred Fount* reached his desk at Scribners, he commented that it was "like trying to make out page after page of illegible writing."[7] In a 1905 article for the *Atlantic Monthly* he attacked the Master's late novels as bloodless theoretical exercises.

Wharton told Brownell she shared his criticisms of James; they were doubly satisfying because of her growing resentment of the frequent comparisons of her work to his by reviewers, implying she had no separate identity as a writer.

"The author has been a faithful student of Henry James" was a typical polite putdown.[8] Wharton complained to Brownell about "the continued cry that I am an echo of Mr. James (whose books of the last ten years I can't read . . .)." Brownell sympathized: "Of course it is unpleasant not to have one's uniquity recognized, but sometimes you seem to have come out of the mix better than he does." As evidence he cited the reviewer who called her "a masculine Henry James."[9] Oddly, James had also noted "the masculine conclusion" in her writings, which tended "to crown the feminine observation."[10]

The reviewers exaggerated her debt to James, basing it superficially on the society milieu in which both their novels were set. She might have imitated him at first, but she was tougher-minded, more attuned to the contemporary world and social change; more interested in manners, morals, science; possessed of a more sensuous feminine perspective. He thought her promising, but was less interested in her work as literary art than in the woman he envisioned behind the prose. As he told a friend, what was best in her stories was "her amiable self" and what was "not best was quite another person."[11]

Having failed to attain a personal audience with James, Wharton pursued him by post. In October 1900, she mailed him a recently published short story that she hoped was up to his standards. He responded by praising the "ironic and satiric gifts" exhibited in her "admirable little tale." The subject (divorce), however, was really too big—was it not?—for a short story? And, really, the story was too "hard," too "derisive," but one forgives her because she was "so young, &, with it, so clever." Then he momentously advised her to stick to "the American life that surrounds you," and to "use to the full" her satiric gifts.[12] James told Minnie Jones that "the little lady . . . *must* be tethered on native pastures, even if it reduces her to a backyard in New York."[13]

Despite James's friendly invitation to visit him when next she was in London, Wharton rightly smelled a whiff of condescension. Her resentment flared up a few months later when she wrote a friend regarding *The Sacred Fount,* bemoaning the "ruins of such a talent."[14] She even attempted to purge her anger in a parody of James, but she lacked the skill or sympathy to bring it off.

In August, James instructed his publishers to send her his new novel, *The Wings of the Dove,* and wrote Wharton apologizing for its long-windedness and praying (condescendingly?) that she wouldn't find it "hopelessly heavy"—grandly unaware that she would find it precisely that, as she had the previous novels of his "late" period. Self-deprecation was one of his masks, as Wharton would discover. (She later spoke of his "pride that apes humility.")[15]

But out of pique she had ignored James's request that they exchange future work and had not sent him a copy of her new novel, *The Valley of Decision,* which appeared in early 1902. Or was she reluctant to have him read it after his exhortations to write about American life? Her first novel was, in fact, a two-volume historical chronicle set in eighteenth-century Italy.

James obtained a copy of *The Valley of Decision* on his own and sent her some tepidly polite words of praise. But he repeated more emphatically his advice to pursue "the *American Subject*"—"the immediate, the real, the ours, the yours, the novelist's that it waits for." Moreover, he introduced a personal note: She must not follow his unwise example of living abroad, which had left him abysmally out of touch with vital developments in American upper-class society. He was planning an extended American lecture tour to brush up on his homeland. He closed with the ringing exhortation: "DO NEW YORK!"[16]

She forwarded his missive to her editor, Brownell, explaining with a disingenuous casualness, "I never send Mr. James my books and should not have expected him to be in the least interested in 'The Valley.' " Brownell said James's letter was nice but added in his possessive way that she was going to "do" New York anyway so her close admirers, such as himself, "had no need to speculate about her plans."[17]

Brownell was referring to an embryonic Wharton New York novel called "Disintegration," which she soon abandoned. She was also considering another European historical novel, but she dropped that project too. Instead, she heeded the advice of Henry James. It was, writes her Pulitzer Prize–winning biographer, R.W.B. Lewis, "the most important and the wisest literary advice Edith Wharton ever received, and it could not have come at a better moment." She had reached a crucial fork in her development as a novelist: Should she go ahead with another European historical novel or should she write of the New York world she knew?

James's letter gave her a firm push on the road that led to *The House of Mirth,* which she began in September 1903, put off for a year on account of Teddy's illness, and completed by November 1904. This tale of the crushing of Lilly Bart by a callous high society was located in the world she and James knew well, but the style and substance were, as Millicent Bell writes, "deliberately and aggressively un-Jamesian."[18] Instead, it was written in a more modern style, closer to Dreiserian natu-

ralism, which was appropriate to a novel showing the implacable weight
of the social order crushing the individual. When it appeared in October 1905, the reviewers recognized the novel as Wharton's declaration
of independence. Commented one: "The marks of her former master's
influence have wholly disappeared. . . ."[19]

The first meeting between James and Wharton took place in late
1903, not long after that auspicious novel had been started. While she
and Teddy were in London, he called at her hotel just before Christmas.
On first impression she thought he looked like "a blend of Coquelin
and Lord Rosebery"; the comparisons to the French actor and the
British politician accurately reflected both his theatrical manner and
commanding appearance. Now almost bald, he had shaved his beard,
revealing a "noble roman mask" and a "big dramatic mouth."[20] She was
relieved to find that he talked "more lucidly than he writes."[21]

To a friend he confessed she seemed a bit *"sèche"*—dry, hard. Perhaps
he judged her to be a bluestocking, which for a man of his generation
meant too intellectual and masculine. But he spoke more positively to
Minnie Jones. He said he found Edith "sympathetic in every way."[22]
They had so much to talk about—art, ideas, mutual acquaintances. The
differences were obvious—gender, age (she was forty, he was sixty),
experience—but they shared a wickedly ironic sense of humor, a passion for literature, and a professional interest in the theory and practice
of novel writing.

Edith was just now witnessing the first stages of her husband's psychological deterioration. In April 1903 they had toured Italy, Edith researching a book on gardens, Teddy trotting after her "like an equerry."
Upon returning home he exhibited appalling symptoms of mental
breakdown, for which the doctors could find no physical cause. In
today's terms, he exhibited the mood swings of bipolar disorder. Living

with a brilliant, intellectually forceful woman who was becoming a famous novelist may have exacerbated latent emotional conflicts; he may
have feared she would abandon him in pursuit of her career. He was already dependent on her financially, but now he faced the prospect of
tagging behind a formidable New Woman with a growing circle of her
own friends, nearly all of them articulate male intellectuals. Most
prominent of these was Walter Van Rensselaer Berry, an international
lawyer and cultivated dilettante whom she had known since 1884 and
whom, some said, she had wanted to marry. Berry remained her closest
male friend, perhaps her lover (see below), certainly for a time her literary adviser, for she ran by him most of her manuscripts. He was also
at her side during various crises in her marriage, a trusted old friend.

Since 1898 James had lived in the English Sussex village of Rye near
the smell of the sea. His domicile, Lamb House, was a charming square
Georgian brick house with Palladian windows looking out on a spacious
garden. There was a separate garden house, which he used as a study
and for dictating to his secretary, Miss Bosanquet (tendinitis had crip-
pled his writing hand). A staff of two or three servants attended to his
needs. He entertained rarely and then only one or two guests. He had
moved to a village far from London to find the solitude he needed to
pursue his sacred vocation. He had written, he believed, his finest novels at Lamb House.

In May 1904 "the Edith Whartons" (whom he also called "the Ted-
dies" and "the rich, rushing, ravishing Whartons") descended on Lamb
House for their first stay.[23] He and Edith talked deep into the night; it
was the beginning of a continuing dialogue. Where, one wonders, was
Teddy during these intellectual conversations? Asleep? It was said he
got on James's nerves. Teddy was a sociable fellow who loved a funny
story, but what could they possibly have had to talk about? One imag-

ines James's strained attentiveness as Teddy chattered about hunting, fishing, golf, tennis, and the society pages. Teddy tried to be sociable; he read *The Golden Bowl*. He thought it clever but rather too long.

Edith would later remark on the "anxious frugality" of James's table, where one might find the remains of last night's meat pie for lunch. He did indeed worry constantly that Edith was suffering from the drabness of his board. In her memoir *A Backward Glance* she writes: "I have often since wondered if he did not find our visits more of a burden than a pleasure, and if the hospitality he so conscientiously offered and we so carelessly enjoyed did not give him more sleepless nights than happy days." He lived, she said, "in terror of being thought rich, worldly, or luxurious, and was forever . . . apologizing for his poor food while he trembled lest it should be thought too good."[24]

Although he was the third-generation heir of a once sizable fortune, James had the exaggerated fear of imminent poverty common among writers, who face the uncertainties of the marketplace. This and his monkish devotion to his art may explain his frugality. Actually, he was not ascetic; he enjoyed the pleasures of the table, as his obesity showed, and the company of friends. His literary work in the early 1900s provided at best a modest return, but combined with his independent income he had a comfortable eight to ten thousand dollars a year. What was galling was not lack of money but the dwindling sales of his later novels in America.

He relished Wharton's visits more than she knew. One of her most lasting memories was of Henry James beaming at his front door, welcoming her with two hearty busses. He had never known a woman quite like her; she was, well, *formidable*. He was the biographer of heroines who stride into traps fashioned by society, but it would take him years to see that Edith Wharton was in some ways like his Isabel Archer or Milly Theale.

· · ·

It was during their first encounter that the Whartons were instrumental in introducing a new dynamic force into James's sedentary life—the motorcar. Teddy had purchased a secondhand French-made Panhard-Levassor in London, and, anticipating his maiden ride, James met them in Folkestone. His first automotive vision was of a huge shiny phaeton with a goggled Teddy sitting high in the open front seat beside the goggled chauffeur. Edith was in the back, swathed in a heavy veil and voluminous duster. The car broke down almost immediately and their first excursion to Rye had to be postponed. Later they had three rainy days of driving.

Edith quickly embraced the new mode of transportation. In her 1908 book *A Motor-Flight Through France,* she celebrated the liberation the motorcar provided—at least for the few in pre–Model T days who could afford them: "Freeing us from all the compulsions and contacts of the railway, it has given us back the wonder, the adventure, and the novelty which enlivened the way of our posting grandparents."[25]

James loved the way the auto enabled the traveler to haul in "a huge netful of impressions."[26] He saw it as a means of expanding his literary horizons. When Edith stayed at Lamb House, they customarily spent the mornings at their desks, then after lunch he would propose an excursion through rural Sussex. On these drives, she recalled, "James was as jubilant as a child. Everything pleased him—the easy locomotion (which often cradled him into a brief nap), the bosky softness of the landscape, the discovery of towns and villages hitherto beyond his range, the magic of ancient names, quaint or impressive, crabbed or melodious."[27]

Her indispensable chauffeur, Charles Cook, performed navigational miracles in those days before highways, road signs, or reliable maps. But James insisted on giving directions to places he was familiar with—usually succeeding only in getting them more deeply lost. Once, in Cook's absence, he attempted to direct a temporary chauffeur to Queen's Acre, the home in Windsor of his friend Howard Sturgis. As he continued to send the driver this way and that, Edith suggested he seek directions, becoming perhaps the first woman in that dawning auto age to tell a man to *ask,* for heaven's sake. James accosted an ancient standing on the roadside and launched into a monologue. As Wharton recalls it in *A Backward Glance:*

> "My good man, if you'll be good enough to come here, please, a little nearer—so. My friend, to put it to you in two words, this lady and I have just arrived here from *Slough;* that is to say, to be more strictly accurate, we have recently *passed through* Slough on our way here, having actually motored to Windsor from Rye, which was our point of departure. . . ."

At this point Wharton cut in: "Oh, please, do ask him where the King's Road is."

"Ah—? The King's Road? Just so! Quite right! Can you, as a matter of fact, my good man, tell us where, in relation to our present position, the King's Road exactly *is?*"

"Ye're in it," replied the ancient.[28]

Some of their most splendid journeys were in France between 1907 and 1909. But the drives they took in the States were also memorable to James—indeed, therapeutic. On his rare American visits he always stayed for a time at the Mount, the château in the Berkshires that Edith had planned and furnished to her elegant tastes. In summer she and her circle of friends, mostly men, settled on the broad terrace looking out on a garden and vast sloping lawn and talked into the fragrant night. On one memorable occasion James read aloud from Walt Whitman's *Leaves of Grass* in his "rich organ tones." Edith had been greatly moved: Whitman was her favorite American poet, as he was James's. He loved driving in Berkshire autumns through hills painted in brilliant reds and golds. Summers, however, could be problematic because of his obesity, which caused him to wilt quickly under the heat. The best relief Edith could provide was to take him on long drives that exposed him to a breeze. One summer he became so uncomfortable that she suggested he sail to England on an earlier ship, leaving Boston in two days. James was appalled at such a sudden and drastic change of plans. What of one's luggage at brother William's in Cambridge? Or one's clothes just sent to the laundry? She depicted him from memory:

> He cowered there, a mountain of misery, repeating in a sort of low despairing chant: "Good god, what a woman—what a woman! Her imagination boggles at nothing. She does not even scruple to project me in a naked flight across the Atlantic. . . ." [29]

Although she loved the Mount, the surrounding countryside was a cultural desert to Edith. A hotel in the Berkshires appalled her:

> Such dreariness, such whining, callow women, such utter absence of amenities, such crass food, crass manners, crass landscape! And mind you, it is a new and fashionable hotel. What a horror it is for a whole nation to be developing without a sense of beauty and eating bananas for breakfast.[30]

This diatribe summed up her view of America. She craved a more civilized existence on the Continent. In England she had discovered that women writers were respected by their families, in contrast to America. The same held true in France. In 1906 the Whartons rented an apartment in Paris in the Rue de Varennes, on the Left Bank, returning to America for summers at the Mount. The city offered her an aristocratic society open to writers and artists—and wealthy American women with connections. Her friend Paul Bourget was a prominent figure in Parisian salons, where the reclusive Marcel Proust appeared like some nocturnal creature and where her *House of Mirth* provided the necessary credentials.

Once settled, she bombarded James with invitations to stay with her. He capitulated in March 1907, confiding his trepidation to friends. As usual difficult to pry loose from his comfortable hermitage, he ritually moaned that she would likely drag him away on a motor tour and introduce him to haughty French duchesses. Actually, he was eager to go. He had finished the grueling work on volumes five and six of the New York Edition—his collected works, rewritten with new prefaces— and a book about his 1904–05 visit to the States, *The American Scene*. He deserved a Paris holiday.

Edith and Teddy had planned for him a three-week auto journey through Bordeaux, Burgundy, Provence, the Pyrenees, and more. Of course, with the rich Whartons it was first class all the way. Their servants preceded the automobilists by train to the night's destination and made ready their rooms in a luxury hotel. James's pride made him insist on paying his own way, but it was a strain. It is "one's rich friends who cost one!" he grumbled.[31] It was well worth it: The "magic monster, the touring Panhard" swept him through incomparable scenery—"a wondrous miraculous motor-tour."[32]

Back in Paris, he lodged with the Whartons "in gilded captivity" for two more months. When it was time to leave, he worried about the expense of tipping seven servants, but during his three-month stay he and Edith had drawn closer. She now saw him as "unfailingly delightful, wise and kind." The more she knew James, she wrote to Charles Norton, the more she admired "the mixture of wisdom and tolerance, of sensitiveness and sympathy, that makes his heart even more interesting to contemplate than his mind." James, who had regarded her with mixed envy and condescension as a female author of best-sellers, now saw her as "sympathetic, admirable, amazingly intelligent."[33]

An odd quirk of their friendship was their shared fascination with the hectic love life of the novelist George Sand. They avidly exchanged books and articles on her. When Wharton earlier visited Sand's home in Nohant, James was beside himself with envy. He demanded, "Do take me!" the next time, "if you have the proper vehicle of Passion," meaning motorcar.[34] And so Sand's home in Nohant became an essential stop on his itinerary.

Their interest in Sand's sex life added an erotic frisson to their relationship. Perhaps this had something to do with the lack of sex in their own lives. James had his young male protégés; he fed vicariously on their youth like an old vampire, but worried that he was becoming fat and unattractive. As for Wharton, she was imprisoned in a loveless marriage. She had never known *la grande passion*—or many of them, as had George Sand!

As they strolled through the echoing rooms, James communed with the ghosts of de Maupassant, Flaubert, Dumas *fils*, and other literary men who had trod these floors. He remembered meeting several of them when he first came to Paris thirty years earlier and listening to their reminisces about George. Outside again, they gazed at the windows of the "plain old house," wondering which famous visitor had slept in which room:

> "And in which of those rooms, I wonder, did George herself sleep?" I heard him suddenly mutter. "Though in which, indeed—" with a twinkle—"in which indeed, my dear, did she not?"[35]

Wharton assessed the place in a more womanly way than James did. She was moved by the contrast between the conventional plainness of the old house and the passionate rebellion of the woman living in it, by the transformation of the timid, abused wife Aurore Dudevant into the famed novelist George Sand with her grand amours.[36]

With all the risqué talk, Edith's auto became a sex symbol for James. He dubbed it "the vehicle of passion" and then "Pagellino" after Dr.

Pagello, another of Sand's lovers. Still later it was "Hortense," after Hortense Allart, another French novelist with whom Edith had become fascinated and who had led an even more openly promiscuous life than Sand.

The car was also a symbol for James of power, potency, and youth. Riding in it, he was "fleeing before fate," outrunning illness, old age, and death.[37] The Panhard also symbolized Edith's power to carry him away from his sheltered hearth. He coined predatory names for Wharton. She was, variously, a bird of prey, an Angel of Devastation, the great bird, the golden Eagle, the Fire Bird, the Bird o' Freedom, the eagle, aquiline. He portrayed himself as a worm or as a poor domestic fowl caught in her prehensile claws.

This image was somehow related to his attitude toward her great wealth, which both fascinated and troubled him. It was a natural force for turmoil in his life; she hit him like a cyclone, uprooting his fixed world. He saw all wealth as somehow corrupting and fretted about the evil effect of her money on her and on her writing. It insulated her, he feared, from the real world. It lent her life "incoherence," made it a nightmare of "perpetually renewable choice and decision" by confronting her with "a luxury of bloated alternatives. . . ."[38]

Leon Edel writes that in her formidable presence James "withered and passively surrendered. He took on a helpless air . . . he who otherwise exuded power."[39] She held the upper hand with her comparative youth, vibrant energy, and money. In his cries of alarm one senses a panicky rejection of her threatening female sexuality, a repressed panic that had made him throughout his life flee women friends who desired intimacy. Edith (in his imagination) he both fled and embraced.

For she also played a more benign, almost maternal role, cosseting him, spoiling him like a favorite uncle, bestowing fairy-wand miracles of pleasure. Reflecting his gratitude for her kindnesses, he called her "the Lady of Lenox" and "the Angel of Paris." And in truth, like the motor trips, her visits gave him great pleasure. He urged her to come even as he was moaning about her imminent arrival to Sturgis or another friend.

Perhaps her strongly affectionate, daughterly ways stirred dormant heterosexual yearnings. She was "Dearest Edith"; she unlocked a tender part of him that is in every man, that responds to woman as mother, sister, daughter, even lover, though there was no possibility of erotic consummation. That side of their relationship was sublimated into their fascination with sexual gossip.

To Edith, he was redundantly "Dearest Cher Maître," the sympathetic, wise friend and confidant. As a motoring companion he was constantly pleasing and saved her from being alone with Teddy. Her motorcar junkets had a darker motivation, James sensed; they were, as Millicent Bell writes, "animated by the frantic energy of escape" from her unhappy marriage.[40] After all, her auto tourism book was called a "motor-*flight*" through France.

As for Teddy, in his automotive attitudes he resembled the American males who transfer sex and aggression into a potency symbol on wheels. These traits surfaced when his mental illness became worse. James left a firsthand description of the onset of one of his manic states: "Every sound of him is the maddest possible swagger and brag about his exploits and conquests, the first with his prodigious and unique American motor car—100 miles an hour—in which it is quite open to him to kill himself; the second by his effect on the ladies especially of the variety theatres. . . .")[41]

In 1907 their friendship shifted into a faster lane when the twosome became a threesome—an erotic triangle.

Morton Fullerton was an American who headed the Paris bureau of the *Times* of London. Raised in Waltham, Massachusetts, the son of a clergyman, he graduated from Harvard magna cum laude and swept the literary prizes as well. After working for newspapers in the States he moved to London and joined the *Times* in 1890. He was slender, dapper, handsome with a full mustache, ornate of speech, fluent in French— and a brilliant journalist who possessed high literary talents in James's view.

Perhaps Fullerton's insatiable libido had something to do with his failure to live up to that promise. Living abroad, the clergyman's son transformed himself into a figure resembling the priapic hero of *My Secret Life*.

He and James met in London in 1890, and they frequently dined at James's club and discussed literature. Fullerton became part of Oscar Wilde's London circle, of which James disapproved, and was the lover of the sculptor Ronald Sutherland (Lord Gower).

James introduced him to the wealthy Margaret Brooke, the Ranee of Sarawak. Fullerton, who was bisexual, quickly charmed and seduced the Ranee, who was fifteen years older. She was the separated wife of Sir Charles Brooke, the white rajah of a small independent state in northwest Borneo. Unable (or unwilling) to consummate a physical relationship with Fullerton, James may have sought vicarious fulfillment through Fullerton's women. As biographer Fred Kaplan speculates, James "showed some taste for playing the role of facilitator-voyeur as a way of furthering his own intimacy with his young friend."[42]

When Fullerton moved to Paris to be the *Times*'s bureau chief, James wrote him passionate letters. The language he used when the Channel separated them suggests the depth of his feeling: "I want in fact more of you. You are dazzling . . . you are beautiful; you are more than tactful, you are tenderly magically *tactile*. But you're not kind. There it is. You *are* not kind."[43] In December 1905, he writes, "I can't keep my hands off you."[44]

In Paris, Fullerton, now exclusively heterosexual, pursued serial affairs, even after his marriage to a beautiful young chanteuse who bore him a child and divorced him after a year because of his infidelities. He became romantically embroiled with another, older woman, who was fiercely possessive. After he left her she threw hysterical fits and threatened to broadcast to the world the contents of letters she had discovered in his desk that described his bisexual affairs.

Fullerton feared she would soil him with scandal unless he mollified her. He wrote to James asking for advice, confessing his past affairs with both sexes. James evinced some jealousy over Fullerton's forays among the Wilde set, hinting he might have himself been interested in such diversions. At any rate he told Morton the woman's threats were mere bluster and suggested he buy her off.

In 1907 Fullerton returned to the United States to visit his parents and to come to an understanding with his adopted sister, who had fallen in love with him. He then proceeded to the Mount to stay with the Whartons, to whom James had introduced him in Paris. Edith's first impression had been "he is very intelligent, but slightly mysterious, I think."[45] At the Mount, however he made himself less mysterious, and she started keeping a private journal expressing her warming feelings toward him.

Before Fullerton left for the States, James had begged him to stop off for a few days at Lamb House. "My difficulty," he said, "is that I love you too fantastically much."[46] But Fullerton once more evaded him.

After both Edith and Fullerton had returned to Paris, Fullerton appeared at the Wharton apartment with increasing frequency. He and Edith held soulful conversations about books and poetry. In March, Teddy sailed for America to take the waters at Hot Springs, Arkansas, which the doctors hoped would cure his mental instability. To Edith this was a relief: The time spent caring for him had kept her from working on her new novel, *The Custom of the Country*—and from Fullerton.

The lovers strolled on the Bois de Boulogne in the blooming

Parisian spring, attended gallery openings, and dined *à deux* at her apartment. They made a pilgrimage to Hortense Allart's home, and she later praised Allart as "a George Sand without hypocrisy." She admired "her frankness, her absence of 'the man tempted me' element, her fearless way of looking life in the eyes."[47] In short, a free woman, independent in her sexuality, unchained by Sand's domesticity.

Edith was deeply in love. Fullerton pressed her for physical surrender; she was torn, wanting only a spiritual union of two kindred souls. But she also felt overwhelming stirrings of physical desire and worried that her capacity for lovemaking had withered from desuetude.

As it turned out, she could not have chosen a more practiced and considerate lover. The violent storm of passion he unleashed must have been a gratifying reward to him, a connoisseur of femininity. Years later, he admonished a biographer not to portray Wharton as sexless; she was, he said, like George Sand in strength of passion and adventurousness in the act of love.[48]

Henry James visited Edith in Paris during the early stages of the affair in April. The three took several motor trips. At first Fullerton bridled at James's coming; he was pressing his seduction at that point and felt the older man would be in the way. But Edith persuaded him to reconsider. She explained to Fullerton that she was in constant fear of not pleasing him, and having James along eased some of the pressure—just as, though in a different way, his presence had made easier the motor junkets with Teddy.

Two old friends of James's also happened to be in Paris—Henry Adams and William Dean Howells—and he had warm reunions. The days with Edith passed "in golden chains, in gorgeous bondage, in breathless attendance and beautiful *asservissement* [enslavement]."[49]

James departed on May 9; Edith sailed for America two weeks later. Fullerton saw her off on the train to Le Havre, and they had a passionate interlude in her compartment. She gave him her journal chronicling their affair. "I have drunk of the wine at last," the latest entry said. "I have known the thing best worth knowing, I have been warmed through and through, never to grow quite cold again till the end. . . ."⁵⁰

As she told Sara Norton, who was worrying that she had not sufficiently devoted herself to her father in his final illness, "Alas, I should like to get up on the housetops and cry to all who come after us: 'Take your own life, every one of you.' "⁵¹ She meant *live* your own life—don't immolate yourself for others, as she had in her marriage. It was a variation of Lambert Strether's cri de coeur in James's *The Ambassadors*: "Live all you can. . . ."

At the Mount, Teddy awaited her. One evening she showed him an "amusing passage" in an article by the philosopher John Locke. He glanced at it and asked: "Does that sort of thing really amuse you?" That night she wrote in her diary: "I heard the key turn in the prison lock."⁵²

Teddy's abuse of Edith became more flagrant that fall. In early October, just before she sailed for Europe with Walter Berry, she wrote James a despairing letter about her marriage and her seemingly hopeless love for Fullerton. She asked if she could visit him in England.

James replied that he was "deeply distressed at the situation you describe & as to which my power to suggest or enlighten now miserably fails me." "Don't *conclude*!" he counseled, meaning don't take any irreversible steps. "Some light will *still* absolutely come to you—I believe—though I can't pretend to say what it conceivably may be. . . . Only sit tight yourself & *go through the movements of life*. That keeps our connection with life—I mean the immediate & apparent life behind which, all the while, the deeper & darker & unapparent, in which things *really* happen to us, learns, under that hygiene, to stay in its place. . . . Live it all through, every inch of it—out of it something valuable will come—but live it ever so quietly . . . waitingly!"⁵³ Work, the daily routine, the *mechanics* of life, kept the demonic unconscious forces at bay.

Rather than proceeding to Rye, Edith left Berry in London and rushed to Paris for a reunion with Fullerton. Then she swept back to England and James. Watching her frenetic goings and comings, an anxious James wrote his friend Sturgis: "*What* an incoherent life! It makes me crouch more dodderingly than ever over my hearthstone."[54]

Edith spent the rest of the year caroming from one country estate to another, for James had transplanted her well into his world. He wrote Berry, now in Cairo serving on the World Court, "She has been having, indeed, after a wild, extravagant, desperate, detached fashion the Time of her Life." He thought the visit had been good for her troubled spirit, but "what a way of arranging one's life."[55]

Back in Paris she found Teddy in a terrible state. He could not adjust to the brilliant salon she had assembled. He had earlier told James, "Puss wants to come over, but I feel much too well to want to stand her crowd."[56] "Poor dear Teddy, poor dear Teddy," James sighed, "so little made . . . for such assaults & such struggles!"[57] Teddy departed again in April for the States, leaving Edith to write passionate poems to Fullerton. They were able to talk openly about their relationship, clearing the air.

In June of that year Edith and Fullerton came to England; he was sailing to America and Wharton came along to say goodbye. They had a rendezvous with James at the Charing Cross Hotel in London, near Waterloo station, where Fullerton would catch a train the next day. The three friends had a festive farewell dinner with much champagne and talk before the lovers returned to their suite for a passionate night.

What a welter of emotions must have stirred in James as he watched the man and the woman he cared for as deeply as any two people on earth ascend to their tryst. Biographer Fred Kaplan speculates: "As James left, he knew that he had come as close as he ever would to holding Fullerton in his own arms."[58] Or Edith.

. . .

Fullerton's former mistress had erupted again and he was worried about her, so after he had sailed, Edith and James held a consultation about his future. They plotted ways to free him from the woman, who was an impediment to his devoting himself to Edith and to his literary destiny. They decided she must be paid off, but Fullerton hadn't the means to do it. Edith could easily afford to give him the money, but he would never accept it from her.

They hatched an elaborate scheme, appropriate to two writers: Fullerton would be offered a contract to write a book about Paris by their mutual British publisher, Macmillan, which was issuing a Great Cities series. (James had signed to do one about London for the same firm.) In addition to paying Fullerton the usual advance, James would ask Macmillan to provide an additional £100 for expenses. He would reimburse the firm, he said, but Fullerton must not know this. Actually, Wharton supplied the £100; James, it might be said, laundered it.

R.W.B. Lewis reminds us of the similarities between the friends' machinations and the situation in James's 1902 novel *The Wings of the Dove,* in which a journalist named Morton Densher (read Morton Fullerton) is offered a large sum of money by a wealthy American woman by whose love he has been "blest and redeemed."[59] This was one of James's novels Edith had been unable read. Now he had prophesied her life.

It should be noted that this was not the only time that art and life tangled in this friendship. It's true that James never had an opportunity to put Wharton in a novel, but he did cast her in a short story called "The Velvet Glove." The plot concerns a playwright-novelist who en-counters a wealthy, glamorous princess, who is a novelist under a nom de plume. She asks him to write a logrolling introduction to her latest effort. The writer finally refuses, telling the woman she should stick to being a princess and let ordinary folk like him do the mundane work of writing novels.

The seed of the story was a proposal James received from an obscure socialist magazine to submit an essay on Wharton. The editor claimed—falsely, it turned out—that she had requested that he do so to promote the publication of her 1907 novel *The Fruit of the Tree,* in which she handled (fumbled) a host of social issues she knew little about, such as euthanasia and industrial reform. James toyed with the idea of writing the article as a kind of recompense for her social kindnesses to him. But after reading *The Fruit of the Tree* and disliking it, he dropped the idea. In fact, far from begging James to write about her, Wharton had expressed alarm about the prospect, fearing he would make mincemeat of her. (Oddly, in her memoir *A Backward Glance,* she gives a false version of the origin of the story, claiming another lady author had propositioned him.)

James's story emerged as an elaborate secret joke on Edith Wharton. Edel shows how his description of the princess's novel subtly mocked *The Fruit of the Tree.* He also drew certain of the princess's character traits from Wharton; for example, her plain nom de plume, Amy Evans, resembles "Edith Jones"; the title of her novel is *The Top of the Tree;* and the heroine takes the novelist for a chauffeur-driven motor trip around Paris at night.

The story was rejected by American magazines but eventually published in England. James deflected his disappointment to Edith, telling her that *she* was the rejected one since the heroine simply *reeked* of her. Whether or not she appreciated the inside jokes is unknown. She told a friend it was "a delightful little story—a motor story!" and congratulated James on it in similar terms.[60] Acutely in need of praise, he replied gratefully: "Your exquisite hand of reassurance & comfort . . . makes me *de nouveau* believe a little in myself."[61]

What James hadn't realized was that *she* had schemed to perform for *him* the service the princess asks of the novelist-playwright. In early 1908, at the time Scribners was bringing out the New York Edition, she had offered to *Scribner's Magazine* a critical article praising James that was written by none other than Morton Fullerton. Charles Scribner was dubious, telling her that the New York Edition was selling poorly because the book-buying public was "frightened by the false impression that the older novels have been rewritten in the later style" that had made James's name poison with the public.[62]

Since Fullerton defended the later style, Wharton, eager to give James's morale a boost, again urged Scribner to publish the essay, confessing that she had "had a hand—or at least a small finger" in it.[63] Scribner would not be enticed by her involvement, however. The article eventually appeared in the April 1910 issue of the *London Quarterly Review*. This version explicated James's literary theories as expressed in his talks with Fullerton and Wharton. It was the first comprehensive summing up of James's career.

By the time the article came out, the affair between Wharton and Fullerton had cooled. He may have come to regard her as just another of his conquests. For Edith, the awakening she had experienced left a sensual afterglow that infused her fiction. As Lewis comments, her love for Fullerton had not only fulfilled her as a woman; it had made her a more deeply human artist. This awakening is evident in the passion of the young lovers in *Summer*; in the morally complicated trio in *The Reef*; and in the tragedy of the thwarted lovers in *Ethan Frome*.

In her story "The Letters," she combined herself and another woman in Fullerton's life and cast Morton as a philandering painter. In the end the heroine decides she loves him despite his infidelities. In a psychological horror tale, "The Eyes," however, the Fullerton stand-in is condemned by his disembodied conscience.

The affair also opened her to future amorous adventures; she had romances with at least two younger men—to both of whom James introduced her. He followed the progress of both liaisons with vicarious avidity. As the scholar Lyman H. Powers observes, such participation "clearly gave James a good deal of stimulation and gratification; it 'completed' the special relationship he enjoyed with Edith Wharton."[64]

Early in 1909, James was felled by heart trouble and jaundice. He told Edith he had undergone "a bad & worried & depressed & inconvenient winter" and felt the "brush of the dark wing."[65] In June she and Morton swooped down on Rye and whisked him away for three days of motoring. Her visit provoked the usual anxiety attack in James, and after she left, he wrote a friend: "The Angel of Devastation has become a mere agitating memory, but nothing could have exceeded the commotion and exhaustion produced by her prolonged stay."[66]

Meanwhile, Teddy had been making a new life for himself—with a vengeance. In December he delivered a shattering confession: The previous summer he had embezzled fifty thousand dollars from her trust fund and used the money to purchase downtown property and buildings in Boston, including an apartment house where he had lived with another woman.

This bizarre conduct may have been revenge for Edith's affair with Fullerton, but it devastated and infuriated her. She confided immediately in James, who quivered that her "beautiful and sad letter" had knocked the breath out of him. He applauded her "gallantry & serenity and lucidity" and was touched that she admitted him into the circle of friends, including her brother and Walter Berry, who were helping her pick through the financial rubble of Teddy's defalcations.[67]

The abject Teddy was ordered by Edith, backed by his family, to make good the entire amount. This he did, wiping out his share of a legacy from his recently deceased mother. He was also relieved of his co-managership (with Edith's brother) of Edith's trust fund.

James reviled the cad. He would henceforth be "the unspeakable Teddy." James could not avoid thinking about the curse of Edith's formidable fortune, the source of all this trouble. "I greatly pity her," he wrote a mutual friend. "I can't help regretting, however that an *intellectuelle*— and an angel—should require such a big pecuniary base."[68] The incident just showed him how her wealth distracted her from her true vocation.

And yet she managed to complete *Ethan Frome* during her ordeal. Into that grim novel, she infused her bitterest, most pessimistic forebodings about her marriage. The cousin-lovers of her story, Ethan and Mattie, are maimed for life by their failed attempt at suicide and sentenced to live out their days under the vicious dominance of Ethan's neurotic wife, a stand-in for Teddy Wharton, writes Lewis.

In Teddy's disgrace, Edith depended heavily on the ever-consoling James with his wise, sympathetic letters: "Sit loose, live in the day— don't borrow trouble & remember that nothing happens as we forecast it—but always with interesting &, as it were, refreshing differences."[69]

Inevitably, James noted the resemblance between Edith Wharton's unhappy marriage and that of Isabel Archer in *The Portrait of a Lady*. In a letter to Sturgis on Edith's troubles he conflated her with Isabel, meditating on her great mistake in marrying Osgood. He spoke of how painfully the thought must come to "poor Edith" in her "dark vigils" that she had done "an almost—rather an utterly—inconceivable thing in marrying him." But her bed was now made—"and such a great big uncompromising four-poster."[70]

In 1910 it was James's turn for trouble. He was plunged into a deep depression, "a black sick state." He feared the loss of his powers: "I'm done! Or all but!" he lamented to Howard Sturgis.[71] He attributed his condition to "stomachic colic" and "food-loathing" brought on by his practice of "Fletcherizing" his food, a voguish dietary quackery that called for chewing each morsel until it was liquid.

Concerned, Edith enlisted Miss Bosanquet as her personal spy, charging her to provide frequent bulletins on the patient's condition and to summon her in an emergency. Miss Bosanquet, whom James cherished because she not only took dictation impeccably but also understood the meaning behind the words, continued to serve as Edith's special agent until the Master's death.

Wharton wrote James almost daily, and delicately expressed concern about his financial situation, since he was no longer writing. He assured her that his income was quite adequate, but she could never understand how he got by on eight thousand dollars a year and believed he was "haunted by the spectre of impoverishment."

Her "beautiful" letters buoyed him. A no doubt rare and expensive basket of grapes sends him into paroxysms of prosody: "The grapes of Paradise that arrived yesterday in a bloom of purple & a burst of sweetness . . . cast their Tyrian glamour about. . . ."[72] The arrival of another cornucopia has him extruding arabesques of fancy: "This very hour—as I sit here solitudinous—there has dropped upon me a basket, or casket, of celestial manna that can only have been propelled to its extraordinarily effective descent by the very tenderest & firmest, most generous & most unerring hand in all this otherwise muddled world."[73]

In one of his letters he thanks her for her letter thanking *him* for his encouragement over the years. And he adds: "But the great thing is that we always tumble together—more and more never apart . . . we may trust ourselves & each other to the end of time."[74] Compressed in those words was the story of a friendship.

In 1910, James's beloved brother William died; Henry had been at the philosopher's bedside at his summer home in New Hampshire, where he had gone to die after visiting Henry in England. He stayed on into the following year, visiting Edith at the Mount that summer. He arrived in time to witness a furious battle between Edith and Teddy over Edith's decision to sell the summer home, which had become too much for her to manage. Making a kind of last stand for his self-respect, Teddy fought her, but the stronger will prevailed, leaving him stripped of all pretense of purpose in life. (She would divorce him in 1913, and he would spend the rest of his time in and out of sanatoriums.)

In December Edith descended on Rye and spirited James to friends' houses. "Our great Edith has been with us—came and went, with a great flap of her iridescent wings," he reported to Minnie Jones. "She seemed very brave and bright and did, in her ten days, exactly 9000 separate and mutually inconsistent things, but she liked it all."[75]

She returned for her annual visit in 1912, when James was trying to work on an autobiographical volume begun as a tribute to William. Back in stride after so many bad times, he trembled at Edith's imminent arrival, warning Howard Sturgis to sound the alarm: "The poor old Rye-bird" fears that she will carry him off "struggling in her talons."[76] And yet after the visit he wrote Minnie Jones: "She was never more brilliant and able and interesting."[77]

While in Paris, Edith undertook a campaign to secure for him the 1911 Nobel Prize in Literature. The honor was overdue, she felt, and the prize money would ease his last years. She lobbied tirelessly on both sides of the Atlantic, enlisting in Britain the eminent critic, author, and librarian of the House of Lords, Edmund Gosse, a friend of James's, and in America the equally distinguished critic and author William Dean Howells, also an old and loyal friend. But the Swedish judges awarded the laurel to Maurice Maeterlinck, the Belgian playwright. James's failure was in some part attributable to his lack of a world reputation, particularly in Sweden, where his books were considered too difficult to translate.

Two years later, Edith got wind of a campaign under way in England to present James with a suitable gift on his seventieth birthday,

April 15, 1913. A large number of friends and admirers—three hundred in all—subscribed £5 each. The money was used to purchase a handsome antique golden bowl and to commission a portrait of the Master by John Singer Sargent.

Wharton launched her own parallel campaign in America, soliciting contributions from American friends to an old-age fund of five thousand dollars. When James got wind of this, he was furious. He ordered that it be stopped immediately and the money refunded. He did not reprimand Edith; instead, he tactfully included her name on the list of donors whom he formally thanked for the British campaign.

Still worried about his finances, Wharton devised a scheme that could have served as a plot for another James story. She persuaded her publisher to agree to pay James eight thousand dollars for a new novel, half of that due on signing. The money would come from her swollen royalty account; James was not to know, of course. Happy to please his star author (Wharton, that is), Charles Scribner wrote to James, inquiring about a new novel he had begun just before his 1910 illness. "As the publishers of your definitive edition," he continued, referring to the New York Edition, "we want another great novel to balance *The Golden Bowl* and round off the series of books in which you have developed the theory of composition set forth in your preface."[78] Scribner lied that he was eager to get the novel as soon as possible; therefore he would advance four thousand dollars at once.

James could not quite believe this sudden, favoring shift in the winds of fortune. The failure of the New York Edition was still a raw sore. But he quickly convinced himself of what he badly needed to believe—that the offer was legitimate. Edith's ruse had the desired effect of boosting James's morale. He set to work with renewed energy, happily dictating to Miss Bosanquet like the Master of old.

The ultimate Jamesian irony was that the novel he was working on (which he might *not* have been working on but for the Whartonsubsidized advance), called "The Ivory Tower," had been at least in part inspired by Edith and her world. His underlying theme was the American "money-passion" and the nation's penchant for "frenzied acquisition."[79] The action shuttles between New York, Newport, and a mansion much like the Mount—the world of the superrich. The hero, a young man raised abroad, comes into a large inheritance from his American uncle, which he comes to see as representing "the black and merciless things that are behind the great possessions."[80] He returns to Europe—the ivory tower—abandoning America and its frenzied finance. So the book was, in part, James's final attempt to justify his own decision to expatriate himself—a fate he had warned Wharton to avoid a decade earlier. Edith is not a character in the novel, but there is an heiress, and James comments on "her wealth, which is, by all the mistrusts and terrors it creates, the deep note of her character and situation."[81] Here he implicitly expresses his disapproval of Edith's wealth, which he had, of course, enjoyed in small ways but sternly judged to be the enemy of art, of the spirit. But he was primarily thinking of the post–Civil War financial and industrial mega-fortunes of Gould, Rockefeller, Carnegie, and other robber barons, which seemed to him corrupt and evil compared with the landed wealth of the plain Republican America in which he grew up.

He started making notes for the novel in December 1909 and began dictating the following January—around the time Teddy's embezzlement was revealed. This corrupt, even evil behavior, which amounted to sabotage of Edith's work, demonstrated to him the validity of his theory about the curse of great wealth and its hostility to a literary vocation.

"The Ivory Tower" might have been a great novel, but the Henry James that could have written it was no more. He was old and ill and lacked the staying power for the job. He had trouble grasping the present. In a letter in November 1914 he told Wharton, "It's impossible to 'locate anything in our time.' "[82] As Powers notes, "The Ivory Tower" was "of 'our time,' and he no longer had a sense of it." He turned to an old manuscript fittingly titled "The Sense of the Past."

In June 1913, the last peacetime year, he wrote Wharton, "I should so like one of our fine old-fashioned motor days—just one."[83]

The slaughter unleashed in Belgium and France in August 1914 cast a black cloud over Wharton and James's Edwardian world of sun-washed green lawns and summer afternoons: "The plunge of civilization into this abyss of blood & darkness," wrote James, "is a thing that so gives away the whole long age during which we had supposed the world to be . . . gradually bettering. . . ." He had lived to see a "triumph of evil."[84] Germany represented the recrudescence of barbarism; France and England defended the ramparts of civilization.

Now dwelling in London, James visited wounded soldiers in a hospital as his favorite, Walt Whitman, had done in the Civil War, and sheltered refugees at Lamb House. Wharton started a factory in Paris for impoverished wives of soldiers and hurled her bottomless energy into relief efforts. She visited the front lines and sent back to James vivid pictures of battle and suffering. Those letters were the only ones of hers that have survived, for in 1915, in a fit of depression, he burned his correspondence. Then, to protest America's failure to enter the war at Britain's side, he renounced his citizenship. Wharton severely disapproved of his gesture, but later came to understand.

The useless life of the observer weighed upon him; he could only visit wounded soldiers and give them oranges and candy. Yet the reign of blood and iron did not make him renounce the religion of Art. Yes, he had lived for Art, but what was Art but heightened life? As he told H. G. Wells, in a debate about the topical or journalistic novel, of which Wells was the leading practitioner: "It is art that *makes* life, makes interest, makes importance . . . and I know of no substitute whatever for the force and beauty of its process."[85]

In 1915, he suffered a stroke and heard a voice saying, "So here it is at last, the distinguished thing!"[86] He was bedridden; he lived in hallucinations, including one that he was Napoleon. Edith fretted in Paris; Miss Bosanquet told her she need not come. Wharton feared that James would interpret a visit from her as signifying that he was at death's door. (The Angel of Devastation's final visit to spirit him away?) Further strokes incapacitated him, and the two women prayed he would die quickly rather than survive with his great intellect dimmed.

The distinguished and merciful thing came on February 28, 1916. Edith Wharton, who had always preferred the older man to his later novels, wrote to Miss Bosanquet, "We all who knew him well know how great he would have been if he had never written a line."[87]

CHAPTER 5

FROM HEART TO HEART

Willa Cather and Sarah Orne Jewett

We like a writer much as we like individuals; for what he is, simply, underneath his accomplishments. . . .
It is the light behind his books and is the living quality in his sentences.
—WILLA CATHER, "MISS JEWETT" (1925)[1]

You do need reassurance,—every artist does!—but you need still more to feel
"responsible for the state of your conscience" . . . you must find your own quiet centre of life . . .
you must write to the human heart.
—JEWETT TO CATHER (1908)[2]

I N FEBRUARY 1908, Willa Cather, escorted by the wife of future Supreme Court justice Louis D. Brandeis, ascended the wide carpeted stairway to the second floor of 148 Charles Street in Boston, the home of Annie Fields, widow of the publisher James T. Fields and premier hostess of Boston's golden age.

She entered the famous long drawing room, which ran the depth of the house, its shelves and walls displaying hundreds of books and pictures and other memorabilia of some of the distinguished authors whom the Fieldses had entertained—Dickens, Thackeray, Matthew Arnold, Hawthorne, Emerson; the actors Edwin Booth and Joseph Jefferson; the painters Winslow Homer and John Singer Sargent. Thackeray had completed *Henry Esmond* in the guest room on the fourth floor; Matthew Arnold had read aloud his poem *Tristram and Iseult* in this room; Charles Dickens had held forth in the first floor dining room with comical stories about American lecture audiences. (When a friend later speculated that the young and beautiful Mrs. Fields had been in love with Dickens, Cather laughed. No, he had more likely fallen in love with her.)

The thirty-five-year-old Willa Cather, a New York magazine editor raised in Red Cloud, Nebraska, could not fully have comprehended Annie Fields's central position in an earlier Boston, when all those great living names, now entombed in school anthologies, had gathered at her home and bantered over James Fields's excellent wines and fine cuisine. But she retained an indelible first impression of that room. At the far end, the great windows opened on a sunken garden; beyond it lay the Charles River, dully gleaming like pewter in the pale winter light, stippled by the orange glow of the setting sun. In the light from the window, she discerned two ladies having tea. The white-haired Mrs. Fields reclined on the sofa beneath a portrait of the young Dickens. Her friend Sarah Orne Jewett sat in a chair.

Annie Fields in her late sixties was still pretty, with youthful skin, rosy cheeks, and ruby lips—the mobile mouth of a young woman, Cather recalled—and a tinkling laugh that could shift to a lower, reproving register when a guest strayed into forbidden areas. Miss Jewett, fifty-nine, was tall and somewhat plumper and grayer than her picture on the card in the *Authors* game Cather had played as a girl. She had a gentle but arch wit; her face mirrored an inner childish sweetness. A carriage accident six years ago had so traumatized her physically and psychologically that she had stopped writing fiction. But she had always valued living higher than writing.

That afternoon, Willa Cather trod quietly, reverentially, as if visiting a historic church. And she was, in a way. She later wrote: "At that house the past lay in wait for one in all the corners; it exuded from the furniture, from the pictures, the rare editions, and the cabinets of manuscript. . . ." Longfellow, Whittier, Lowell, Holmes, and others, who had gathered half a century earlier to exercise their wit or read their latest poems, seemed to haunt the room. "It was at tea-time, I used to think, that the great shades were most likely to appear; sometimes they seemed to come up the richly carpeted stairs, along with living friends."[3] They were restored to flesh and blood in the oral home movie Annie Fields unspooled while reclining on the sofa before the windows lit by the setting sun.

Hearing Annie Fields reliving the old days, Cather said she became aware for the first time that America *had* a literary history of its own. She believed a "noble past" dwelled in this house, and whenever she visited again she directed the conversation away from modern topics to the old days in an attempt to open the floodgate of Annie Fields's memories. As a Midwesterner who had grown up starved for the culture of the East, she felt that here she held it in her hand, tangible, *alive.*

Annie Fields's "at homes" were a gathering place for intellectual Boston, particularly the women. Mrs. Fields and Miss Jewett would be stationed before the windows at the far end of the great drawing room, the tea table between them, greeting guests as co-hostesses. Their women friends, many of whom were linked in similar arrangements, considered them a couple.

The term "Boston marriage," meaning a long-term domestic partnership between two women, might have been coined for Mrs. Fields and Miss Jewett. It was assumed by polite society that sex did not enter into the relationship, since having children was the only admitted reason for sex. Certainly, friendship and practicality were major factors. Lillian Faderman, who studied female friendships in the Victorian era, posits that Boston marriages were most prevalent among an elite of educated women who had a profession such as medicine or law, or taught, or held a government post.[4] Such women realized that marriage would mean obeying their superior husband's commands and bearing children, effectively canceling their career. On the other hand, living alone could be depressing; it was better to pool one's emotional and economic resources with a congenial female in similar circumstances. As the Irish writer Edith Somerville, who collaborated on novels with her partner, Violet Martin, said, "The outstanding fact . . . among women who live by their brains, is friendship. A profound friendship that extended through every phase and aspect of life, intellectual, social, pecuniary."[5]

Observing such a stable, socially accepted relationship between two independent literary women was another first for Willa Cather during her visit to 148 Charles Street. Her own preference for female friendships was long established, but she worked out her sexual life by trial and error, with blunders and grief along the way.

Those began with her gender identity crisis as a teenager in Red Cloud, Nebraska. She cut her hair short, donned men's clothes, and called herself William C. Cather. It wasn't that she disliked boys; she wanted to be one of them. Her boyish ways drew little comment; Tomboys were not considered "deviant" or unchristian in 1880s Nebraska.

Wearing trousers, she arrived in 1891 at the University of Nebraska in Lincoln. Like Jewett, she had considered only two careers, medicine or writing. Unlike Jewett, she regarded both to be occupations women were unfitted for because they were too emotional. Her own solution to this disability was to reject the trappings of femininity and adopt those of masculinity—to become a boy.

As her biographer Sharon O'Brien has shown, she expressed contempt for most women authors in her critical writings for the university literary magazine and extolled the macho males like Rudyard Kipling. She fell in love with touring actresses and lent them money. Men avoided her because she was mannish and standoffish. A friend's mother took her in hand, however, and helped her purchase women's clothes. Actually, she preferred wearing feminine things.

In her freshman year she formed a crush on a beautiful upper-class woman named Louise Pound (who would carve out a brilliant academic career as a philologist and folklorist). Two surviving letters indicate that Willa had a desperate infatuation with Pound. In one she declares that it is unfair that society should consider female friendships to be unnatural.[6] And indeed there had been a social shift away from tolerance of such liaisons—especially in academe, where faculty women had frequently entered into Boston marriages and students developed passions for teachers or classmates. The male-dominated society had become alarmed. Such liaisons were condemned as a threat to traditional patriarchal marriage. What would men do if women refused to cosset and comfort them and bear their posterity, and chose instead to live with other women? There was also a wider recognition of the phenomenon of sex relations between two women, known by the new word "lesbianism." The Oscar Wilde scandal in England had spread the shocking news that men had sexual relations with one another.

Awareness of society's disapproval of same-sex relations apparently shattered Willa Cather's innocence. In the university literary magazine, *The Hesperian,* she published a gratuitous attack on Louise's brother Roscoe, calling him a "notorious bully" who "quit growing when he graduated" from the Harvard Law School (Pound went on to become a famous legal philosopher). Cather biographer Phyllis C. Robinson speculates that the attack was in retaliation for something Roscoe had said about her; possibly he called her attachment to his sister unnatural. At any rate, Willa's attack in print provoked the Pound family to declare Willa persona non grata at their home in Lincoln.[7]

Around this time, Cather wrote a story about a young man who had a tendency to plunge "hotheaded and rapacious into friendship after friendship, giving more than any one cared to receive and exacting more than any one had leisure to give. . . ."[8] That, one suspects, was a self-portrait of the artist as a young man.

Her stories written in college reveal a precocious literary talent.

Her essays and book reviews appeared frequently in the Lincoln newspaper. After graduation in 1895 she moved to Pittsburgh to edit a housewives' magazine. She lost that job, but made a living doing freelance book and theater reviews, columns, and feature stories for the magazine. In her spare time she worked on her own writing and began selling stories and poems to leading New York magazines. In 1899 she met Isabelle McClung, the beautiful daughter of a wealthy judge. A stern, forbidding man, he was a hero of Pittsburgh's industrial elite for presiding over the conviction of the anarchist Alexander Berkman, the attempted assassin of steel magnate Henry Frick. Isabelle was three years younger than Willa, a "sumptuous" aristocratic beauty.[9]

A passionate worshipper of literature, Isabelle devoted herself to helping Willa become a great writer. In 1901 she arranged for her friend to live in the McClung mansion in Pittsburgh's wealthy Squirrel Hill section and fixed up a study for her in the attic sewing room, where Willa could work on her stories in solitude. After dinner the two women retired to the bedroom where they read European novelists—Tolstoy, Turgenev, Balzac, Flaubert. In 1902 Willa and Isabelle traveled as a couple in Europe.

The friends parted in 1906 when Cather migrated to New York to become an assistant editor at *McClure's Magazine*. McClung, who was dependent on her father and would never have a career of her own, stayed home. She would, however, visit Cather frequently in the city. Once she came to nurse her friend when she was sick. Willa returned to Pittsburgh often and worked on several of her novels in the sewing-room study (it appears in her novel *The Professor's House*). When McClung married a violinist-composer in 1916, Cather was emotionally devastated and wrote some stories laced with anti-Semitism (the husband was Jewish); later she made her peace with him. In 1923 he and Isabelle invited her to spend the summer with them in France, where they had moved in 1921, promising her a study of her own. She came but devel-

oped neuritis in her right arm and was unable to write. The malady may
well have been psychosomatic. She returned to New York in a state of
depression.

In the introduction to *Not Under Forty,* a collection of essays published in 1922, she wrote: "The world broke in two in 1922 or there-
abouts," probably a private allusion to the pain caused by Isabelle's
move to Europe.[10]

But the two women continued to be close friends. After Isabelle's
death in the late 1930s, Willa plunged into suicidal grief but recovered.
She said everything she had ever written had been for Isabelle. The
friendship and the room of her own that McClung had provided at the
dawn of her career had been invaluable to her.

It's possible that Annie Fields's primary emotional orientation had always been toward women. In her happy marriage to the much older
Fields (whom she called Jamie), she mainly played the role of hostess-
companion and editorial assistant. She had wed him at the age of nineteen; a widower, he had previously been married to her cousin. They
had no children, and she appeared to prefer literary and philanthropic
activities to homemaking. She was attractive to women, including
Sophia Hawthorne, wife of her good friend Nathaniel. After her husband's physical ardor faded, Sophia transferred her worship to Annie,
once writing to her, "I love you with a mighty love. You embellish my
life."[11]

Annie had met Sarah Orne Jewett while Jamie Fields was still alive;
in addition to playing hostess to visiting Ticknor & Fields authors, she
dealt with the women contributors to the *Atlantic,* of whom Jewett had
been an early one, encouraged by William Dean Howells. According to
biographer Mark De Wolfe Howe, as they grew closer, the much older
Mr. Fields approved. The relationship fulfilled "the need of [Annie's]

nature for an absorbing intimacy," he believed, and he expected them to continue their partnership after he was gone.[12] After Fields's death in 1881, the women traveled as a couple to Europe, and their lives remained intertwined for nearly thirty years.

Sarah Orne Jewett was not the stereotypical sour, cloistered old maid. As a child she had been adventuresome and tomboyish. She accompanied her physician father on his rural rounds and wanted to be a doctor too, but her health was frail, so she chose writing as an alternate profession. Like Nan Prince in her novel *The Country Doctor,* she advocated that women be free to choose a profession and not marry.

In her own life there had been no broken engagement, no lover tragically killed in the Civil War. When her friend the poet James Greenleaf Whittier asked her if she had ever been in love, she replied that she needed a wife, not a husband. She had lived all her life in the large family home in South Berwick, Maine, in which she was born and which she shared with her sister and several servants. She had friends there who dated back to her childhood, but Boston and the *Atlantic* opened a window on the world. She cultivated an international circle of friends, male and female (Rudyard Kipling and Henry James were admirers and correspondents), as well as interacting with her fellow townspeople, some of them friends from childhood. The house, with its ample garden and carriage house behind, was located in South Berwick's heart. From her front window Jewett could glance out at her neighbors on their daily rounds.

She demanded privacy for her work, but lived very much in the world. The same was true for Annie Fields, a brilliant hostess who worked among Boston's poor. She was also a writer, mainly of tracts, memoirs, and sentimental poetry, and Jewett was her faithful first reader. For part of the year they lived apart. Sarah spent spring and fall in South Berwick, winter in Boston, and summer at Annie's place in New Hampshire. When they were apart, they wrote each other daily—

long, affectionate letters on Jewett's part. When Fields collected some of them into a book published in 1912, Mark De Wolfe Howe advised her to excise passionate declarations, leaving only a few tame endearments: "This is the first morning in more than seven months that I haven't waked up to hear your dear voice and see your dear face. I do miss it very much. . . ."[13] Perhaps that was all, as far as their intimacy was concerned: tender, even romantic friendship, sex sublimated into hugs and kisses.

In 1908, when Willa Cather passed through the door at 148 Charles Street and met the two ladies who would change her life, her editorial career was thriving at *McClure's Magazine.* A long-term editorial assignment, fact-checking an article on Mary Baker Eddy, had landed her in Boston, the Vatican City of Christian Science. She spent her time hunting down former Scientists, who confirmed anecdotes or provided fresh ones about "Mother" Eddy's eccentricities. On top of this research, she rewrote the series from top to bottom, making it publishable as well as libel-proof.

Her boss, the neurotic, hard-driving S. S. McClure, progenitor of muckraking journalism, was a fanatic for accuracy, and the Eddy story was touchy. His choice of Willa to vet it showed the trust he placed in her. He could be said to have discovered her. In 1903 he had read some of her early stories, including "Paul's Case," "The Wagner Matinee," and "The Sculptor's Funeral"—now considered classics—and immediately wired the author. The unknown's work was blazoned to the world in his magazine, and his publishing house, McClure, Phillips, brought out a collection of her stories, *The Troll Garden,* in 1905.

McClure lured Cather permanently to New York in 1906 following the wholesale resignation of his editorial staff, including the star investigative journalists Lincoln Steffens, Ray Stannard Baker, and Ida

Tarbell, and his business partner, John Phillips. They had become fed up with his autocratic, inefficient ways. They thought they could run the magazine better than he could and demanded he sell it to them. He refused, and they left to found their own magazine. The upheaval might have warned Cather off, but she was anxious to make the move to New York. A woman who deeply valued loyalty and filial respect, she would never repudiate Sam McClure.

Hurrying to rebuild his empire after the mass exodus, McClure drove his people all the harder. As an employee said, working for "the Chief" was like "working in a high wind, sometimes of cyclonic magnitude."[14] But an innate courtesy and kindness tempered McClure's manic energies, and it was this part of him that Cather undoubtedly clung to so loyally. Sam McClure might be considered the only male love interest in Willa Cather's life—other than her father and an obscure suitor in Pittsburgh.

He repaid her devotion by piling on more responsibilities. He told his wife, Hattie, that she was "the best magazine executive I know."[15] He regularly sent her complimentary letters. On his deathbed many years later, he smiled when a visitor mentioned her: "She was wonderful, a wonderful girl."[16]

Upon her arrival in New York she had taken rooms in a shabby building on Washington Square South in the Village the bohemian side of the park. By 1908, her salary was enough to enable her to move to a better apartment building, where Edith Lewis lived. Lewis was from Lincoln, Nebraska. She became a devoted admirer of Willa's while in college and undoubtedly fell in love with her. When she moved east after breaking with her family, Cather helped her obtain a job at *McClure's* as a proofreader.

In that capacity, she traveled regularly to Boston to go over the latest article in the Mary Baker Eddy series. The two of them drew closer during the year Cather spent in the city. The series, which stretched out to fourteen installments, caused a sensation and boosted the magazine's newsstand sales.

To the ladies at 148 Charles Street, it must have seemed that this smart young woman was leading a successful life, holding a responsible, high-paying job. She was thirty-five years old, five feet three inches tall, a stocky woman with a confident smile, candid blue eyes, and reddish-brown hair parted sensibly down the middle. Energetic, with boyish mannerisms, she exuded straightforward, small-town friendliness. On the job she wore utilitarian middy blouses or sport coats and heavy tweed skirts. Going out at night to the opera or the theater, she indulged her taste for finery—jewels, plumed hats, and deep-woven fabrics.

Inside, however, she was seething with frustration. After she returned to New York and the *McClure's* offices on East Twenty-third Street, she and Jewett corresponded, and Cather increasingly confided in the older woman. Jewett urged her to visit them at Annie's summer villa in Manchester-by-the-Sea, New Hampshire, for "more than a night or as long as you could stay."[17] And that fall when Jewett was back home in South Berwick, Cather visited her.

Jewett was drawn to Cather both as a spirited young friend and as a writer of great potential. She was egalitarian in her friendships; differences in age, class, or experience were irrelevant to her. She was humble, and "never made pronouncements," Cather noted. Although she was a well-read, well-traveled woman, she called herself a country person. She had gathered her ideas from the gossip of townswomen she'd known since childhood, just as Willa had listened to the life stories of immigrant women in Red Cloud.

Cather addressed Jewett as "Dear, Dear Lady." For she regarded her as "a lady, in the old high sense."[18] She developed deep-seated crushes on elegant, beautiful women, from Isabelle McClung to opera singer Olive Fremstad, the inspiration for the heroine of *The Song of the Lark,* and Red Cloud's own Lyra Garber, wife of former governor Silas Garber and the model for Mrs. Forrester in *A Lost Lady.* This proclivity traced back to her haughty, elegant Virginia-born mother, whom she believed she could never please. Jewett, by contrast, emanated the serene security of tradition and deep ancestral roots. She had an independent income and lived in an old home furnished with Chippendale chairs, oil paintings of ancestors, mahogany bedsteads, Wedgwood china, an antique spinet, and Oriental rugs and vases.

Cather envied Jewett's social assurance. In her own childhood, faded gentility had vied with economic insecurity. She had been rudely uprooted in her ninth year from green rural Virginia and deposited in the windblown emptiness of the Nebraska prairie. Her gentle father had struggled to support a wife and seven children in a raw new town.

She also respected Jewett's writings. Back in the mid-1890s she had called Jewett America's finest woman writer. At one point she ranked Jewett's book of linked Maine stories, *The Country of the Pointed Firs,* with *Huckleberry Finn* and *The Scarlet Letter* as the greatest American novels.

Like many in her generation, she fell under the sway of Henry James; "the mighty master of language," she called him, "the keenest mind any American ever devoted to the art of fiction." She appropriated his recurring themes of the plight of the artist and the conflict between beauty and commerce in the American soul. Her greatest challenge as a writer would be to free her pen from James's telepathic guidance. It was years before she understood that James "was interested in his countrymen chiefly as they appeared in relation to the European scene,"[19] and that she was interested in her countrymen chiefly in relation to the *American* scene.

What had Jewett to do with all these problems? First, she had entered Cather's life at a crucial moment in her identity crisis. Second, she was a writer whom Cather admired on the printed page who was now a friend. Finally, as a woman artist and professional, she was Willa's only link to America's sparse female literary tradition. In her own younger days, Jewett had also sought female role models—in particular Harriet Beecher Stowe, whose novel *The Pearl of Orr's Island,* Jewett said, taught her to write "about people of rustic life just as they were."[20] Jewett was a distant descendant of the earliest published American woman writer, Anne Bradstreet.

During Willa's visits to Berwick, Jewett provided a sympathetic ear as Cather talked excitedly about Nebraska people and the stories she wanted to mine from the native sod. She extolled the husky, bawdy immigrant women, as much pioneers as the men whose plows broke the plains or who platted the towns, chartered the banks, and built the railroads in the new country.

Nebraska was a very long way, Willa knew, from the pine-forested, sea-girt Maine of Jewett's stories, a land of crumbling old towns and barren farms from which the men had fled to the cities or the West seeking a better living, or had been lost at sea or killed in the Civil War.

In Jewett's stories, female characters are often depicted as independent, self-reliant, and tenderhearted, like the widow Almira Todd in *The Country of the Pointed Firs.* Jewett wrote about girls on the brink of adulthood, countrywomen running farms, widows eking out frugal lives, or threadbare daughters of the gentry clinging to their social position. She gathered her tales from, as she put it, "simple scenes close at hand," like Mrs. Todd harvesting healing herbs from her backyard garden.[21]

Cather was deeply affected by Jewett's interest. The older woman became a mother figure, supplying the emotional sustenance Cather had lacked in her unresolved conflict with her real mother. Jewett, unable to do her own writing, may have poured her latent maternal energies into Willa. Her letters to Cather contain some of the most

generously helpful words ever written by one American writer to another.

There is one from Jewett that contains personally tailored advice.
She had just read Cather's latest story in *McClure's*, "On the Gull's
Road." It was a tale about a young man who falls in love with a beautiful older married woman on a ship bound from Italy to the United
States. Her husband, the ship's engineer, is a philandering boor; the
young man attracts her. But she has a serious heart condition and
knows she will die young. Rather than inflict this grief on her admirer,
she parts from him, leaving him a few mementos he treasures for the
rest of his life.

Jewett praises the "writer's young and loving heart" and the way she
drew "the wife and her husband with unerring touches and wonderful
tenderness for her." Then she comes to what mattered most to her: "The
lover is as well done as he could be when a woman writes in the man's
character,—it must always, I believe, be something of a masquerade—
you could almost have done it as yourself—a woman could love her in
that same protecting way—a woman could even care enough to wish to
take her away from such a life, by some means or other."[22]

These words have been read as Jewett's urging Cather to be honest
and express her sexual inclination (which Jewett presumably sensed or
had heard about from Willa) through a female character. Cather, however, could not do that because, remembering her unhappy experience
with Louise Pound, she feared that such a love would be branded abnormal. Jewett belonged to an earlier time when a woman could love
another woman without being called perverse.

Yet Cather may have taken from this letter of Jewett's some sort of
validation for her romantic attraction to women. In another surviving
letter she enthuses about Jewett's "Martha's Lady," the story of the love
of one woman for another, a love so strong that it triumphs over class,
time, separation, and marriage to another.

The woman who loves another woman is Martha, a drab, awkward country girl. Noting her inexperience, the rich, vivacious Helena teaches her how to perform the delicate services that her employer, Miss Pyne, requires, such as arranging the table flowers or brushing her hair. After a long visit, Helena goes away, but Martha has fallen in love with her. When Helena marries an English diplomat, Martha is badly shaken.

Forty years pass and Helena returns, an old woman bent by the cares of her marriage. Martha is shocked, but she quickly grasps that because they are old they are at last one. She serves Helena with the same tenderness, and suddenly Helena senses her love. Jewett ends the story with Helena's exclaiming: "Oh, my dear Martha! Won't you kiss me good-night? Oh, Martha, have you remembered like this, all these long years!"

Sharon O'Brien theorizes that Cather identified with the Martha character, with Jewett representing Helena, the "dear lady." Cather told Jewett she thought it the saddest and loveliest of her stories and reread it many times. She said it left her feeling humble and desolate; she felt the way she did after her mother had whipped her as a little girl, wanting a new chance to be good.[23] The story thus triggered a flashback to her relationship with her own mother, whom she desperately tried to please and whose love she despaired of ever winning.

Of course Jewett wasn't whipping her; she was kind and gentle. And yet she was the teacher and there was probably steeliness under her teasing, humorous manner. Jewett once criticized Harriet Beecher Stowe's weak ending to her novel *The Pearl of Orr's Island,* which tells of a young woman struggling against the confines of the traditional feminine role. The problem was, Sarah wrote to Annie Fields, that a woman like Stowe, whose primary involvement was with her husband and children, could not "bring herself to that cold selfishness of the moment for one's work's sake. . . ."[24] Rather than face the full implications of her proto-feminist tale, Stowe hastily eliminated her heroine in a senti-mental death scene.

Jewett's kid-gloved toughness shows in her letter of December 19, 1908, which Willa Cather read over and over. First, Jewett expresses concern about the creative energy Willa is dissipating on her job. She must conserve her energy for writing more short stories as fine as "The Sculptor's Funeral," which should be a "starting-point" for all her future work. This work will surely be finer, if only she has "time and quiet to perfect" it. If she does not, she will never achieve her potential.[25]

Jewett tells her what she must do to progress artistically. First, she must cultivate detachment and live, read, experience so she can envision her material from a broader perspective. Cather had acquired in her lifetime an ample storehouse of experiences to draw on, but she must gain "the standpoint of the looker-on who takes them each in their relations to letters, to the world."[26]

Second, she must stay true to her "literary conscience"; she must universalize her experience—"write for the world," not her office friends. She must find a "quiet centre of life, and write from that to the world that holds offices, and all society, all Bohemia; the city, the country—in short, you must write to the human heart, the great consciousness that all humanity goes to make up."[27] "Otherwise," says Miss Jewett, "you can write about life, but never write life itself."[28]

Jewett sums up: "To work in silence and with all one's heart, that is the writer's lot; he is the only artist who must be solitary, and yet needs the widest outlook on the world."[29] She closes by assuring Willa that she has been thinking about her a great deal and urging her to write before too long.

Cather replied by return mail. Jewett's letter had unlocked problems stored up inside her involving her present job and her personal life. Her career thwarts her creative instincts; reading stacks of ill-written manuscripts deadens her spirit. Her personal life is barren and stressful. She straggles home exhausted, longing to crawl inside herself and sleep. She is tired all the time and repelled by anything to do with words.

On top of all this, McClure had appointed her co–managing editor with more executive responsibilities. Her mind had become a card file, crammed with notes of future articles and plans intelligible only to her, making it impossible for her to delegate her job to anyone else. And McClure frequently traveled in Europe, leaving her in charge. Journalism gives her no emotional satisfaction; it's a mental exercise, like solving a math problem. She fears she is becoming trapped in editorial work. McClure even tells her she does not have it in her to be a successful writer. (Cather apparently didn't realize he probably was manipulating her insecurity because he didn't want to lose her.)

She sends part of her salary to her parents and brothers in Red Cloud. She has saved some money and will have enough to take off three or four years if she lives simply. She has been working without a break since she was fifteen. Perhaps she can devote some time to herself and her own writing. She wonders if she is not a split personality: the efficient editor clashing with the artist.[30]

On March 9, 1909, Jewett suffered a stroke that left her paralyzed on one side. Cather rushed to 148 Charles Street the next day to help Mrs. Fields; they stayed out of Jewett's room to avoid exciting her. In May, Cather sailed for London on an author-scouting trip; and while she was abroad, on June 23, Jewett died. Willa immediately wrote to Annie Fields, telling her she couldn't help but think that somehow Miss Jewett was with her. She remembered how Sarah had been fearful of suddenly losing Annie, who was nearly ten years older, but life had spun the wheel the other way. She said she often dreamed of Annie and Sarah together.[31] Perhaps in one of those dreams she saw Mrs. Fields and Miss Jewett seated at the tea table before the window at 148 Charles, as they were that first February afternoon.

Jewett's spirit remained a vibrant presence in Cather's life. She told her friend Elizabeth Sergeant that it guarded her from temptation. She said she had felt "the lure of big money rewards in the crude sense—for cheap work—letting all the people who wanted you steal your energy and time."[32] Then she remembered Miss Jewett's admonition that she must avoid writing for money.

In 1925, in a tribute to Jewett, Cather set down what she had learned from her. First, she had come to understand the essential difference between a journalist and a creative writer. The former can write on any subject, while the latter "can do his best only with what lies within the range and character of his deepest sympathies." Jewett had her "fisher-folk and seaside villages";[33] Cather would find their equivalent in the farms and railroad towns on the Great Plains, in the Swedish farmwives and Bohemian hired girls.

Another of Jewett's maxims that deeply impressed Willa was "You must know the world before you can know the village."[34] She meant that a writer must move in the greater world and read the best literary works before writing about his or her own patch of earth.

Third, write simply and directly, staying true to one's voice, one's vision. "Write it as it is, don't try to make it like this or that," Cather paraphrased her mentor. "You can't do it in anybody else's way—you will have to make a way of your own. If the way happens to be new, don't let that frighten you. Don't try to write the kind of short story that this or that magazine wants—write the truth and let them take it or leave it."[35] The writer must do this even if she risked rejection and failure.

Next, Jewett had "early learned to love her country for what it was. What is quite as important, she saw it as it was."[36] Brilliant as Cather's early Nebraska stories were—like "The Sculptor's Funeral" (which raked over small-town philistinism) and "The Wagner Matinee" (recounting a careworn farm woman's transfiguration while watching an opera in Boston)—they are arrows dipped in anger at the mediocrity and cultural aridity of her native heath. She told herself that her resentment at the cultural starvation of her girlhood had pinched and narrowed her art. She vowed she must see her native place, as Jewett saw hers, sympathetically.

Another thing: She must develop an ear like Jewett's for the way people talked. A writer "must be able to think and feel in that speech— it is a gift from heart to heart."[37] Cather in 1908 was writing stories in which characters talked like people in a Henry James novel. Jewett's example would turn her to writing about characters that talked like the people she had grown up with.

Sympathy—that was the crux of Jewett's art, Cather felt. She gave herself "absolutely to her material," immersed herself in it until *it* was telling the story. She wrote stories that "melt into the land and the life of the land until they are not stories at all, but life itself."[38]

Jewett's example inspired Cather to reclaim her birthright subject: Nebraska. For two more years, while at *McClure's,* she continued to write fiction almost exclusively in her Jamesian mode. Her first novel, *Alexander's Bridge,* completed in 1911, was set in Boston and was Jamesian in its drawing-room dialogue and Eastern characters. But then she opened a new chapter in her writing life. Her first effort in this new vein was called "The Bohemian Girl." Then came a story called "Alexandra," about a Nebraska farm woman.

In March 1911, Cather traveled to South Berwick. Then she joined Elizabeth Sergeant in Gloucester for a holiday. Sergeant was a platonic friend, a Bryn Mawr bluestocking who had arrived in Cather's office in 1910 with a story about tenement life. But they had talked books rather than social problems.

That day in Gloucester, Sergeant noticed, Cather looked "morose." She had been staying at Miss Jewett's home and had used her writing desk in the small green second-floor bedroom. She had a strong feeling that Miss Jewett's spirit hovered there, gently warning her that time was running out. Sergeant also remembered her praising the older woman's "gift for revealing in ordinary country people the treasury of life and feeling that lay below the pinched surfaces."[39] The final push came in 1912 when Annie Fields published her tribute to her life companion, *The Letters of Sarah Orne Jewett;* it contained the two letters to Cather, quoted above, that had so moved the younger author. Reading Jewett's admonitions in cold type, Sergeant believed, roused Willa to start writing her novel about immigrant farmers and rural life in early Nebraska, O *Pioneers!*

Cather said she felt as though she were "taking a ride through familiar country on a horse that knew the way. . . ."[40] In a copy of her novel that she presented to a Red Cloud friend, Willa scrawled this inscription: "This was the first time I walked off on my own feet—everything before was half real and half an imitation of writers whom I admired. In this one I hit the home pasture and found that I was Yance Sorgeson [a character in the novel] and not Henry James."

She said she had written O *Pioneers!* in defiance of the remark of a critic, "I simply don't care a damn what happens in Nebraska."[41] He was a stand-in for the condescending East that cowed her into meek deference—or drove her to emulate Henry James. Jewett, with her stories peopled by Maine folk, predominantly women, had heartened her to accept and affirm who she was. No wonder she dedicated the novel to Jewett.

Of course Cather could not have become the writer she did if she had not also disregarded some of Jewett's maxims. Jewett represented a different literary generation. In her country of the pointed firs, much stayed hidden. Or as Cather delicately observed: "There are many kinds of people in the State of Maine and neighboring States, who are not found in Miss Jewett's books."[42]

To write truly about Nebraska, Willa had to tap dark memories of blighted lives. She remembered, she said in a 1905 letter to a colleague, the poet Witter Bynner, that in the 1880s a lengthy drought ruined scores of Norwegian farmers in her county. Many of them were driven by debt to madness or suicide. Such stark rural tragedies, so common on the Great Plains, were only hinted at in Jewett's stories.[43]

Cather also found it impossible to follow Jewett's advice to portray her women characters through a woman's eyes. She felt more natural seeing her women characters through male eyes, as with the title characters of My Ántonia and A Lost Lady. Expressing Jim Burden's love for Ántonia Shimerda or Niel Herbert's for Mrs. Forrester through a woman's eyes would have resulted in an entirely different book and drawn her into the controversial arena of same-sex affection, which she feared openly expressing.

The women in Cather's novels are sometimes eroticized, of course. She caressingly visualizes Alexandra Bergson's gleaming white skin in O Pioneers! She describes through a male character's eyes the beautiful singer's nudity in her Greenwich Village story "Coming, Aphrodite!" Paradoxically, although Cather could not write about same-sex affection as openly as Jewett did, she could write of women as objects of erotic desire, which Jewett could not. But she did this as if through male eyes and in the context of the franker realism of her generation.

Meeting Fields and Jewett in Boston, observing their contented Boston marriage, also encouraged Cather to make a dramatic change in her personal life. After returning to New York from her Boston sojourn in 1909, she moved in with Edith Lewis, beginning a lifelong companionship. In a letter to Jewett written in October, Cather gives an ebullient description of her new arrangement with Edith, sounding as though she had talked about it in advance with Miss Jewett and Mrs. Fields. They are, she boasts, reveling in their new apartment. Mrs. Fields will be surprised to learn that they have been cooking their own meals, which takes their minds off the stress of their jobs.[44]

Practicality rather than love seems to have been a prime mover in this relationship. Elizabeth Sergeant compared Edith to a first mate who performs necessary and useful tasks while the captain steers the ship. Edith paid the bills, dealt with the maid, bought tickets, shopped for groceries. What Cather had needed most up until then was the "quiet centre of life" that Jewett had urged her to find. She also adopted, wittingly or not, Jewett's remark about needing a wife more than a husband, for she was the dominant partner in this relationship.

For Cather, work came first, and she needed a guardian to create the ideal setting. She was ruthless in asserting her privacy—in exercising what Miss Jewett called "that cold selfishness of the moment for one's work's sake." She told Sergeant that her primary requirement was "to be alone . . . to work in a corner protected by someone who knew what it was all about." In Edith Lewis, and earlier in Isabelle McClung, she found those protectors. Although Lewis pursued a career of her own in publishing and advertising, she devoted herself to serving Willa. She fiercely guarded Cather's legacy after her death in 1947, aggressively enforcing the terms of Cather's will—forbidding movies to be made of her books, destroying letters, barring biographers from quoting from the surviving few.

When Edith died, she was buried next to Willa in Jaffrey, New Hampshire, where they had spent many summers, under a smaller stone.

CHAPTER 6

THE BELIEVER AND THE SKEPTIC

Theodore Dreiser and H. L. Mencken

*As for Doctor, Professor Mencken . . . [he] seems to me to lack faith
in anything and everything save the futility of everything.*
—DREISER TO MENCKEN (1943)[1]

*The truth about Dreiser is that he is still in the transition stage
between Christian Endeavour and civilization, between Warsaw,
Indiana and the Socratic grove.*
—H. L. MENCKEN, "THEODORE DREISER" (1917)[2]

IN 1908, when Henry Louis Mencken met the novelist Theodore Dreiser, who would have such a decisive effect on his career, he was twenty-eight, a native Baltimorean, the son of a prosperous German American cigar manufacturer. He spent his childhood, he said, "as a larva of the comfortable and complacent bourgeoisie."[3] His father's early death freed Henry from working in the family business, which he hated, and with unholy haste he obtained a job as a reporter on the *Baltimore Herald*. After the *Herald* went out of business, he moved to the *Sun*, where he had a quick rise, becoming managing editor, Sunday editor, and author of a regular column, "The Free Lance," which punctured local stuffed shirts.

Journalism was the gaudiest, bulliest life a young man could ever want, he said. But he had literary ambitions. He wrote mooncalf verse, and he turned out competent short stories, some of them published, but his heart inclined toward loftier expression. He burned to write a book on Nietzsche, whose aristocratic philosophy appealed to a part of him linked to his autocratic Prussian ancestors. He was also enamored of Henrik Ibsen's wintry realism. And he longed to write plays with the coruscating wit and contrarianism of George Bernard Shaw. As a Tory and Social Darwinist, though, he had no use for Shaw's socialism. In the meantime, he hired out his typewriter for magazine work, which brought him to Dreiser's doorstep.

Dreiser, then thirty-seven years old, had grown up in far different circumstances than bourgeois Baltimore. Born in Terre Haute, Indiana, in 1871, he was the son of a failed woolen mill operator, a German immigrant and strict Catholic. One of nine children, he knew bleak poverty, picking up coal along railroad tracks for the stove, eating cornmeal mush three times a day, bouncing from house to house and town to town, his precociously sexy sisters ensnared in scandals with callow seducers. It was an education in the injuries inflicted by class in America. He left school in the ninth grade and later spent a year at Indiana University, thanks to the generosity of a former teacher who sensed his talent. He worked as a reporter in Chicago and St. Louis, he turned out magazine "specials" as a freelancer in New York, but, like Mencken, he aimed higher. Reading Balzac, who seemed aware of how the world worked, implanted the dream of being a novelist. His first effort, *Sister Carrie,* appeared in 1900. Though it is now recognized as a seminal work of American realism, at the time only a few scattered critics discerned the novel's greatness. Among its 456 buyers was Henry L. Mencken, who said it deeply affected him.

Dreiser's brooding about the failure of his first novel and his inability to make progress on his second, *Jennie Gerhardt,* drove him to a nervous collapse. After he recovered, he abandoned novel writing for editorial work, at which he was very successful. Within a few years, the author of the "immoral" *Sister Carrie* had become editorial director of Butterick Publications, overseeing an empire of three genteel ladies'

magazines led by *The Delineator,* whose slogan was "Human Betterment."
Peering over his shoulder was George Wilder, the caustic, hard-driving
president of the Butterick Company, who often suggested uplifting
features to Dreiser. One of his ideas was for a series on baby care (he
was the father of four). Dreiser snapped to and signed up Dr. Leonard
Hirshberg, a Baltimore pediatrician who wrote popular articles, to do
a series, with ghostwriting help from his friend Mencken. Indeed,
Mencken ended up writing much of the childcare series, and Dreiser
corresponded with him. The great joke is that the friendship between
these two men, neither of whom ever had or wanted children, began
with solemn exchanges on the meaning of various kinds of crying and
the virtues of bottle over breast feeding.

Mencken produced the clear, practical, and ingratiating prose
Dreiser wanted. He turned out to be able and punctual, and Dreiser
came to depend on him, asking him for editorial advice and article
ideas. Eventually, he offered him a staff job at $50 a week. But Mencken
would not leave Baltimore, where he still lived a comfortable bachelor's
life with his mother in his boyhood home at 1524 Hollins Street.

In the spring of 1908, Mencken ventured to New York and to the
Butterick building at Spring and MacDougall streets. He ascended to
Dreiser's baronial office on the twelfth floor, all dark paneling, drapes,
and Tiffany lamps. The great editor was seated behind a vast desk on a
raised platform; chairs for visitors were positioned so that they had to
look up to him (as Dreiser himself confessed). He recalled that first encounter:

> There appeared in my office a taut, ruddy, blue-eyed, snub-
> nosed youth of twenty eight or nine whose brisk gait and ingra-
> tiating smile proved to me at once enormously intriguing and
> amusing. . . . With the sang-froid of a Caesar or a Napoleon he
> made himself comfortable in a large and impressive chair . . . and

beamed on me with the confidence of a smirking fox about to devour a chicken.4

Mencken's recollection was of "a rich magazine editor with six or eight secretaries," who "had on a suit made by Hart, Schaffner and Marx . . . costing at least $27.50, and used a gold lead pencil."5

Dreiser was an imposing man, over six feet tall, with sensuous, cruel lips and a cast in his right eye. As it happened, Dreiser liked people who stood up to him, and the cocksure Mencken amused him. By the time their meeting had ended, Dreiser recalled, "I counted him among those whom I most prized—temperamentally as well as intellectually."6

Each man was using the other in a friendly way. Mencken sought to make some extra money by extending his range beyond Baltimore. Dreiser wanted to please his boss and boost circulation.

Dreiser also enlisted Mencken to submit his own writings to a publishing company in which he was a silent partner (he didn't want Wilder to know about his outside projects, which were inappropriate for the editor of a ladies' magazine). Mencken proposed books on Nietzsche and Ibsen, and Dreiser recommended them to his colleagues. He also offered to help Mencken place his writings with other editors he knew around town. Then he secretly purchased a failing magazine called *The Bohemian* and bombarded Mencken with pleas for articles, once wiring him close to press time that he needed "3 funny editorials bad" by Monday.7 He got them Monday, and they were gems.

Mencken eventually begged off Dreiser's requests for articles. He told Dreiser that he was nearing thirty and felt keenly his failure to write the great work he had planned to do—a couple of philosophical books and a satirical play "that now encumbers and tortures my system. You will understand what a stew I am in."8

Dreiser indeed understood, because he was growing restless in his current job and yearned to write more novels. He worked on *Jennie Gerhardt* sporadically, but he enjoyed the money and power of his present post. He was still haunted by his past failure, even though the excellent reviews of a new edition of *Sister Carrie* in 1907 had in a sense vindicated him and made him a hero to young people.

Although Mencken was ebullient and witty and Dreiser ponderous and given to brooding, their personalities actually complemented each other's. Perhaps because of his depressive tendencies, Dreiser found that Mencken's buoyant irreverence had a tonic effect on his spirits. He shared the younger man's cheerfully cynical view of human nature, acquired by hanging around police stations, night courts, saloons, and whorehouses.

There was also their mutual Teutonic heritage, especially their liking for good German beer. Dreiser showed Mencken the New York *Brauhäuser* like Luchow's and the Hofbrau. What they talked about on these pub-crawls was unrecorded, but since Mencken was a Nietzschean and Dreiser a Schopenhauerian, they certainly engaged in spirited philosophical arguments. When Mencken sent Dreiser a copy of *The Philosophy of Friedrich Nietzsche,* which he finally wrote for another publisher, he inscribed it, "In memory of furious disputations on sorcery and the art of letters."[9]

Dreiser had a Teutonic craving for the Absolute as well as a superstitious streak handed down by his fey, adored mother, a fount of Old Country lore. He had recently published a controversial series on spiritualism in *The Delineator* that had raised hackles among Bible Belt readers. Dreiser pretended to be objective on the subject, but a part of him wanted to believe in Ouija boards and table-rapping and superstition. Mencken gave the horselaugh to such superstition. He was a materialist to the soles of his high-top shoes. He regarded Dreiser's trust in Christian Science as an abomination. A dedicated hypochondriac, he was a firm believer in conventional medicine: He checked himself in to

Johns Hopkins Hospital at the drop of a symptom. He had doctor friends whom he affectionately referred to as "quacks."

Their first real quarrel was over religion; it was the old clash between the believer and the skeptic. Mencken contributed an article to *The Bohemian* in which he dismissed prayer as superstition. Dreiser objected, saying that the scientific method was a form of prayer. He apparently meant that scientists trying to discover how nature worked were seeking to control it, just as a priest or shaman was trying to influence human destiny by pleas to the gods. Mencken disputed that: "When a man seeks knowledge he is trying to gain the means of fighting his own way in the world, but when he prays he confesses that he is unable to do so." He said the practical man makes efforts to save himself rather than propitiating a putative divinity that may not even exist.[10]

That said, Mencken told Dreiser to change the editorial as he wished. The quarrel created a hairline fracture in their friendship that would in time become a major fault line. Mencken had been raised in an irreligious home; his father was a freethinker. Dreiser's father was a rigid German Catholic, who described the torments of Hell in terrifying ways to his children, implanting lifelong fear and guilt. In his early twenties, Dreiser rebelled, violently rejecting his childhood indoctrination. He devoured Darwinists like Herbert Spencer and Thomas Huxley, renounced Catholicism, and proclaimed the gospel of Spencer, who taught of a God that was unknowable and a universe governed by scientific laws. Dreiser would later write that he could find no meaning to life and sometimes believed that the universe was run by the Devil. Nevertheless, though splenetically anti-Catholic, he carried on a lifelong search for a Creator. Mencken regarded Dreiser as an emotional, credulous man who would eventually return to the Church.

· · ·

In 1910, Dreiser's fortunes drastically changed. He had fallen in love with Thelma Cudlipp, the eighteen-year-old daughter of a Butterick employee. Fearing a scandal, George Wilder ordered him either to give her up or to resign. He resigned, but then Thelma's mother whisked her off to England; he brooded, alone, folding and unfolding his handkerchief, for a decent interval, then went back to his unfinished novel. He told Mencken he was going to write four or five novels he had in mind and if he couldn't make a good living he would return to editing.[11] Mencken urged him to "give the game a fair trial; you have got the goods."[12]

Dreiser completed *Jennie Gerhardt* in 1911. He sent it to Mencken, who threw his hat in the air: "I get a powerful effect of reality, stark and unashamed," he wrote Dreiser. "It is drab and gloomy, but so is the struggle for existence. It is without humor, but so are the jests of that great comedian who shoots at our heels and makes us do our grotesque dancing."[13]

Dreiser's vision of his characters as pawns in an amoral and meaningless chess game, and his view that the question of life had no answers, meshed with Mencken's philosophy. This mature, tragic vision, Mencken believed, was the hallmark of all great European novelists, and Dreiser was the first American novelist to inflect his novels with it. He swam against the dominant literary currents of romanticism and idealism, with a few exceptions over the years such as Hawthorne and Melville, Mark Twain in his blackest effusions, Howells (minus the bourgeois propriety), Frank Norris, and Stephen Crane. All those writers were dead or antiquated. Mencken hitched his wagon to Dreiser's rising star.

By the time *Jennie Gerhardt* was published, Mencken was in a position to give a push to both of their careers. With a recommendation from Dreiser, he took over as book critic of *The Smart Set,* a magazine with a disreputable past that published "society" fiction. Most of the popular novels he read presented life as the preachers thought it should be rather than the grim, morally ambiguous affair it often was. It was against this idealistic fiction that Mencken was whipping up rebellion, and Dreiser was his stalking horse.

In his letter praising *Jennie Gerhardt,* Mencken had said, "Perhaps I read my own prejudices and ideas into" the novel. That was accurate. He would later say, "Dreiser simply gave me a good chance to unload my own ideas, which were identical with his."[14] To Mencken, literary criticism was a personal judgment on the author's character and values.

Over the next three or four years, Mencken was content to serve as Dreiser's loyal factotum and booster. Dreiser was anxious, worried about his marital problems and money; Mencken sent him jocular letters and downed endless seidels of Würzburger with him in New York. Once a book was out, he became a Paul Bunyan of literary logrolling. He reviewed *Jennie Gerhardt* in three different publications, hailing it as the finest American novel he had ever read, save *Huckleberry Finn.*

Dreiser had responded a little uneasily to Mencken's review of *Jennie Gerhardt:* "It sounds too good to be true but it is a great comfort nonetheless."[15] But he gradually became dependent on Mencken's critical judgment and encouragement, having few other peers who were doing what he was doing with the novel.[16] Now he had a friend and rising young critic to tell him.

Mencken's public stand for Dreiser rode the growing wave of rebellion among younger writers and artists against the Genteel Tradition; they had looked to the Continent for their manifestos, and now here was an American painting realistically the American scene. But Mencken's radical views also exposed him to the crossfire Dreiser was drawing from the moralizers in academe and the book review sections. Dreiser told him: "It looks to me as though your stand on Jennie would either make or break you."[17] It made him—and Dreiser too.

Mencken began making regular trips to New York after he was

named co-editor of *The Smart Set.* Not long after *Jennie Gerhardt* appeared in 1911, Dreiser separated from his wife and moved to a shabby apartment on West Tenth Street in Greenwich Village, where he wrote prolifically. Mencken performed double duty, editing Dreiser's manuscripts and then reviewing them in his regular outlets. These books included *The Financier* and *The Titan,* two novels in a projected trilogy about a robber baron, and *A Hoosier Holiday,* a nonfiction account of a motor journey Dreiser made back to the Indiana of his boyhood.

Dreiser's novels, with their pessimistic realism and frank (for the times) sexual themes, regularly drew fire from the moralists, and sales were dispiriting; Dreiser constantly feared he was teetering on the brink of poverty. He wailed to Mencken that he must give up the writing game and return to magazine editing. Mencken, now his main friend and champion, continued to buck him up. "Certainly you'll reach the place where your novels will keep you,"[18] he assured him. He told a friend, "Dreiser is a sensitive fellow and easily dashed."[19]

Then World War I broke out. Mencken and Dreiser's German heritage placed them on the side of the Fatherland and strengthened their mutual Anglophobia. With America officially neutral, but tilted toward Britain and France, Mencken flaunted his pro-German views in his column. As the Kaiser's troops advanced on Paris, he crowed, "In Paris by Christmas!"[20]

Mencken's vociferous pro-German sympathies stemmed from ethnic heritage and a snobbish loyalty to high *Kultur.* At times he seems the voice of Old World superiority, a Teutonic Mrs. Trollope scolding the colonists' bad manners. He differed from the Europhiles in that he enjoyed the show and had no desire to reform anyone. Asked why he lived in America in view of his criticisms of the country, he quipped, "Why do men go to circuses?" On the literary battlefront he led the charge against the entrenched Anglophiles and puritans. He said they marginalized writers from immigrant "stocks" and enforced, through literary criticism, Anthony Comstock's blue laws. Dreiser lacked Mencken's aristocratic bias, his ancestral identification with the Prussian Junkers, but he shared Mencken's Anglophobia and hatred of the censors and moralists.

And so the anti-German sentiments of the time pushed them closer together in the early years of the war. As Thomas Riggio, editor of their correspondence, notes, "Their letters became a secret weapon, a form of defense against an escalating sense of social marginality. The old formulas took on new meaning." Thus, that satiric bogey the "Puritan" was expanded to connote political as well as literary intolerance; Mencken wrote Dreiser about "the Puritan mind" with its "maniacal fear of the German."[21]

Nevertheless, a personal rift was opening up beneath their feet. Mencken harbored a gnawing disapproval of Dreiser's lifestyle and of the avant-garde direction his writing was taking. After moving to Greenwich Village, Dreiser, in line with the "free love" spirit of the Village, conducted a hectic, duplicitous love life. He wrote in his diary during this period, "I believe it would almost kill me—be absolutely impossible for me to be faithful to one woman."[22]

Mencken was a worldly man; he had sexual affairs of his own and a longtime mistress, Marion Bloom, whom he came close to marrying until she converted to Christian Science. But honor and decorums were central to his personal code. He upheld the conventions; adultery was dishonorable, a low blow. "In all matters of manners I am, and have always been, a strict conformist. My dissents are from ideas, not decorums," he once rationalized.[23] The Greenwich Village scene outraged his bourgeois soul; he considered its denizens a bunch of no-talent spongers and phonies. He pictured Dreiser seated in his shabby flat with the huge abstract nudes on the walls, heavy red curtains over the windows, and lugubrious Russian music on the phonograph, composing avant-garde obscurities by candlelight while an attending houri fanned him.

After he and George Jean Nathan took over *The Smart Set,* Mencken begged Dreiser to send him chapters from his next novel. Dreiser instead sent him several experimental dream plays; one, *The Blue Sphere*, tells of a deformed child lured to its death by supernatural forces. Mencken and Nathan published the dramas, but Mencken rejected a short story—"The Lost Phoebe," one of the best tales Dreiser ever wrote. He longed to "blaze out" with an excerpt from a big, naturalistic Dreiser novel, but he complained to Nathan that Dreiser had fallen prey to the arty ideas of his Village seraglio. Relations were further strained by Dreiser's complaining about *The Smart Set*'s low rates.

Mencken's hostility toward the Village baffled Dreiser; he resented the innuendoes that he was becoming a bohemian layabout. Financially pinched, he was working harder than ever, trying to pay the rent and his estranged wife's alimony by writing stories for the tired businessman's bible *The Saturday Evening Post*. He generally remained aloof from the Village counterculture, though, unlike Mencken, he savored its colorful and eccentric characters.

When Dreiser finally did forward the manuscript of his latest novel, Mencken was shocked to discover that it confirmed all his worst imaginings about the Village's corrupting influence. The novel was *The "Genius,"* an autobiographical apologia about an artist torn between commerce and art. Mencken thought the writing sloppy and self-indulgent. And there was too much sex. Mencken feared stirring up the censors—with good reason. He had recently had a run-in with John Sumner, successor to the deceased smut smiter Anthony Comstock as head of the New York Society for the Suppression of Vice. Sumner, an earnest, plodding soldier of the Lord, had been shocked by a harmless magazine that Mencken and Nathan cynically concocted to make money, *La Parisienne*. It was edited for the rubes who thought anything French was naughty. Actually, its contents consisted of fiction from *The Smart Set* rewritten by the editors to transplant the stories to a French setting. When Sumner banned it, Mencken and Nathan fought him in court and won. But the episode left them wary of the censors.

They met in Dreiser's flat to discuss the *"Genius"* manuscript. Mencken's demands for cuts of sensitive material collided with Dreiser's autobiographical realism. When Mencken objected to a scene in which the hero puts his hand on his sweetheart's knee, Dreiser protested, "But that's what happened!" They had words, which became so heated that Dreiser's resident girlfriend fled into the night. For the first time in their relationship, Dreiser spurned his friend's editorial advice and Mencken washed his hands of a Dreiser novel.

Then, perhaps as a peace offering, Mencken asked Dreiser to send him a critique of the contents of *The Smart Set* under his and Nathan's stewardship. Dreiser replied that the editors had "tamed down" the magazine to mere "persiflage and badinage . . . which not even the preacher in Keokuk will resent seriously."[24]

Dreiser provided a list of radical writers connected with *The Masses*, such as Max Eastman and Floyd Dell, whom he thought Mencken and Nathan should feature in their magazine. Mencken replied that he wanted no "red-ink boys"; their stuff was "empty . . . hollow-headed and childish."[25] Dreiser suspected something was "eating" Mencken, and he knew what it was—his bohemian lifestyle was "not suitable for the home streets of Baltimore."[26] The allusion to "the home streets of Baltimore" drew blood. Mencken resented being called provincial, even though he preferred the comfortable ambience of his hometown to the hectic, money-grubbing New York scene.

Dreiser was unhappy that Mencken wasn't measuring up to his high standards, and Mencken was unhappy that Dreiser wasn't measuring up to his. Each stubbornly clung to expectations the other refused to meet.

In 1915, Sumner turned his attention to the nonpornographic effusions of the literary Village, including the proliferating sex manuals. He decided that *The "Genius,"* with its sexual frankness and unpunished seductions, would lead American girlhood astray. He threatened to prosecute Dreiser's publisher for obscenity unless he withdrew all copies of the book.

Mencken's instinct was to rally to his friend's side, whatever his opinion of the novel or Dreiser's personal behavior. The puritans had gone too far. The issue was freedom of speech for all authors. Seeking to mobilize the literary community, he launched a petition drive and obtained the signatures of some 450 prominent American writers.

But when Dreiser collected the signatures of several radicals, Mencken was furious. He believed the most effective protest against censorship would involve respectable authors, including some household names. The radicals' presence muddied his message. He now regarded himself as the master strategist of the petition drive—Ober-General Von Mencken sweeping to Paris. He considered Dreiser a loose cannon, naive, clumsy, and impolitic.

Dreiser countered, reasonably enough, that it was no sin to add to the petition the names of some prominent avant-garde intellectuals who lived in the Village, like Eastman and Dell, who had joined Mencken in praising *Jennie Gerhardt*. Also, to challenge the de facto ban, he proposed selling a copy of the novel and getting himself arrested. This would force the courts to decide whether the book was obscene or not. Spending time in jail would also save him money, which he badly needed.

Mencken was against the test-case strategy. He told Dreiser his timing was bad, given the wave of anti-German sentiment sweeping the country: "A man accused of being a German has no chance whatever in a New York court at this time."[27]

Mencken was running the show, and Dreiser began to chafe under what he called his "dictatorial tone." In Mencken's defense it must be acknowledged that Dreiser was not the most politic of men. At this delicate time, when he was caught in the censors' sights, as it were, he sent Mencken a play he had just written, *The Hand of the Potter*. It was a tragedy; the central character was a sexual pervert.

Mencken erupted: "You have a positive genius for doing foolish things."[28] The censors would fall on this play with knives drawn; in the wake of its inevitable banning, the distinguished authors who had signed the petition would feel morally tainted and back out. Dreiser had double-crossed him.

Dreiser was baffled and hurt: Why the fuss, why the outrage? He had simply followed his natural artistic inclinations, as he always did. He was expressing a personal theory of human nature in this play, derived from his own anarchic sexual desires. He believed that he had been born with a strong sex desire—that desire was a "chemism." It drove people beyond their control. The same held true for the pedophile in the play, whose behavior was criminal but beyond the control of willpower because it was part of his bodily chemistry. The hand of the potter—God—had slipped.

To Mencken, it was the hand of the playwright that had slipped. The thing was wretchedly constructed, a botch, a disaster. Dreiser replied that if it was a failure, the critics would so judge it; he would deserve their condemnation.

Mencken also contended that the very subject of perversion was unsuitable. "It is all very well enough to talk of artistic freedom," he declared, "but it must be plain that there must be a limit in the theatre, as in books. . . . I often have to leave a high-class social gathering to go out and piss; you, at least, have been known to roll a working girl on the couch. But such things, however natural, however interesting, are not for the stage. The very mention of them is banned by that convention on which the whole of civilized order depends."[29]

Dreiser having none of this moralizing from Mencken, of all people. The civilized order indeed! What was unsuitable about the subject matter of his play? Newspapers regularly reported such crimes—and far more sensationally than he had depicted this one. He had soberly, almost clinically (he was accurate there), dramatized a social problem in a restrained way, never showing the perverse acts on stage. He concluded defiantly: "Current convention will not dictate to me where I shall look for art—in tragedy or comedy. My inner instincts and passions and pities are going to instruct me—not a numbskull mass that believes one thing and does another."[30]

The letters rumbled back and forth between New York and Baltimore like artillery barrages on the Western Front. Finally, Dreiser called an armistice. The two met for a beery farewell dinner, and Mencken headed off to cover the war for the *Sun*.

Despite the authors' petition, *The "Genius"* remained suppressed. A New York court later ruled that since Dreiser's timid publisher had voluntarily withdrawn the book the moment Sumner threatened to ban it, there had been no official declaration of obscenity under New York law, and thus Dreiser could not claim his contractual or constitutional rights had been violated, and his suit was thrown out. His novel sank into a kind of legal limbo, effectively banned by the threat of legal action, costing him needed royalties. Dreiser's test-case approach was probably a better legal strategy than Mencken's petition campaign. Yet the latter did produce the first declaration against censorship in American history by a wide range of American authors and the Authors League.

On the surface, the waters were calm, but tensions swirled beneath. They bubbled up in 1917 when Mencken wrote a long critical essay on Dreiser for his first *Book of Prefaces*. It was mainly a tribute, a profound, definitive critical statement of Dreiser's importance, but he sounded his reservations as well. He felt he had become too closely identified with Dreiser for his own good as a critic and needed to distance himself. So his sweet encomiums were soured by his matchless invective, as in this passage, attacking once again Dreiser's excessive credulousness:

> There come moments when a dead hand falls upon him, and he is once more the Indiana peasant, snuffling absurdly over imbecile sentimentalities, giving a grave ear to quackeries, snorting and eye-rolling with the best of them. . . .[31]

Dreiser wrote in his diary that he felt "horribly blue and sad, feeling eventual failure staring me in the face."[32] Having had so much faith in the power of Mencken's criticism when it was deployed in his defense, he was totally devastated when it was turned on him—and in a major essay that Dreiser believed would define his place in American literature.

A frozen silence set in between them. Mencken wrote a friend that Dreiser was "full of some obscure complaint against me."[33] If anything, he was angry that Dreiser would hold the review against him—expecting him to say what he did not believe.

Dreiser did not have Mencken's iron pride; once when they met in a restaurant, he offered to shake hands. Mencken was having none of it: "My excommunication still holds," he told a friend. He claimed to be relieved: He was tired of defending Dreiser. He told a publisher who was trying to mediate their quarrel that Dreiser was too susceptible to the flattery of his Village harem. But he had no intention of carrying on a vendetta against Dreiser: "He has his own work to do, and I may be wrong."[34]

At the same time, he felt isolated and lonely. There was no one in New York with whom to drain a seidel: Nathan was on the wagon. He'd had a falling-out with the feckless writer Willard Huntington Wright, onetime editor of *The Smart Set,* who had come under suspicion of being a German collaborator. When he learned that his secretary was a plant of the British, he dictated a wildly pro-German letter to her as a joke.

All hell broke loose, and the man to whom the letter was addressed, a friend of Mencken's, was interrogated by police and the Secret Service. Mencken, himself suspected as a German spy, was brought in for questioning by the authorities. Showing his unbending sense of honor, he "excommunicated" Wright, an unstable person and a drug addict, despite the latter's apology. "When I am done with a man, I am done with him," he later wrote the friend who had suffered by Wright's reckless act. "He deliberately betrayed my confidence. Such things are not forgiven."[35] Mencken could tolerate Wright's deadbeat ways and his drug addiction, but for him to betray a friend of his, and especially to act stupidly, was over the line. (Wright would reform and, in the 1920s, become author of the Phil Vance detective novels.)

A suffocating miasma of patriotism and repression descended upon America after it entered the war in April 1917. Mencken had given up his *Sun* column because his pro-German opinions were no longer welcome, and he found few outlets elsewhere. He published a couple of books that were denounced by reviewers as Hun propaganda.

Dreiser was also feeling isolated. He told friends that Mencken did not appreciate the experimental work he was doing and wanted him to keep mining the same vein of tragic realism he had worked in *Sister Carrie* and *Jennie Gerhardt*. But he also said: "I am overly fond of Mencken, literally. He is and always will be to me a warm, human, boyish soul, generous, honest and superior—so far above the average run that I cannot even think of him in connection with it."[36]

In the wartime mood of anti-German hysteria, Dreiser had also become a literary untouchable. Critics gave him both barrels: pro-German as well as immoral. His novels were called "barbaric" examples of animalistic Teutonic savagery. This hostility blocked him on his new novel about a religious zealot. Why bother? It would be cursed by critics and banned by the censors, he figured. He turned out short stories to support himself. *The Saturday Evening Post* purchased one for a good sum. Then its super-patriotic editor, George Horace Lorimer, whose editorials inveighed against subversive aliens, decided it (or rather Dreiser) was unsuitable for his 100 percent American audience.

He was ready to make peace with Mencken, but a hidden factor complicated their relationship. Dreiser's current lover, Estelle Kubitz, known as "Gloom" because of her liking for tragic Russian novels, was the sister of Marion Bloom, Mencken's girlfriend, now serving in France as an army nurse. In times past, the two couples had gone out together, but the situation made Mencken vaguely itchy. More troubling, Estelle confided to him how Dreiser mistreated her—his infidelities, his stinginess, his boorishness. Yet, to Mencken's disgust, she kept trotting back to him.

When Estelle was offered a good job but decided to stay with Dreiser, Mencken dressed her down for being Dreiser's "doormat."[37] He was disgusted by what he saw as Dreiser's caddishness, and his distaste for Dreiser as both a man and a writer fused sourly. Still, Dreiser kept making overtures, and Mencken retained a lingering affection for him from the early days. The battle against the puritans, the fight against the censors, their wartime exile, had made them ethnic blood brothers.

The healing balm of humor gradually returned to their letters. At Christmastime, Dreiser sent Mencken a sentimental novel by Bertha M. Clay. Thanking him, Mencken claimed he had read it avidly in the bathroom while suffering the aftereffects of an accidental overdose of castor oil.

Actually, the quarrel signified that their relationship was undergoing another redefinition. Dreiser's rebuff of Mencken's opinions about The "Genius" meant that he wanted to go his own way. That was fine with Mencken, who wanted to go his. Their relative stations in life had changed. Mencken had emerged as an influential critical voice, and he knew it. He told the journalist Burton Rascoe, "We remained on good terms so long as I was palpably his inferior—a mere beater of drums for him. But when I began to work out notions of my own it quickly appeared that we were much unlike."[38]

Once Dreiser told Mencken that he had never really known him. Mencken replied with one of his scatological jokes, of which the punch line was "Well, you ain't missed much."[39]

In 1919, fleeing the Village and his romantic and publishing problems, Dreiser moved to Hollywood, where he hoped to make money writing for the movies. He was accompanied by a woman he had recently fallen for in an epic way, a beautiful, aspiring actress named Helen Richardson, with skin that he compared to blue-veined marble. She satisfied him sexually as no woman ever had. Dreiser had been estranged from his first wife, Sara White Dreiser, since the affair with the Butterick employee's daughter in 1910. She refused to give him a divorce, and he owed her alimony. Helen's marital status was the same, so they kept their whereabouts secret to avoid nosy lawyers and process servers. When he gave his address as General Delivery, Mencken grumbled that it was the "address of a pickpocket."[40]

Dreiser revealed no more. Their letters during this time were taken up with Dreiser's publishing affairs; Mencken edited his manuscripts and acted as his occasional New York agent. He negotiated with the censorious John Sumner on a new, bowdlerized edition of The "Genius." Dreiser grumpily accepted some of the expurgations Sumner demanded, but later, without telling Mencken, he backed out of the deal. He had found a more liberal publisher, Horace Liveright, who was eager to challenge the censors and brought out the complete novel. Mencken was irate but let it go, and Dreiser was perhaps vindicated. In the anything-goes twenties, a flood of steamier sex novels drowned out Sumner's protests. Dreiser's book sold more on its literary merits than its prurient appeal. Dreiser was once more rehabilitated.

He and Mencken were now of an age when they reminisced about better days and complained about creeping decrepitude. When Mencken issued a mock warning against excessive venery, Dreiser replied that every ten years or so someone sent him that very warning, and it always proved to have been exaggerated. Now here was Mencken doing the same, so he could be confident of his potency for another decade.

More tomfoolery: Dreiser proposed that they draw up their last words, something suitably literary. For himself he fancied "Shakespeare I come."[41] A query from Mencken as to the late Theodore Dreiser's resting place drew a reply on the stationery of the "Theodore Dreiser's Widows and Orphans Relief and Aid Association."

Convinced that Dreiser was wasting his time in California, Mencken badgered him to return to civilization: "How long are you going to stay out there among those swamis, actors, tourists, and whores? . . . You are so damned securely buried that thousands of boobs are growing up who have never heard of you."[42] He wanted a heads-up on Dreiser's novel in progress (it was *An American Tragedy*), but the latter would tell him nothing; actually, he was stuck on the book.

Mencken tried to make amends for calling Dreiser a peasant by praising his "proletarian viewpoint," which enabled him to evoke feeling, to appeal to the emotions. But he confided to a friend that while Dreiser was a "great artist," he was a "very ignorant and credulous man."[43] In other words, he was irrational, unintellectual. He felt that Dreiser was regressing in his work, doing inferior stuff. No doubt Mencken's disdain for the peasantry, traceable to his pride in his Prussian Junkers ancestors, had made it a term of contempt—and Dreiser probably sensed it.

Dreiser had his off-the-record view of Mencken as well. He told a friend that the Baltimorean lacked a "sense of beauty"; he was too materialistic, interested only in the visible facts of life. As for himself, he was searching to ascertain the immutable laws of the universe, seeking answers to the eternal questions of why we are here and where we are going.

Some of Dreiser's philosophical ruminations were collected in a book of essays titled *Hey, Rub-a-Dub-Dub!* issued around 1920. In his review, Mencken concluded: "Dreiser is no more fitted to do a book of speculation than Joseph Conrad, say, is fitted to do a college yell."[44]

Dreiser didn't allow his friend's shafts to wound him, and Mencken laid down some advice for keeping the peace between them. Henceforth, he said, "When I write of you as an author, I put aside all friendship; when you write of me as a critic, do the same. In this department I am a maniacal advocate of free speech."[45]

It was a good rule, and one they found impossible to follow.

In 1922, Dreiser returned from California with Helen and the unfinished manuscript of *An American Tragedy.* He continued to be very secretive about this book, the story of a young man who falls in love with a rich girl and plans to murder his pregnant working-class girlfriend. While researching his final chapters, Dreiser wanted to view the death row at Sing Sing prison, and he asked Mencken to use his influence with the *New York World* to wangle him a pass. Mencken did so, but unbeknownst to him, the newspaper requested that Dreiser write up an interview with a convicted murderer. This condition annoyed Dreiser, and he demanded a high fee. When he heard about this demand, Mencken felt Dreiser had once again betrayed him by putting him in an awkward position with people from whom he obtained a favor. The quarrel left a lingering bad taste in Mencken's mouth—another example of Dreiser's boorishness.

Dreiser finished the novel in December 1925. Exhausted and debilitated by a bronchial cold, he and Helen set out for a vacation in Florida.

On the way they stopped in Baltimore at 1524 Hollins Street. At the time Mencken was upset because his mother, to whom he was deeply attached, was in the hospital, seriously ill (she died the next day). By Mencken's recollection Dreiser offered no words of sympathy and talked of other matters. Before departing he asked for a bottle of scotch from Mencken's well-stocked pre-Prohibition cellar and insisted on paying for it. For years Mencken resented his seeming callousness.

Yet Helen remembered that on the way to the car Dreiser expressed great affection and sympathy for Mencken. Why he had offered no consoling words is a mystery. Many years later, Mencken suggested to Helen a possible explanation for Dreiser's behavior: "There was a curiously inarticulate side to him, and it often showed up when he was most moved."[46] These were not men who ordinarily confided their affections.

Dreiser eventually learned of Mrs. Mencken's death and sent belated condolences. He had been traveling and Mencken's letter hadn't reached him. Mencken thanked Dreiser and warned him, by the way, that he was operating on *An American Tragedy* in the next issue of *The American Mercury* "without anesthetics" but "*with* reservations."[47]

The surgery was major. Mencken called *An American Tragedy* "a shapeless and forbidding monster—a heaping cartload of raw materials for a novel . . . a vast, sloppy, chaotic thing of 385,000 words—at least 250,000 of them unnecessary!" But a preponderance of reviewers hailed Dreiser as the Great American Novelist. Even Stuart P. Sherman, the conservative critic who had leveled anti-German attacks at Mencken and Dreiser during the war, praised the book. (Mencken had never forgiven Sherman and spurned his offer to shake hands when they met at a party after the war.)

This time Mencken was in the minority, a company of dissident mossbacks, many of whom thought Dreiser's novel immoral. Concentrating on social and political writing, Mencken had lost touch with the latest literary movements and the young writers, while Dreiser had moved into the mainstream.

Punitive Comstockery was on its last legs—witness the unimpeded sales of The "Genius" and the defeat of a so-called clean books bill in New York's state legislature. True, Boston's Watch and Ward Society banned An American Tragedy the following year—not long after Mencken had gone up there to get himself arrested on the Common for selling The American Mercury, which had also been banned for obscenity. Mencken won his test case, unlike Dreiser's publisher.

Dreiser reacted as badly to the review as he had to Mencken's 1918 essay ridiculing him. In a letter that starts out with an invitation to dinner, he suddenly explodes in spluttering fury: "As for your critical predictions, animosities, inhibitions—et cetera. Tush, who reads you? Bums and loafers. No goods. We were friends before ever you were a critic of mine, if I recall."[48]

Later he told Charles Angoff, Mencken's assistant at The American Mercury, "that boss of yours ought to stay in Baltimore on the Sun and keep out of writing about books. [Eugene] O'Neill is luckier than the rest of us. He has George Nathan to write about him."[49]

Mencken disdained a reply, and for seven years they did not communicate. It was Dreiser who first called for a truce. He corrected an erroneous story about Mencken's work in the "Genius" petition campaign that was to appear in a history of The Smart Set. Mencken wrote to thank him, and Dreiser leaped at the opportunity to revive the friendship. He proposed a meeting in New York "white flags in hand . . . with all knives under the table."[50]

Mencken agreed; he wrote in his diary that he couldn't think of any way to get out of it. Lubricated by two bottles of vodka, they were soon squabbling as in the old days. Only this time the subject was which German restaurant served the best beer and bratwurst.

So the wound healed. They met infrequently and corresponded. There were inevitably disputes over this or that, mainly politics, none serious. Mencken, the Tory, felt the backlash of the leftward shift on campuses as the Depression deepened. In the twenties, irreverence was in, and collegians had flaunted his magazine as a bible of sophistication. No more. Youth was fearful of the future and needed answers, not skepticism. Already weary of editing *The American Mercury* and of contending with his publisher, Alfred A. Knopf, as to its future course, Mencken resigned as editor in 1933.

Dreiser asked Mencken for his thoughts on the Nazi takeover in Germany. Mencken opposed Hitler, yet thought him a political quack, more crazy than dangerous. They both clung to the Teutonic nationalism of World War I, and it clouded their vision of the evils of Nazi Germany. In May 1933, Dreiser came out with some stupid anti-Semitic pronouncements that took him years to live down.

Like many intellectuals in the 1930s, Dreiser became more radical. Mencken avoided the subject but finally asked him point-blank if he was a Communist and swallowed the bunk they were peddling these days. Dreiser fired back a passionate avowal of his political and philosophical credo, including his belief in both God and Stalin. The difference between him and Mencken, he said, was that he had been born poor and wanted a political system that would make life better for the poor. He chided Mencken for being a cynic and a skeptic.

Mencken countered that his first memory of Dreiser was of a rich magazine editor. He pointed out that he (Mencken) had worked for a living since he was a teenager. As for Communism, Stalin's butcheries before the war had exceeded Hitler's.

They agreed not to disagree. After Dreiser moved permanently to California in 1938, Helen still at his side (he would marry her in 1944), they maintained a sporadic correspondence. When he hadn't heard from him for a while, Mencken would send an inquiring letter, checking if Dreiser was still extant. He warned him not to do a deathbed conversion to Catholicism. When Dreiser announced that he had joined the Communist Party, six months before his death, Mencken privately wrote it off to his friend's congenital credulousness. If not Catholicism, then Communism: What was the difference?

They never met again. In 1944 Dreiser traveled to New York to accept the Award of Merit and a $1,000 prize (money he needed) from the National Academy of Arts and Letters. Mencken had attacked that organization in the twenties as a bastion of untalented literary conservatives who had scorned Dreiser as an immoralist. He declined to come to the ceremony despite Dreiser's pleas, accusing him of betraying the cause they had fought for thirty years ago.

Dreiser died in December 1945 of a heart attack. He never returned to his Catholic faith, as Mencken predicted, nor indeed joined any organized religion. He announced to friends that he now believed in a Creator who imposed an intelligent design on the universe.

When Helen wired Mencken of Dreiser's death, he wrote her that it "leaves me feeling as if my whole world had blown up. We had met only too seldom in late years, but there was a time when he was my captain in a war that will never end, and we had a swell time together. No other man had a greater influence upon my youth."[51]

His diary entry closest to the event was more equivocal. He says, "We were never really close friends, for I was a congenital skeptic and he was of a believing type of mind."[52] He probably recalled their first quarrel nearly forty years ago over prayer, with Dreiser defending belief and Mencken skepticism. That rift had run like the San Andreas fault through their friendship, though other cracks opened between them—over literature, decorum, women. Mencken never could accept Dreiser's uninhibited sex life and his search for an answer to the "why are we here" conundrum. Or his passionate quest for social justice, driven by his boyhood poverty. Yes, he was a peasant, a proletarian, but he knew it and was not ashamed. Unlike Mencken, he declared, he believed in the common man.

But he would always be deeply grateful for Mencken's help. In 1943 he wrote: "You arrived in my life when, from a literary point of view, I was down and out, and you proceeded to fight for me. Night and day, apparently. Swack! Smack! Crack! . . . It was lovely! It was classic."[53]

With Dreiser's books to champion in the early days, Mencken was able to perform a signal literary service, while making a name for himself. In a dangerous time for artistic freedom, he stepped up and challenged the censors, articulating, with Dreiser as his test case, a vision of a more mature, truthful, freer American literature.

When Helen wired Mencken the news of Dreiser's death, she closed: "He loved you."[54]

CHAPTER 7

POOR SCOTT,
POOR ERNEST

F. Scott Fitzgerald and
Ernest Hemingway

*I met Gerald and Sara who took us for friends now and
Ernest who was an equal and my kind of idealist. I got drunk
with him on the Left Bank in careless cafés.*
—F. SCOTT FITZGERALD TO ZELDA FITZGERALD (1930)[1]

*. . . you are the best damn friend I have. And not just—oh hell—
I can't write this but I feel very strongly on the subject.*
—HEMINGWAY TO FITZGERALD (1927)[2]

IN APRIL 1925 Scott and Ernest met at Le Dingo (The Crazy)
American Bar in Montparnasse. Hemingway was drinking with
Lady Duff Twysden and Pat Guthrie, the real-life prototypes of Lady
Brett and Mike Campbell in *The Sun Also Rises,* a novel as yet unwritten.
Scott probably initiated the meeting; he had been looking for Heming-
way all over Paris.

In *A Moveable Feast*, a memoir Hemingway wrote in the late 1950s, he
says that the Princeton baseball star Duncan Chaplin was with Fitzgerald. But Chaplin was not even on the Continent in April 1925, and had
no recollection of ever meeting Ernest Hemingway.[3] Like some other
factoids in *A Moveable Feast,* Hemingway summoned Chaplin from a twi-
light zone between memory and imagination—as fiction writers with a
scene to set, a tale to tell, are wont to do.

Hemingway asserts that Chaplin was more likable than Scott, who
is portrayed as a bit of a poseur in his Guards tie. Hemingway warns

Fitzgerald that the Brits on the premises might object to it, establishing his superior savoir faire. Right from the start he was competing.

As the two excellent books devoted to the Fitzgerald-Hemingway relationship by Scott Donaldson and Matthew J. Bruccoli have shown, *A Moveable Feast* is a mélange of fact and fiction. Fitzgerald is a character named "Scott," a pale, blond man with a feminine mouth—the "mouth of a beauty." He is at times a pest, at times a naive, unstable fool who needs to be taken in hand. He starts by asking Hemingway what he was asking everyone at the time: Had he slept with his wife before they were married?

Hemingway also reports that after downing several drinks and a glass of champagne, the pale skin of Scott's face grew tight and waxen, then he passed out. Fitzgerald's tolerance for alcohol was low, but something about this snapshot seems a bit staged. It smells of what they call "foreshadowing" in the writing game.

So Hemingway's recollection, the only eyewitness account of the meeting, is unreliable. What do we know for a fact? We know that Hemingway was twenty-six. And we know that he had a reputation among Americans in Paris as a writer with a future.

We know that Fitzgerald at twenty-nine was a rotogravure-section celebrity with the profile of the Arrow Collar Man and the aura of the eternal collegian about him. His two novels, *This Side of Paradise* and *The Beautiful and Damned,* were considered exposés of the younger generation's wanton behavior, which involved petting in rumble seats and drinking from flasks between Charlestons.

His wife, Zelda, mirrored his public image, the quintessential flapper, kittenishly Southern yet impulsive and shockingly direct, with a cupid's-bow mouth and wild-hawk eyes that darkened to pools of inscrutable anger. The two felt themselves to be twins and they sometimes dressed alike. They were reputed to drink recklessly, trash hotel rooms, insult hosts, pass out on couches, jump clothed into fountains, dive unclothed into the Mediterranean, and toss money around like *merde*.

Hemingway was a promising novice, a handsome, husky chap with a mustache and wide grin and the macho air of a white hunter. He had a knack for winning the love of men and women. He was considered the Real Thing by the American colony, which included more than the statistical norm of phonies, though he had to his name only two slender volumes of stories and poems, published by avant-garde presses in print runs of two hundred copies. His personality and style placed him in the tradition of roughneck American realists like Stephen Crane and Jack London.

After a brief service at the front as an ambulance driver with the Italian army, in which he enlisted at the age of nineteen, he had been wounded in the leg by shrapnel and spent the rest of the war in a Milan hospital recuperating. There he had an affair with a tall, twenty-six-year-old nurse named Agnes von Kurowsky. After the war he married Hadley Richardson, also tall, also several years older than he, whom he met in Chicago. An amateur musician of some talent, she had a modest but useful trust fund.

He was from Oak Park, Illinois, the son of a dominant mother and a recessive father, a doctor. He was thus a fellow Midwesterner to the Minnesota-born Fitzgerald. They'd taken different escape routes. Scott's had been via a Catholic prep school in the East, then to Princeton, a gentlemen's preserve. Hemingway had gone to work for the *Kansas City Star* straight out of high school.

Throughout his early life, Fitzgerald's ambitious mother pushed him into superior social circles. Her inheritance supported the family, allowing the bluer-blooded father to fail respectably. Scott had been, he said, "a poor boy in a rich town; a poor boy in a rich boy's school; a poor boy in a rich man's club at Princeton."[4] He failed his serious courses, and the war came as a relief. After passing the army's second lieutenant's exam in 1917, he left college, confident he would die gloriously in battle. To his chagrin, he remained in the States for the duration. He always regretted missing the show, which Hemingway, who had passed the martial test of manhood, was transmuting into violent vignettes and stories.

Hemingway had studied writing in the city room university with postgrad work in Chicago under Sherwood Anderson, who had been a father and mentor to him, teaching him a simple, unliterary prose style that Anderson had learned from Gertrude Stein in Paris. Hemingway used Anderson's *Winesburg, Ohio* as a model. Anderson had probably also passed on his love of Mark Twain's *Adventures of Huckleberry Finn,* which Hemingway read in the winter of 1925 and ever after considered the headwaters of American literature. The older writer urged him to move to Paris, which he did in 1923 as foreign correspondent of the *Toronto Star.* Anderson had slipped him letters of introduction to Parisian lights including Sylvia Beach and James Joyce.

He and Hadley and their son, John (Bumby), shared a small apartment above a sawmill in Montparnasse. They lived off Hadley's trust fund after Hemingway quit the paper and started writing full time. He earned very little from the literary magazines and small presses that provided the only outlets for his experimental work.

Hemingway was an expatriate reverse snob who sneered at Jazz Age frivolity in distant America. Fitzgerald's feverish lifestyle encompassed all that—New York speakeasies and shiny Duesenbergs and baronial Long Island estates. He wrote stories exclusively about the very young and very rich for the big-money *Post.* He had a romantic tendency to hero worship, glamorizing even as he criticized. He admired aggressively masculine men because he wasn't one himself, and once wrote, "When I like men I want to be like them. I want to lose the outer qualifiers that give me my individuality and be like them."[5] He envied Hemingway's glamorous decoration, the Italian army's Silver

Medal of Military Valor—actually awarded for wounds rather than the valorous deeds Hemingway sometimes added to his citation. Hemingway had passed the test. Now he appealed to Fitzgerald as an idealistic young artist, his poverty a testament to his integrity.

Hemingway made a literary mentor of Fitzgerald, an older, more experienced writer. But there was an undercurrent of challenge; he was already feeling him out for weaknesses, like a club fighter jabbing his opponent. He did that to everyone worth anything.

Matthew Bruccoli writes: "Hemingway needed a claque, Fitzgerald needed heroes."[6] Hemingway needed to dominate and be deferred to; Fitzgerald needed to charm and be loved. When drunk he insulted people as though testing the limits of social tolerance, and then the next day abased himself begging for forgiveness. He had a few leftover friends from his Princeton days, along with a few later ones who admired his mind, talent, and charm. These ties were sometimes strained by his need to borrow money (though he regarded them as debts of honor) and his alcoholic outbursts. Fitzgerald held on to his writer friends like Hemingway, Ring Lardner, John Dos Passos, and John O'Hara. He once said of Dos Passos: "We never quite understand each other & perhaps that's the best basis for an enduring friendship."[7]

Longing to write the artistic novel he had in mind, sick of cranking out stories about debutantes for the *Post,* Fitzgerald spent the summer-fall of 1924 in Cap d'Antibes, on the French Riviera, where life was cheaper than in America. There he completed *The Great Gatsby,* "living in the book" so deeply that his bored, golden-haired Zelda, tanning on the beach, flirted dangerously with handsome French airman Edouard Jozan. Scott forced her to break off the budding affair, but the dalliance had shaken their marriage, unmanned him, made her suicidal. They moved to Paris in late April with their three-year-old daughter, Scottie.

The meeting with Hemingway at the Dingo happened by chance, but Scott had been looking for him. He had first heard of Ernest from his Princeton friend Edmund Wilson. Hemingway had approached Wilson, a rising young critic, and cajoled him into doing a double review of his first two slender books, *Three Stories and Twelve Poems* and *in our time*. Wilson praised the stories in the October 1924 issue of *The Dial*.

Fitzgerald reported to his friend that he had met "Hemminway," who could introduce him to Gertrude Stein.[8] When he wrote Perkins six months later, he still mispelled the young genius's name: "This is to tell you about a young man named Ernest Hemmingway. . . . I'd look him up right away. He's the real thing."[9] Perkins quickly tracked down a copy of *in our time*, which was not easy to do since only 170 had been printed in Paris.

Perkins told Hemingway he admired the volume of stories but could not publish it because it was too slender. He sent a second letter after hearing that Hemingway had a novel in progress. His letter, addressed care of Sylvia Beach's Shakespeare & Co. bookshop, missed Hemingway, who was skiing in the Austrian Alps. By then he had signed a contract with Boni & Liveright for a collection of stories, called *In Our Time* with capitals because B&L was a real publisher.

Hemingway's stories were shipped to Liveright by a vice president of the firm visiting in Paris. He had been given them by Robert McAlmon, whose small press had hand-printed *Three Stories and Ten Poems*. The B&L editors, including T. R. Smith, editor in chief, and the flamboyant Horace Liveright himself, had been enthusiastic about the stories and were eager to sign Hemingway. In February Liveright cabled an offer of $200 for his book and an option on his next two books. Hemingway accepted; it was by far the largest sum he had ever earned from his writing.

Not long after meeting Hemingway, Fitzgerald received a letter from Tom Smith, inviting him to move to Boni & Liveright if things didn't work out at Scribners. Fitzgerald swore his loyalty to Max Perkins and observed that for Liveright to add him to its list would create "a monopoly in restraint of trade" since it already had in its stable two of the other most promising American writers of his generation—e. e. cummings (*The Enormous Room*) and Ernest Hemingway. He added that he would be glad to review *In Our Time* "for any paper you might select."[10]

Smith's letter had already stirred a hornet's nest of rumors in the publishing community. Perkins wrote Fitzgerald to ask if he was jumping to Liveright. Fitzgerald replied that Max was his editor for life. Perkins, whose deep personal loyalty to his authors would become legendary, had dug Fitzgerald out from the slush pile and launched his career with *This Side of Paradise* in 1919.

By this time Fitzgerald was extolling his editor to Hemingway, who had already promised Perkins that he would be the first to know should he ever be free from his contract with B&L. His only reservation was that Scribners was a conservative house, and his instinct was to push the limits for sex and four-letter words. Charles Scribner, Jr., it was said, would as soon allow obscenities in his books as permit someone to use his living room for a latrine.

A few days after their encounter at the Dingo, Fitzgerald met Hemingway for drinks at the Closerie des Lilas, a café frequented by neighborhood people, including some ex-soldiers mutilated in the war. Hemingway recalled Fitzgerald downing two whiskeys and being "cynical and funny and very jolly and charming." He impressed the acolyte with his knowing observations on "writers and publishers and agents and critics and George Horace Lorimer [the autocratic editor of *The Saturday Evening Post*], and the gossip and economics of being a successful writer."[11] He also spoke cynically about writing for the *Post*, claiming that his method was to write a good story, then use his technical skills to dumb it down so Lorimer would accept it. Hemingway objected to this kind of whoring. Scott replied that he had to make enough money so he could write chancy artistic novels. Hemingway vowed to keep his talent inviolate.[12]

Inside Fitzgerald, the highly paid *Saturday Evening Post* artisan, was a serious artist whipped on by a strong ambition. As he wrote in his notebook: "An inferiority complex comes simply from not feeling you're doing the best you can."[13]

The artist within had emerged in April 1925 when Charles Scribner's Sons published *The Great Gatsby,* the definitive novel of the Great Bubble. Artistically it was perfection. Gilbert Seldes, among the highbrow critics, lauded Fitzgerald's use of "irony and pity," and said, "He has mastered his talents and gone soaring in a beautiful flight," leaving the rest of his generation on earth.[14] T. S. Eliot called *Gatsby* the first advance in the American novel since Henry James. Edith Wharton praised the progress Fitzgerald had made over his previous novels and said that *Gatsby* augured "even greater things."[15]

Commanding *The Saturday Evening Post*'s highest rates and buoyed by the critical success of his novel, he considered himself the "biggest man in my profession."[16]

Yet he was constantly plagued by money worries. From Scott's perspective, *The Great Gatsby* sold "only" twenty thousand copies. He had earned "only" $37,000 from the three novels he wrote between 1920 and 1926, an average of $5,300 a year. The problem was that his expenditures were $30,000 a year (perhaps $360,000 in today's dollars). Hemingway and Perkins blamed Zelda for the extravagant lifestyle that kept Scott tethered to the magazine millstone. But it was a folie à deux. "We ruined ourselves," he told Zelda; "I have never honestly thought that we ruined each other."[17]

·   ·   ·

At their meeting at the Closerie des Lilas, Fitzgerald invited Hemingway to join him on a trip to Lyon to pick up his car, which he had left with a mechanic. Hemingway accepted.

Scott overslept, missing the train, so Ernest went to Lyon without him. The following day Scott turned up at the hotel. They had breakfast and Scott ordered the chef to pack an elaborate lunch. Then they picked up the auto, now minus its roof (Zelda wanted a chop-shop convertible) and set off for Paris. They made frequent stops en route to crack bottles of Mâcon and raid the picnic hamper. It rained constantly, making the lack of a roof more unpleasant. Scott worried that the exposure would cause congestion of his lungs (he believed himself tubercular) and pneumonia, of which there had been a recent outbreak that wiped out scores of Frenchmen.

They stopped at a hotel and he took to his bed, insisting that Hemingway take his temperature. Room service delivered a bath thermometer. Rather than tell Fitzgerald the truth and prolong the whole process, Hemingway says he placed it under the patient's armpit. After a solemn interval he extracted it and pronounced Scott normal.

The next day was balmy and they drove to Paris in good time. On the way Fitzgerald lectured Hemingway on the novels of Michael Arlen, recommending that he study *The Green Hat,* an international best-seller. Ernest said he couldn't stand Arlen's chic novels (though later critics say Lady Brett Ashley shares some traits with Arlen's heroine). Then Fitzgerald recited the plots of all of Arlen's books.

In *A Moveable Feast* this trip is blown up into a comical set piece, lampooning Scott's childish incompetence. (The thermometer escapade may have remotely inspired Hemingway's story "A Day's Wait," in which a little boy with a fever learns fear of death.) At the time, though, Hemingway wrote Max Perkins: "We had a great trip together driving [Scott's] car up from Lyon then the Cote d'Or. I've read his Great Gatsby and think it is an absolutely first rate book."[18]

Fitzgerald told Gertrude Stein, also an admirer of *Gatsby*, that he had had a "slick drive through Burgundy" with Hemingway, who is "a peach of a fellow and absolutely first rate."[19] He later included the journey in a list of his "Most Pleasant Trips."[20]

The friendship warmed in the Paris summer. Fitzgerald regarded Hemingway as "an equal and my kind of idealist" in literature.[21] The summer would be a dead loss as far as his new novel was concerned—"1000 parties and no work," he complained to Bunny Wilson.[22] Inhaling the modernism in the air, Scott conceived a novel that would be "something really new in form, idea, and structure—the model for the age that Joyce and Stein are searching for, that Conrad couldn't find."[23] But he succeeded only in completing a long story, "The Rich Boy," one of his finest but not the new note he was searching for.

He seemed more devoted to café hopping than to writing—or so Zelda charged. She was jealous of Hemingway, who had formed an instant dislike for her. He always describes her in asexual language—wan, neurotic, hawklike. She was given to saying bizarre things like "Ernest, don't you think Al Jolson is greater than Jesus?"[24]He was not alone in thinking she was crazy. He also thought she had lesbian traits, but he was fascinated by the lesbians he knew in Paris, like Stein and her partner Alice B. Toklas, and the elegant Sapphists tea dancing at Natalie Barney's salon, and he may have been projecting this fascination on Zelda. In fact, she was or would be attracted to women; revulsion at a macho man may have been an early sign. She said things such as no man could be "as male as all that."[25] (Scott loyally protested when she put down Hemingway, once telling her to "lay off Ernest" after she quipped that *The Sun Also Rises* was about "bullfighting, bullslinging and bullshit.")[26]

Hemingway believed that Zelda was jealous of Scott's writing and that she made him take her partying so he would be in no condition to write the next day.[27]

But Zelda claimed that Hemingway encouraged Scott's careless drinking. Her intuition that Hemingway was dominating Scott was perceptive. Hemingway "lorded it over [Fitzgerald] from the start," writes biographer Kenneth Lynn; Bruccoli says much the same thing.[28] He had been tested in the war; he was stronger, more macho, more sexually experienced, a heroic drinker. In a letter to Fitzgerald written two months after their first meeting, he fantasized about their different versions of Heaven. Fitzgerald's would be "filled with wealthy monogamists, all powerful and members of the best families all drinking themselves to death." Hemingway's Heaven would provide ringside seats for the bullfights and two houses in town, one for his wife and children and the other for his "nine beautiful mistresses on 9 different floors."[29] He would, of course, satisfy all those women.

Zelda believed that Scott was neglecting his career to promote Ernest's. The Wisconsin-born novelist Glenway Wescott, in Paris at this time, acquired the same impression. He recalled Scott insisting that his *Gatsby* and Wescott's latest novel were inferior to Hemingway's work. He called Ernest the "one true genius" of their generation.[30] To Wescott (whose homosexuality Hemingway cruelly caricatures in *The Sun Also Rises*), Fitzgerald's deference seemed "a morbid belittlement and abandonment of himself."[31] It was as though helping Hemingway were a kind of expiation for the waste of his own talent. Helping Hemingway's career was also a way for a commercial American writer to gain admission to the clannish expatriate scene.

So Fitzgerald busied himself on Hemingway's behalf, urging his agent, Harold Ober, to take him as a client, writing a review of *In Our Time* for *The Bookman,* trying to persuade H. L. Mencken, whom he regarded as the greatest American critic, to publish Hemingway in *The American Mercury.* (Mencken stereotyped Hemingway as one of the expatriate set, whom he disdained as poseurs. He had dismissed *In Our Time* as the "sort of brave, bold stuff that all atheistic young newspaper reporters write.")[32]

In August or September, Fitzgerald finally did start a new novel, about an expatriate who kills his mother. It would take him eight years to finish what became *Tender Is the Night.*

Hemingway wanted to leave Liveright; Scribner's pasture looked greener. His disillusionment peaked in October 1925 when *In Our Time* was published and fell considerably short of selling out its modest first printing. He felt Liveright had not adequately believed in his stellar potential. He criticized the small print run, the dearth of advertising, the boring jacket with blurbs from writers like Anderson. This last was standard procedure with an unknown's first book, but Hemingway felt it belittled his talent.

He felt no gratitude to Horace Liveright for publishing his first book. Why should he? He knew damn well he was the real thing. Liveright had not promoted him as he deserved to be promoted. And he was still fuming about censorship. Liveright had insisted he drop the story "Up in Michigan," about a young man's seduction of a Northern Peninsula girl. He had also excised from another story references to a married couple's efforts to make a baby.

Hemingway's contract gave Liveright an option on his next two books; the agreement would be terminated if the publisher rejected either of them. What Hemingway did was to write a book Liveright was bound to reject. It was a parody of Sherwood Anderson's *Dark Laughter.* It was called *The Torrents of Spring.* As he admitted to Scott, "I have known all along that they could not and would not be able to take it as it makes a bum out of their present ace and best seller Anderson. I did not, however, have that in mind when I wrote it."[33] This may have been true: What he had in mind was demolishing Anderson. He was damned if he was going to stay in his paternalistic shadow. Besides, in the best-selling *Dark Laughter,* Anderson's naive style (influenced by Gertrude Stein) and Greenwich Village Freudianism verged on self-parody.

Time for the disciple to jump ship. He overrode Hadley's protests that he was sucker-punching a kind man who had helped him.

But to say he deliberately composed a book-length parody just to goad Liveright into breaking the contract is to make him too Machiavellian. He was willing (he wrote Liveright) for B&L to publish his next two books—if it did so on *his* terms and not the terms of his unfair agreement, which for a paltry $200 gave Liveright an option on them. He demanded more support, more money, more personal attention, more advertising, *and* no quotes on the jacket. And he wanted an immediate reply.

Fitzgerald had nothing to do with the writing of *Torrents*. He does appear in it under his own name. He had turned up drunk at the Hemingway apartment and stumbled into the (empty) fireplace; Hemingway immediately dropped that misadventure into his shaggy narrative. In a letter dated November 30, Fitzgerald apologized to Hemingway: "It is only fair to say that the deplorable man who entered your apartment Saturday morning *was not* me but a man named Johnston who has often been mistaken for me." He was eager to read "the comic novel."[34] Scott did write a testimonial to Liveright calling *Torrents* the funniest novel ever written by an American. Praising it to Liveright seems inconsistent with plotting to break Ernest's contract.[35]

Hemingway sent the manuscript of *Torrents* to Liveright with a cover letter that sounds like a cocky young writer pitching his new work. He points to the tradition of parody in the English novel—comparing it to Henry Fielding's satire of Richardson's *Pamela*. He assures him it will sell twenty thousand copies. Though he should ask for $1,000 he'll take an advance of only $500—the minimal amount he can accept and still be sure Liveright will push the book. As for hurting Anderson's feelings, no one "with any stuff can be hurt by satire." He goes on: "It should be to your interest to differentiate between Sherwood and myself in the eyes of the public and you might as well have us both under

the same roof and get it coming and going."[36] There is no doubt about
who is the comer and who the goer.

On December 30, 1925, Liveright wired a rejection, followed by a
breezy letter: "Really, old top, even admitting that Torrents of Spring is
great American satire, who on earth do you think would buy it?" It was
a "bitter . . . almost vicious caricature" of Anderson, and its satire was
"entirely cerebral." He scoffed at the charge that he had not advertised
In Our Time; Hemingway needed to write a successful novel, then his
short stories would sell.[37] He patiently awaited said new novel under
their contract.

Hemingway replied that with the rejection of Torrents he considered himself free to pursue other attractive offers. "I also know that I
will . . . eventually make a great deal of money for any publisher," he
bragged.[38]

Acting as his friend's official go-between, Scott telegraphed
Perkins: "YOU CAN GET HEMINGWAY FINISHED NOVEL PROVIDE YOU
PUBLISH UNPROMISING SATIRE."[39]

Fitzgerald had learned that the publisher Harcourt, Brace had offered $500 for Torrents and $1,000 for the new novel. This intelligence
was useful to Perkins. Knowing how high the competition would go
would help him in bargaining with Hemingway. Fitzgerald warned him
that Hemingway, though "one of the nicest fellows you'd ever meet,"
was naive about publishing and very excitable.[40] So Max should be sure
to get a *signed* contract. Perkins agreed to publish *Torrents of Spring* (which
was indeed unpromising in terms of sales), and Hemingway's next
novel (which was, in fact, unfinished).

Fitzgerald asked Perkins to destroy his Hemingway letters.[41] He
had walked a tightrope between his friend and his editor, trying to play
fair with both, without a shred of deviousness. He wanted no misunderstandings on Hemingway's part.

In February, Hemingway sailed to New York, where he had a

friendly farewell drink with Horace Liveright and then met with Perkins, who offered him Harcourt, Brace's terms: $1,500 for both *The Torrents of Spring* and the second novel he was now working on. Harcourt would not up the ante, so Hemingway signed with Scribners, who would henceforth be his only publisher.

Perkins also wanted to publish Hemingway's boxing story "Fifty Grand" in *Scribner's Magazine.* The story recounts an aging prizefighter's last bout. Fitzgerald had played an editorial role, suggesting that Hemingway cut a true anecdote that leads off the story on the grounds that it was too well known. Hemingway dropped it. Perkins and the editor of *Scribner's* liked the story but asked Hemingway to trim it further to fit the magazine's maximum length of eight thousand words. Hemingway refused. "Fifty Grand" would be published in the *Atlantic Monthly* with Scott's cut but otherwise intact.

After Hemingway departed, Perkins wrote Scott: "I am extremely grateful to you for intervening about Hemingway. He is a most interesting chap about his bull fights and boxing."[42]

Hemingway spent the spring revising his novel and shipped it to Perkins, who was enthusiastic, though worried about profanity. Accompanied by Hadley, Bumby, and his new love, Pauline Pfeiffer, a *Vogue* fashion editor in Paris, Hemingway joined the Fitzgeralds on the Riviera. Gerald and Sara Murphy, a gilded young couple who maintained a home that was a guesthouse for visiting Americans, were on the scene. Just that winter they had taken up Ernest and were enthusiastic about *The Sun Also Rises,* which he'd read to them in manuscript. They welcomed the Hemingway ménage with a party in a restaurant. Scott and Zelda came late and very drunk. Perhaps jealous of Ernest's starring role, Scott was on his worst behavior, breaking ashtrays, leering at a pretty girl until she called the headwaiter. Gerald Murphy was so disgusted he left early.

Scott put jealousy aside when Ernest asked him to read his manuscript. He spent several days on it and gave him tough, intelligent criticism. And he did so in a tactful way that avoided offending Hemingway.

He strongly disliked the first two chapters, in which Hemingway provides biographies of Jake Barnes and Brett Ashley. Fitzgerald told him he was surprised to see these passages, knowing Hemingway's belief "in the superiority . . . of the *imagined* to the *seen*." Here he was explaining rather than showing. He proposed several cuts throughout. After his sharp criticisms of the first two chapters, though, Scott said he had been too enthralled to do any more faultfinding: "The novel's damn good."[43]

Fitzgerald was right. The first chapters contain too much "elephantine facetiousness" and violate what would become Hemingway's signature technique of showing only the tip of the iceberg.

Hemingway's respect for Scott was such that he accepted his suggestions and cut even further; as a result, the published book begins with the sentence: "Robert Cohn was once middleweight boxing champion of Princeton." In a letter to Perkins accompanying the revised manuscript, Hemingway mainly invokes Scott as an authority in defending what he represents as his changes. Thus, it is "Scott agrees with me" rather than "Scott suggested."

And Fitzgerald remained involved in the editing process as an intermediary between author and editor. On first reading, Perkins had pronounced the book "a most extraordinary performance . . . astonishing."[44] But he confided to Scott that it still verged on being "unpublishable" because of four-letter words and possibly libelous portraits of real people. He'd already gone to the mat with Scribner over whether to accept the book at all. Then there was Jake's reference to "Henry James's bicycle," referring to an accident that possibly rendered James impotent. Henry James was a venerated Scribners author who still lived in the memories of some people there.

Fitzgerald saw no problem with the James allusion. He said he did have reservations about a hero with Jake's incapacity. Impotence was a fit subject only for humor, he said. Also, Hemingway was so hung up on the taboos surrounding the subject that he had "edited the more vitalizing details out." As far as Scott was concerned, the only censorable passage was one that repeated the word "balls." He added a plea: "Do ask him for the absolute minimum of necessary changes, Max—he's so discouraged about the previous perception of his work by publishers and magazine editors."[45]

Perkins thought Hemingway had handled the hero's impotency problem with sufficient delicacy; it was the four-letter words that could get the book banned. Ultimately, Hemingway cut "balls" and left a blank where "shitty" occurs in an improvised song Jake's friend Bill sings, about "irony and pity . . . when you're feeling ——."[46]

In that scene Hemingway was mocking Gilbert Seldes's review of *The Great Gatsby,* which had praised Fitzgerald's use of "irony and pity." Fitzgerald's influence shows up in other passages. Jake says that impotence can be treated only humorously. There are allusions to writers in the States who write articles about whether a flapper should bob her hair—a dig at Fitzgerald's popular *Post* story "Berenice Bobs Her Hair." He grafted some of Zelda's traits onto Brett.

Hemingway would later erase from the historical record Fitzgerald's contributions to *The Sun Also Rises.* In *A Moveable Feast* he says he did not show the manuscript to Fitzgerald until after he had edited and cut it. He similarly fouled the record on Fitzgerald's help with "Fifty Grand," claiming Scott had "mutilated" the story by his inept editing.[47]

In the 1930s, in a letter to John O'Hara, Scott deprecated his role in shaping the novel. He said, "The only effect I ever had on Ernest was to get him in a receptive mood and say let's cut everything that goes before this. The pieces got mislaid and he could never find the part I said to cut out. And so he published it without that and later we agreed that it was a very wise cut."[48] The last sentence is odd. Scott may be confusing what Ernest actually cut with his suggestions at the time for smaller trims.

The Sun Also Rises was published in October to smashing reviews and robust sales. Fitzgerald was still struggling with his next novel. He and Zelda sailed for the States in December 1926. Aboard ship he wrote reassuring words to Hemingway, who had recently separated from Hadley and intended to marry Pauline. He said their friendship had been "the brightest thing" about his stay in Europe. He promised to look after Ernest's interests at Scribners but guessed his help was no longer needed, given the success of The Sun Also Rises.[49] The balance had shifted: Scott was no longer the insider.

Receding with the shores of France were the best days with Hemingway. There would be no second act in this friendship.

In January 1927, Scott went out to Hollywood for a lucrative scriptwriting stint. His bank account restored, he rented a large white-elephant mansion called Ellerslie outside Wilmington, Delaware. He wrote Ernest briefly about his Hollywood experiences and added that he was glad the novel was "such a brilliant success" and also selling. He closed, "For God's sake come and visit us this summer. Always your devoted friend."[50] Ernest insisted that Scott was his friend too: "Oh shit I'd get maudlin how damned swell you are."[51]

That November Ernest came to the States with his new, pregnant wife, Pauline, whose comparative advantages included being wealthier than Hadley. They settled in Key West for a while, then proceeded to Arkansas, where her father was a big landowner, and then Kansas City, where Patrick Hemingway was born. On a roundabout swing through the East, before returning to Florida to spend the winter, they called on Scott in Delaware. He took them to the Princeton-Yale game and got drunk and disorderly. When Hemingway told him he was nearly finished with his new novel, *A Farewell to Arms,* Scott was devastated and claimed he was working eight hours a day on his, which was a lie. He had failed to meet the delivery dates he promised to Perkins.

Pauline returned to Key West, where Hemingway's sister Sunny was caring for their new baby, Patrick. Ernest went to New York to meet Bumby, his son by Hadley, who had arrived by ship for a stay with his father. Then, on December 6, Hemingway, accompanied by Bumby, boarded a train for Key West. In transit, Hemingway received a telegram saying his father had died (depressed over failing health, he had shot himself); finding himself temporarily short of cash to buy a ticket to Chicago, he wired Scott for help. Scott met him in Baltimore with a hundred dollars.

Whatever Scott's own financial situation, whenever Hemingway was in a financial pinch, he would send him a hundred dollars or two. Hemingway still lectured Scott about wasting his talent on magazine stories to make money when he should be working on his next novel. Yet Scott, whose definition of "genius" was the ability to hold two contradictory thoughts at the same time, was able to separate his hack work from his novels. The problem was that the potboilers took up too much of his time, and also he often needed infusions of gin to write them.

The Fitzgeralds spent the summer of 1928 in Paris, and Scott began another draft. Zelda, now twenty-eight, was feeling the chill of her onrushing thirties. (Scott, too, was obsessed with growing old. When he had turned thirty the previous year, he had moaned, "It is tragic. What is to become of me, what am I to do?" Hemingway once scolded him: "You put so damned much value on youth it seemed to me that you confused growing up with growing old.")[52] Seeking a physical outlet, Zelda took ballet lessons.

In March 1928, Scott and Zelda were back in Paris. Ernest and Pauline had returned from Key West, but Ernest told Perkins not to reveal his address to the Fitzgeralds; he was feeling the "horrors" at the prospect of their arrival. Pauline disapproved of them as well. The drunken scenes had lost their charm. There had been more late-night visits the last time. Scott abused the concierge when he wouldn't admit him, and pissed on the steps. Hemingway feared that Scott's destructiveness would queer things with his landlady.

When Scott heard about the ban, he was hurt. It was humiliating not to know Ernest's address while other people did. Hemingway later relented, but damage had been done. Thus began what would become the Dangerous Summer of their friendship—1928.

Scott's drinking was dragging him to the lower depths—quarrels, brawls, arrests. Zelda told him that he'd been "literally eternally drunk the whole summer."[53] She complained that he no longer slept with her; he hit back that she was frigid because she was a lesbian and had fallen in love with her teacher, Mme. Egorova.

According to *A Moveable Feast,* he consulted Dr. Hemingway for advice on his sexual problems. In a chapter called "A Matter of Measurement," Hemingway writes that Scott confessed fears about the adequacy of his equipment. They adjourn to the *pissoir* where Hemingway pronounces him perfectly normal and gives him fatherly advice on sexual technique.

To Matthew Bruccoli, it was "a gauge of Fitzgerald's capacity for self-abasement that he revealed this problem to Hemingway."[54] Kenneth Lynn says the tale reveals Hemingway sadistically making Scott submit to Papa's verdict on his manhood.[55] But something doesn't add up about the story. Zelda was complaining about Scott's neglect of her, not the inadequacy of his member. So why would he go through all that humiliation with Ernest to find out if he was normal in size?

A more bizarre sexual wrinkle in their friendship, which Hemingway doesn't mention in *A Moveable Feast,* was the rumors that they were homosexual lovers. Zelda was one source of these allegations. After the Fitzgeralds had dined with the Hemingways, Scott and Ernest had gone carousing. When Scott came home, he fell into a drunken sleep. Just before he dropped off, Zelda heard him murmur, "No more, baby." She instantly interpreted this as evidence that Scott and Ernest had been lovers. The morning after, she confronted Scott with her suspicions; he was enraged. He later told her he had nearly walked out "when you told me that I was a fairy."[56] At a time when she worried about her own sapphic tendencies, her accusation seems a hysterical displacement of her fears on Scott. Or perhaps she was paying him back for saying she was in love with Mme. Egorova. Whatever her motives, it was a castrating charge.

Another source of rumors was Robert McAlmon, who spread the word that Hemingway was queer. Max Perkins heard this from McAlmon himself, whom Hemingway had sent with a manuscript of short stories. When Fitzgerald learned about it, he told Perkins that McAlmon was a failure and a congenital liar who had once told Hemingway that *Scott* was queer.

Some biographers suggest that these rumors drove them apart. They cite a passage in Scott's notebook: "I really loved him, but of course it wore out like a love affair. The fairies have spoiled all that."[57] But Fitzgerald was simply saying that friendships, *like* love affairs, run their course—one party tires of the other. The line about "the fairies" spoiling "all that" is a separate thought; he was thinking about McAlmon but also saying that one can no longer speak of loving another man. Fitzgerald, who had a keen eye for manners and morals, observed that the language of male friendship had become eroticized compared to the Victorian era. In the 1920s, when a man said he loved another man, it was assumed he meant sexually.[58] At the same time, being called a fairy was a fighting insult. If you were a man, you punched out the creep who made the charge. When Hemingway later caught up with McAlmon in a bar, he decked him.

In the 1930s, Scott would tease Hemingway about the rumors of their being gay. For instance, he wisecracked about "your days with

MacCallagan or McKisco, Sweetie," a reference to the McAlmon rumors (McKisco was a fictional character Fitzgerald had based on McAlmon).[59] On another occasion, Hemingway warned him to be careful in
kidding about this subject—somebody might take him seriously.

Scott's friendship with Ernest was not queered, so to speak, by the
homosexuality rumors. There were more than enough misunderstandings between them to do that. There were, for example, the repercus-
sions generated by the boxing match in Paris that summer of 1928
between Hemingway and Morley Callaghan, the Canadian writer.
Fitzgerald, acting as timekeeper, let the round go on too long when
Callaghan was winning. Hemingway accused him of deliberately extending the round because he enjoyed watching him being beaten up.
It's more likely that Scott became so wrapped up in the fight that he
forgot his job; he felt terribly guilty about his lapse.

Later that fall, a gossip columnist for *The New York Herald Tribune* reported a garbled account of the fight that had Callaghan knocking
Hemingway cold after he challenged Callaghan's knowledge of the
sport. Hemingway was furious about the story and ordered Scott to
write Callaghan a letter demanding he publicly retract it, which Scott
meekly did. Eventually, the truth came out: Callaghan had had nothing
to do with the newspaper story, which originated in Latin Quarter
gossip.

Hemingway wrote and apologized to Fitzgerald. He insisted he had
never believed that Scott would deliberately let the round run over.
After mentioning two good friends of his who had recently died, he
closes: "I'll be damned if I'm going to lose you as a friend through some
bloody squabble."[60]

Yet Hemingway did not purge the betrayal he felt; it smoldered
into a generalized distrust of Scott's literary counsel. Also, the success
of *The Sun Also Rises* acted like steroids on Hemingway's ego. The apprentice was taking over the shop.

He refused to show Scott the manuscript of *A Farewell to Arms* until after a serialized version began to appear in the June issue of *Scribner's Magazine,* presumably feeling that by then his friend's advice would have been rendered superfluous. But Scott was not about to be silenced. He read the typescript carefully and sent a nine-page letter bristling with comments: Pages such and such move slowly and need cutting, pages such and such are dull. The depiction of Catherine as the courageous little mother-to-be was trite and sentimental. If Ernest insists on retaining the word "cocksuckers" the book will be suppressed. At one point Scott writes: "Our poor old friendship probably won't survive this but there you are—better me than some nobody in the Literary Review that doesn't care about your future."[61]

Hemingway scrawled on Scott's letter: "Kiss my ass. E.H."[62]

Scott had abandoned the diplomatic tone he had used in his critique of *The Sun Also Rises.* Hemingway read into Scott's notes a presumption of superiority. This would be the last time he let Scott read a manuscript. In the 1930s he retailed false anecdotes about Scott's asinine advice on *A Farewell to Arms.* When Perkins wanted to bring Scott with him on a visit to Hemingway's home in Key West, Ernest forbade it because he was revising a book and didn't want Scott on the premises bothering him with his crazy opinions.

Fitzgerald was floundering, his novel adrift. Hemingway began ragging him. Fitzgerald felt so abashed he would exaggerate his progress. At first he promised it would "be finished July 1st" [1927]." That date passed and then others, turning like leaves of the calendar in old movies. Yet he was working and reworking it when he had a chance. He changed its focus several times until it was completely different from the book he had started in Paris in 1926. At some point Hemingway read excerpts and encouraged him.

Hemingway told him he was trying too hard. In a letter in September 1929 he harked back to his old view that the Gilbert Seldes review praising Scott's "irony and pity" had "constipated" Scott by making him think he had to "write a Masterpiece." From what he'd read of it, the new novel was as good as the best of The Great Gatsby, but he scoffs at Scott's latest claim of progress and suspects he's sending out "glowing reports."[63]

Scott made a maudlin confession: He had written twenty thousand words and they weren't any good. He was going through throes of depression; he had crying jags. "My latest tendency is to collapse about 11:00 and with the tears flowing from my eyes and the gin rising to their level and leaking over, & tell interested friends or acquaintances that I haven't a friend in the world and likewise care for nobody." Hemingway was "too kind" in not mentioning the deleterious effect of booze on his work. He feared he had written himself out: In the five years after getting out of the army in 1919 he'd done three novels, fifty stories, a play, and some articles. P.S.: "The Post now pays the old whore $4000 a screw," but she's had to "master the 40 positions—in her youth one was enough."[64]

Hemingway wrote back that his depression was just the letdown every artist feels after creation. He was sure the novel was "damned good." He wasn't finished as a writer; he had a lot left in him. He added: "They never raise an old whore's price . . . so either you aren't old or not a whore or both. . . ."[65] Hemingway's sympathy was real but it was congealing into pity, which would harden into contempt.

Meanwhile, Zelda's inner demons had come screaming in the night. She had been increasingly erratic for the past summer, obsessed with ballet practice and her aging body (though she had been offered a job as a chorus girl). In April 1930, she entered a clinic near Paris, later transferring to one in Switzerland, where Scott joined her. They sailed for America in September 1931 and never returned to Europe. She would be in and out of institutions for the rest of her life. Scott, struggling against alcoholism, ill health, and crack-ups as well as the faltering of his powers, spells of creative sterility, the indifference of editors, and the reading public's amnesia, would devote the rest of his writing life to paying for her care.

As he wrote in his notebook: "I left my capacity for hoping on the little roads that led to Zelda's sanitarium."[66]

A Farewell to Arms sold some eighty thousand copies the first year, despite the Crash of '29. The Jazz Age was over, John Dos Passos announced as he moved to the political left. Ernest was now Scribners' rising star and Scott its fallen angel. In 1931 Scott read critic Gorham Munson's obituary for his career in *The Bookman:* "Mr. Fitzgerald has not published a novel since 1925 and his vogue has been succeeded by the vogue of Mr. Ernest Hemingway."[67]

He was still at his novel and bought time to work on it with another cash refill in Hollywood. Encouraged by her doctors, Zelda was writing her own novel, *Save Me the Waltz.* Scott advised Perkins not to bring it out the same year he published a book by Hemingway, because of the tensions ("subtle struggle") between Ernest and Zelda.[68]

Following the Fitzgerald saga from afar through bulletins from Max, Hemingway quipped that Scott "should have swapped Zelda when she was at her craziest but still saleable. . . . He is the great tragedy of talent of our bloody generation."[69]

He was now on intimate terms with Max, discussing Scott's follies from their superior perch. As early as 1926 or 1927, Bruccoli writes, Hemingway's letters to Perkins conveyed "patronizing observations on Fitzgerald, as though an older brother [were] advising his father about a worrisome younger son."[70] It was a case of sibling rivalry, Hemingway competing for the father's exclusive favor, forging a bond of complicity between them. Max the good father divided his attention equally, trying to keep the friendship of both, and out of friendship he mediated their quarrels or patched over misunderstandings between them when he could.

In 1934, Scott at last finished *Tender Is the Night,* now a novel about a good man's ruination in the draining care of his mad wife. He sent a copy to Ernest, but the reply was slow in coming. Finally, he wrote: "Did you like the book? For God's sake drop me a line and tell me one way or another."[71]

Ernest responded airily: "I liked it, and I didn't like it." His main complaint seemed to be that Scott had based the main characters, Dick and Nicole Diver, on their mutual friends Gerald and Sara Murphy, but had slandered them by ascribing to them his and Zelda's traits. He insisted that Gerald would never have become a drunk as Dick does at the end, and that Sara was never as crazy as Nicole is when Dick meets her. The effect was to deprecate Scott's fictions, seemingly out of protective preference for the Murphys (who nevertheless remained friends with Scott), and to personally attack Scott.

He added kindly that Scott really should forget about his personal tragedies, for "we are all bitched from the start and you especially have to be hurt like hell before you can write seriously. . . . You know I never thought much of Gatsby at the time. . . ." He signs it: "Always your friend."[72]

Scott turned the other cheek, writing that "the old charming frankness of your letter cleared up the foggy atmosphere through which I felt it was difficult for us to talk any more." He went on politely to say his admiration for Ernest's work was "absolutely unqualified." Discussing technique, he credited him with partly inspiring the ending of his novel—a dying fall rather than a dramatic climax.[73]

Five years later—too late—Hemingway would express the opposite opinion about *Tender Is the Night.* He wrote Perkins: "It is amazing how <u>excellent</u> much of it is. . . . If you write him give him my great affection."[74]

Perkins passed along the praise and Scott pasted the letter into his scrapbook. He was by then bruised by Hemingway's slighting public references to him. In his memoir *Green Hills of Africa,* Hemingway sneered at writers who let themselves be pressured to feel they must write masterpieces. He had the decency to cut a line from the manuscript that went "Scott was a coward of great charm."[75]

Hemingway wasn't a complete monster; he was aware of his compulsion to denigrate Scott. In the 1939 letter to Perkins he confesses: "I always had a very stupid little boy feeling of superiority about Scott— like a tough little boy sneering at a delicate but talented little boy."[76] But he couldn't stop for the life of him. And Scott at times played the willing victim.

Hemingway once had showed tenderness to Scott, but he had changed, become another person. He had to be the alpha male—"Papa Hemingway." As Edmund Wilson, Ernest's loudest champion in the early days, said in a review of *Green Hills of Africa,* Hemingway was being affected "by the American publicity legend which has been created about him." The bloated "I" of *Green Hills* was "his own worst-drawn character" and "his own worst commentator. His very prose style goes to pot."[77]

But he continued to write masterly stories like "The Snows of Kilimanjaro," in which the hero thinks about "poor Scott Fitzgerald," who once wrote, "The very rich are different from you and me." (That was in Fitzgerald's story "The Rich Boy.") Someone had commented, Hemingway goes on, "Yes, they have more money." Max Perkins knew who the someone was, and it wasn't Hemingway. Over lunch one day Hemingway had said in a kind of bragging way that he was "getting to know the rich." The Irish writer Mary Colom had commented: "The only difference between the rich and other people is that the rich have more money."[78]

Hemingway's gratuitous slap hurt Scott, but he wrote with quiet dignity: "Please lay off me in print. . . . Riches *never* fascinated me, unless combined with the greatest charm or distinction" (which was true; he had always been a critic of the rich).[79] Although he closed that letter with his usual "Ever Your Friend," he now considered the friendship in its dying fall. Scott was through with playing the eternal patsy in a sado-masochistic duo.

Hemingway's reply to Scott's reproachful letter has been lost, but Arnold Gingrich, editor of *Esquire*, where "Snows" appeared, saw it. He recalled it as being "brutal, language you'd hesitate to use on a yellow dog."[80] As one of the few editors who published Scott, Gingrich might have had the decency to ask Hemingway to cut the derogatory allusions, especially since Scott had a story in that same issue; but he claimed that the gibe had slipped right past him. (At Fitzgerald's urgent request, Max Perkins cut it from a hardcover collection of Hemingway stories.)

When Scott's articles about his nervous breakdown, so beautifully written and drenched in wisdom wrung from suffering, appeared in *Esquire*, Ernest raged to Max: "He's gone into that cheap Irish love of defeat, betrayal of himself etc. . . . He's so damned perverse about wanting to fail—it's damned bloody romanticism."[81]

Hemingway was primed for success, though it took him a long time. *For Whom the Bell Tolls* was his first real novel in eleven years. Not counting *To Have and Have Not*, an amalgam of two stories, his dry spell had been longer than Scott's. The book was a huge success—Book-of-the-Month Club, best-seller list, movie sale, and so on—and Scott wrote him a friendly letter of praise he didn't mean a word of. In his notebook he called it "a thoroughly superficial book which has all the profundity of [Daphne du Maurier's] Rebecca."[82]

He was changing. "I talk with the authority of failure—Ernest with the authority of success," he confided to his notebook. "We could never sit across the table again."[83] He was on the ropes financially, his work no longer in demand. He was envious but also critical of Ernest's success. He consoled himself by believing that he was the artist, now, ahead of his time, to be vindicated by posterity: "I don't want to be as intelligible to my contemporaries as Ernest."[84]

Hemingway was "a long cry from his poor rooms over the sawmill in Paris," he wrote Zelda in her last sanatorium.[85] He and Ernest had completely swapped roles since they met fifteen years before at Le Dingo American Bar in Paris.

In 1940, while in Hollywood eking out a living doctoring screenplays, Fitzgerald compiled a log of his encounters with Hemingway. He could recall only four meetings during the 1930s: "Not really friends since '26."[86]

In May of that same year, musing about unkind things said about him in print by old friends, he wrote Perkins, "Once I believed in friendship, believed that I *could* (if I didn't always) make people happy, and it was more fun than anything. Now even that seems like a vaude-villian's cheap dream of heaven, a vast minstrel show in which one is the perpetual Bones." Later in the letter he asks, "Where is Ernest and what doing?"[87]

In December 1940, Scott Fitzgerald died in Hollywood of a heart attack, leaving unfinished his final novel, *The Last Tycoon*. He had planned, if America got into the war in Europe, on being a battlefield correspondent. Hemingway would be one, covering the Allied invasion of Europe and becoming a combatant. Contrary to his detractors, Hemingway was indeed brave, in a reckless, almost suicidal way. He could still outdrink his rivals, too, though alcohol was taking its toll, deepening the inner black despair it was intended to drown. Had he all along sensed in Fitzgerald's crackup a portent of his own?

After his death, Fitzgerald would, as he had predicted, pull ahead in the posterity sweepstakes. In 1949, as the rustlings of his revival began to be heard, Hemingway spoon-fed disparaging words to Fitzgerald's biographer Arthur Mizener: "I never had any respect for him ever except for his lovely, golden, wasted talent." And to Charles Scribner: "Scott was a rummy and a liar and dishonest about money with the inbred talent of a dishonest and easily frightened angel."[88] It was to be a rivalry unto the death.

Hemingway committed suicide on July 1, 1961.

CHAPTER 8

THREE
FOR THE ROAD

Jack Kerouac, Allen Ginsberg,
and Neal Cassady

We all learn from one another and wail along.
—KEROUAC TO GINSBERG (1950)[1]

Sad paradise it is I imitate,
and fallen angels whose lost wings are
sighs.

—GINSBERG (1947)[2]

There is something in me that wants to come out; something of my own
that must be said. Yet, perhaps, words are not the way for me.
—CASSADY TO KEROUAC (1947)[3]

THE THREE-WAY FRIENDSHIP of Jack Kerouac, Allen Ginsberg, and Neal Cassady formed the nucleus of the Beat Generation before "Howl" and *On the Road* ignited the Big Bang. Kerouac and
Ginsberg's cross-fertilizing discussions and letters—rambling riffs on
their friends, work, travels, ideas—were their first attempts to articulate a Beat aesthetic. Cassady was their muse and model. Kerouac said:
"He inspired every word I wrote."[4] Ginsberg was in love with him. He
and Kerouac competed for Neal, body and/or soul.

But before Cassady, Kerouac was Allen Ginsberg's idol. They met
in May 1944. A seventeen-year-old Columbia freshman, Allen had
heard of Jack from Lucien Carr, a member of the off-campus bohemian
set. Carr was a blond young man from St. Louis whose good looks attracted male as well as female admirers, particularly a hulking, bearded

ex-teacher named David Kammerer, who was in love with Lucien. He had stalked him from St. Louis through prep school and then to New York.

When he needed to escape Kammerer, Lucien would hang out at an apartment on West 118th Street belonging to two hip young women named Joan Vollmer and Edie Parker. Edie, a rebellious product of Grosse Point, the ritzy Detroit suburb, was Jack's girl, and he stayed with her when he wasn't living with his parents in Ozone Park or on sea duty with the merchant marine.

From Carr, Ginsberg learned that Kerouac was a former Columbia football star, sometime merchant seaman, and would-be writer who had dropped out of school after quarreling with Coach Lou Little, costing him his athletic scholarship. Ginsberg, indifferent to athletics, imagined him a "workingman proletarian Jack London redneck" writer.[5]

In 1942 Kerouac had joined the merchant marine and shipped out on the *Dorchester* (later torpedoed and sunk with great loss of life), ferrying construction workers to Greenland through U-boat-infested waters. Later, he joined the navy with the idea of entering the V-12 college program, but he flunked the exam and ended up an ordinary gob at the Newport base. He hated the military regimen. One day during company drill, he dropped his gun and walked to the post library, where he read until the shore patrol hauled him away to the psycho ward; he was quickly discharged.

One afternoon in May 1944 when Ginsberg arrived at the West 118th Street place, he discovered that Kerouac had just got up and was waiting for Edie to bring him breakfast. Allen earnestly tried to engage him on Dostoevsky, his favorite author, but Jack yawned and yelled to Edie, "Where's my food?" Allen, a secret homosexual, thought him beautiful with his "sturdy peasant build," his tousled black hair, his sad, compassionate blue eyes.[6]

Jack would later describe his first impression of Allen as a "spindly Jewish kid with horn-rimmed glasses and tremendous ears sticking out, seventeen years old, burning black eyes, a strangely deep mature voice."[7] At first sight, he didn't like him.

They seemed an unlikely pair. Homely Jewish Allen from Paterson, New Jersey, handsome Catholic Jack from Lowell, Massachusetts; Allen the nerd, Jack the jock; Allen the would-be poet and left-wing labor lawyer, Jack the would-be novelist; Allen the queer, Jack the straight; Allen, the son of Louis, a teacher and published poet who had been a Gene Debs Socialist; Jack, the son of Leo, a hard-drinking, cigar-chomping linotyper, horse player, and Catholic right-winger who believed that "Marxist Communist Jews" had led America into World War II.[8]

In common, they had larger-than-life mothers. Naomi Ginsberg had been an intelligent, pretty young woman, a Communist and a teacher of children with learning disabilities, but a series of nervous breakdowns disrupted her career. Her paranoid delusions made life impossible for Louis, and they separated. Naomi would be in and out of asylums in the years ahead, with Allen and his brother, Eugene, bearing the brunt of her erratic behavior, such as parading seductively before Allen in the nude.

Kerouac's mother demanded endless payoffs of love, guilt, and dependence from her Jacky. Born Gabrielle L'Evescue, she was the daughter of a French Canadian tavern owner who died young. At age fourteen she went to work in a shoe factory. Marriage to Leo gave her a home—a succession of them—and three children: Caroline (known as Nin), Gerard, and Jack, born in 1922. Jack was only four when Gerard died, a little saint, the prayers of rustling black-winged nuns levitating him to Heaven. Gerard's frightening death left him with nightmares; he later communed with his brother's spirit.

In 1946 Leo died agonizingly in Jack's arms of stomach cancer. Jack had promised Leo he would take care of Gabrielle, but she continued working in the shoe factory while he was writing his books at home. He always felt guilty that she had to work into her sixties.

Allen bloomed in the warmth of Jack's sympathy. "I suddenly realized that my own soul and his were akin and that if I actually confessed the secret tenderness of my soul he would understand nakedly."⁹ He would tell Jack about his early memories, tapping a similar vein in Jack, who reminisced endlessly about incidents from his own childhood. As Jack was helping him move to a new dormitory, Ginsberg bade goodbye to the windows, the door, the stairs, the hall, and so on, explaining he had done that when he was a child. Jack said he had too.

Jack treated Allen with rough affection, like a kid brother who is always tagging along. In one letter he writes: "As for you, my little friend, there is always something to talk about because you are so unutterably vain and stupid, and that always leaves a splendid electrically charged gap for argument. Merde à toi! That's what I say."¹⁰ They had a high-flown *literary* way of talking in those pre-Beat days.

Jack and Allen were more intense in their ambition to become writers than were any of the other members of the bohemian set except a tall, snuffling, drawling man named William Burroughs, a St. Louis acquaintance of Carr's and the grandson of the adding-machine Burroughs. He was a Harvard alum and had done graduate studies there in anthropology and archaeology. Now he worked as a bartender and consorted with thieves and junkies in the Times Square underworld, rolling drunks in the subway for drug money.

Jack, Allen, and Lucien Carr talked endlessly of bringing a "New Vision" (a term originally used by the French poet Rimbaud) to America through art rather than religion or politics. As Ginsberg biographer Michael Schumacher summarizes, Carr believed "that self-expression was the highest purpose of art." Jettisoning traditional forms and content, "the writer made literature out of his individual mind and experience."[11] Art was autobiographical—the cardinal precept of the Beat aesthetic. This meant, according to Ginsberg, that each must cultivate "the most individual, uninfluenced, unrepressed, uninhibited expression."[12] Jack added that they all had the new vision—"what we lack is the method."[13] This required new language and new forms.

Rimbaud had called for perceiving reality afresh through the "derangement of the senses." Drugs were the fast track to this state. Burroughs, a morphine user, was their guide at the new Vollmer-Parker apartment on West 115th Street. Allen recalled the drug scene there: "Everybody lost in a dream world of their own making. This was the basis of the Beat Generation . . . the idea of the transience of phenomena."[14] Burroughs found a simpatico brain in Joan Vollmer and married her. Though he preferred boys, he was actively bisexual.

A friend of Bill's, a six-foot red-haired Times Square night person named Vickie Russell, turned Jack on to Benzedrine (Benny) inhalers, which were sold in drugstores as a decongestant. You cracked them open, extracted the cotton wad infused with the bitter drug, and either swallowed it or soaked it in coffee or a Coke. Joan became an avid user and ended up hallucinating and spending time in the Bellevue psycho ward. Kerouac contracted phlebitis, which sent him to Queens Hospital in December 1945.

Jack already knew about tea—marijuana, the drug of choice in the hipster-jazz subculture. He got high in Fifty-second Street clubs and smoky Village joints listening to Charlie Parker, Thelonious Monk, and Jack Teagarden. The jagged rhythms of bop, the new sound pioneered by "Bird," were in the air. You could dig the latest records on Symphony Sid's radio program. Bop was the aural equivalent of the drip-action paintings of Jackson Pollock, who would die in 1956, a suicide by DWI. Kerouac would drink with New York abstract expressionist painters at the Cedar Tavern until he was eighty-sixed from their hangout.

Most of Kerouac's books were written on Benny, tea, or cheap wine. Ginsberg composed much of the poem *Kaddish* on heroin and methedrine; he wrote "Laughing Gas" while high from a trip to the dentist; other poems and visions originated in his experiments with psychedelic drugs, from LSD to ayahuasca.

Subterranean New York in the 1950s was an artistic happening about to spread around the world via the hipsters' underground railroad.

"When I first saw the hipsters creeping around Times Square in 1944," Kerouac recalled, "I didn't like them. . . . One of them, Huncke of Chicago, came up to me and said, 'Man I'm beat.' I knew right away what he meant somehow."[15] Among thieves and con men, the verb *to beat* meant to cheat or defeat someone; Huncke's meaning was that you were the object of the verb. The word connoted the weary, funky cool of hipsters, outsiders, misfits, artists, who could not function in a nine-to-five society and sought escape, kicks, fixes, visions, ecstasy, God, death. Some paid a price of poverty or prison or burnout to pursue their obsessions or addictions, living lives counter to the culture of postwar consumerism and Cold-War conformity. Jack felt something inspiring in their nocturnal monologues in nighthawk cafeterias— "nightlong confessions full of hope that had become illicit and repressed by War, stirrings, rumblings of a new soul." For Allen and Jack, "beat" connoted a perverse state of grace—*beatitude,* as Kerouac would famously proclaim. Ginsberg saw beatness as a path to God: "You get beat down to a certain nakedness—like the dark night of the soul that precedes religious visions."[16]

To live the Beat life meant becoming downwardly mobile, chasing the *nostalgie de la boue* along garbage-can streets of the Neon City. Kerouac's onetime girlfriend Joyce Johnson observed that he and his contemporaries became "deliberately classless." Straight people saw this as "an act of incomprehensible perversity" for young men who "had other options."[17]

Carr, Burroughs, and others came from wealthy families and flaunted a style of destructive rebellion against their class. Jack from blue-collar Lowell marveled at their profligacy with money and possessions; still, he too had other options. His football brilliance put him on the upwardly mobile track. He turned down a football scholarship at Boston College (which would have included a job for Leo) to take Columbia's offer, knowing the Ivy League was higher up the status ladder. Football, Leo preached, was the road to a better life as a professional man. He warned Jack against the criminal-junkie Burroughs and the creep-faggot Ginsberg (whom he called "the Cockroach" because of his shambling walk).[18]

Allen, a scholarship boy for brains rather than muscle, drank with Jack and others at the West End bar until four in the morning. Yet he was such a brilliant student (by sophomore year he had caught the eyes of Mark Van Doren and Lionel Trilling, stars of the English faculty) that he made straight A's. Johnny, the West End bartender, reported his wayward ways to the dean, who let Allen off with a warning.

The next infraction was more serious: Allen invited Jack to sleep over in his dorm room after a late night together. Jack was persona non grata on campus—a disgraced dropout and disreputable bohemian. Early the next morning an assistant dean arrived to investigate the cleaning woman's complaint that Allen had written "Fuck the Jews" on the dusty windowpane.[19] (He had done it to protest her anti-Semitism and her failure to clean the windows.) The dean discovered Jack asleep (though not with Allen), and citing a regulation against overnight guests, suspended Allen and told him to seek psychiatric help. Van Doren appeared as a character witness for the boy; Lionel Trilling spoke up for him as well. In deference to Trilling's sensibilities as the only Jew on the Columbia faculty, the dean wrote "Fuck the Jews" on a piece of paper rather than speak the words. The distinguished teacher, critic, and novelist diagnosed Ginsberg as a self-hating Jew.

Allen moved into the apartment on West 118th Street and took a job as a welder in a shipyard. In his off hours he discussed the New Vision with Jack, explored the Times Square netherworld with Burroughs, took drugs, lost his cherry, cruised for sailors, and read and wrote poetry. Also dwelling in the apartment at that time were Carr, Burroughs and Joan, Jack and Edie, and Hal Chase, a straight, clean-cut anthropology student from Denver.

Jack called this 1944–45 period his "year of evil decadence," a time of experiments with drugs, writing and then burning what he'd written, bull sessions at the apartment, balling Edie, and cruising the Turkish baths with Burroughs. The latter, a couch veteran, psychoanalyzed Jack and Allen. He ordered Jack to make a clean break with his mother. When Allen burst out in real anguish, "Nobody loves me!" Bill talked him through to his real feelings. Allen decided his "faggishness" made him feel "guilty and inferior."[20] Bill and Jack collaborated on a novel in the tough-guy style of Dashiell Hammett. The plot was based on a sensational campus murder.

Around this time occurred the celebrated (in Beat lore) Night of the Wolfeans. One evening Bill, Jack, Hal, and Allen were lazing in the bedroom, coming down from Benzedrine highs. Hal started talking about Wolfeans and non-Wolfeans. He said he and Jack were Wolfeans because they were wholesome, heterosexual all-American boys in the spirit of Thomas Wolfe's intensely American novels. Bill and Allen were non-Wolfeans—homosexuals, decadent Euro-intellectuals.

Nonetheless, Allen and Jack bridged their cultural divide and moved to a deeper friendship. One night Allen confessed to Jack his desire to sleep with him. Jack groaned; the thought repelled him. But after about six months he responded to Allen's advances. They mutually masturbated in a truck parking lot off Christopher Street under the elevated West Side Highway (an area that would later become a "meat rack" for gays).[21] Like many young American males, Jack had probably had homosexual experiences and felt guilty about them. Some say his closest boyhood friend, Sammy Sampas, had been his first love, the one person in Lowell who shared his postwar dreams and idealism. Sampas went to war as an army corpsman and was fatally wounded at Anzio beach in 1943. Their song was "I'll See You Again." Jack grieved for him and stayed in touch with his older sister, Stella.

Allen came to realize that Jack's sex games with him were a mix of transitory lust and kindness. As Allen recalled: "He was bending and stretching quite a bit to accommodate my emotions. That's why I've always loved him, because I was able to completely unburden myself and he was able to take it."[22] Jack still preferred women, starting with Edie, whom he married in August 1944.

Allen sensed that Jack was conflicted about gay sex and looked for a more responsive lover. He found him in Neal Cassady, who hit New York around this time. The Columbia gang had been hearing a lot about Cassady from Hal Chase and another Columbia student from Denver, Ed White. The two conjured up the vision of a "mad genius of jails and close raw power," "a reader of Schopenhauer in reform schools, a Nietzschean hero of the pure snowy wild west."[23]

Cassady had been "born on the road," not literally but while his parents were en route to Hollywood, where his father, Neal senior, opened a barbershop, then lost it through drunkenness. The parents returned to Denver and separated, the wife keeping her six children by a previous marriage and Neal staying with his vagrant father. Pop worked Saturdays at a barbershop catering to bums and spent the rest of the week as a self-employed wino. Neal lived with him in flophouses and walked himself to school. When his mother died, her people took him in. His half brother liked to shut him for hours in a Murphy bed. He passed through a series of Catholic institutions and reformatories.

He claimed he stole five hundred cars between 1940 and 1944, but only to joyride in them. He was an ace parking-lot attendant who could jockey a car into a vacant slot at forty miles per hour.

The Columbia students who knew Cassady from Denver pegged him as a fast-talking con man, but to Jack he was a romantic outlaw who brushed aside squares in his rush for kicks. He wore his sideburns long and combed his hair into a pompadour. He had a broken Roman nose that kept him out of the draft and a lean, hard body. He drove like a stock-car racer and could go twenty-four hours without sleep, talking all the way. He could meet a woman at a party and sweet-talk her into bed the same night (her place). He was a multiorgasmic sex "machine in the night," women said.[24] He would have three wives and multifarious girlfriends by whom he fathered four children, three by his wife of longest duration, Carolyn, who followed a pattern of throwing him out and taking him back. Probably because of his horrendous childhood, he craved a stable home life; yet when he had it, he would get itchy and walk out—as if home-wrecking were tattooed on his DNA. That was his way—walking out and hitting the road. Or retreating into some cold empty space inside.

Cassady arrived in gray, snowy New York in December 1946 with his sixteen-year-old bride, pretty little LuAnne Henderson, every man's jailbait fantasy. They had run away from dead-end lives in Denver to Nebraska, where she worked for an uncle as a maid; then they skipped to New York. When Jack found them in their cold-water flat in Spanish Harlem, Neal answered the door in the buff, while LuAnne hid her luscious body under the covers.

The three of them became friends, and Neal shared LuAnne with Jack, making them sex brothers. Describing a threesome in *Visions of Cody*, Kerouac portrays Neal as the liberated lover teaching the repressed Jack to throw off his inhibitions, to swing, to go! Jack's romantic view of him grew to resemble that of another novelist, Ken Kesey, who befriended Cassady in the 1960s. Kesey said, "Cassady did everything a novel does, except that he did it better because he was living it and not writing about it."[25] Cassady articulated his life as a quest for "IT." IT meant, as his biographer William Plummer writes, "ebulliency," high, "a state of exhilaration that could be induced in any number of ways: through sex and jazz and drugs; above all, by going on the road."[26]

One day Neal showed up in Ozone Park and asked Jack to teach him how to write. Jack knew he was being conned for food and bed but didn't care, for he believed Neal was a great man. They spent time talking about writing. He began recording the story of Neal's life for his next novel.

Neal had far more influence on Jack's writing than vice versa. He urged Jack not to think before writing—it killed feeling. In a December 1947 letter that deeply impressed Jack, Cassady wrote: "I have always held that when one writes, one should forget all rules, literary styles, and other such pretentions as large words, lordly clauses and other phrases as such." Much later Jack said that he had "got sick and tired of the conventional English sentence, which seemed so ironbound in its rules, so inadmissible with reference to the actual format of my mind."[27] Neal stoked his muse with Benzedrine, putting down the first word that popped into his head and letting the words stream in free-association overdrive from there.

Jack was in the throes of writing a big Wolfean family saga set in Lowell. Out of his grief for his dead father sprang a determination to write "a huge novel explaining everything to everybody," justifying the Kerouacs and the Sampases.[28] Trying to write in formal literary English, he made difficult headway. (Kerouac was not a natural writer of English prose: His first language was *joual,* a French Canadian dialect.)

During visits to Ozone Park, Neal would stand behind Jack at the typewriter and cheer him on: "Go! Grab that ball! Don't fumble it! Keep going!"[29] Jack said that he "went on blasting away at it just to impress and more to please you. That was the turning point of that novel. . . . Others may criticize . . . but you yell and gab away and fill me with a thousand reasons for writing and getting a big story done."[30]

In talks with Neal, Jack formed a determination to leave home and go west to see the saloons and flophouses and poolhalls of Neal's Denver boyhood, then on to golden California. Neal was feeling trapped in New York parking lots; he needed to drive free on western highways. His rejection of the city firmed up Jack's determination to leave. He was chasing a myth almost as old as America: That life would be better in the West.

Jack set out to re-create Neal as an iconic Western hero. He was "a young Gene Autry . . . a sideburned hero of the snowy West" and "a western kinsman of the sun."[31] Twinned with the Man of the West was the natural literary genius-seer, whose visions flashed "a kind of holy lightning."[32] He'd spent "a third of his time in the poolhall, a third in jail, and a third in the public library."[33] "All my other current friends were 'intellectuals,' " he writes in On the Road. "But Dean's [Neal's] intelligence was every bit as formal and shining and complete, without the tedious intellectualness."[34] He also reminded Jack of his dead brother, Gerard.

In late 1946 Neal and Allen became lovers. By January, Allen wrote in his journal that he had enjoyed a "wild weekend of sexual drama with Cassady."[35] They spent so much time together that LuAnne grew jealous. So did Jack. He was not sexually jealous; his relationship with Neal was always platonic, according to Allen. Rather, he missed Neal's cheerleading. In March, when Neal headed back to Denver, Jack put aside his rivalry and accompanied Ginsberg to the bus station to see him off.

They squeezed into an automatic photo booth two by two for farewell pictures, each of which they sliced in half and gave to the other two. They agreed to meet in Denver.

Back in that city, Neal's heterosexual libido reasserted itself. He fell for a platinum-blond Bennington graduate from Tennessee, an art instructor at the university, named Carolyn Robinson. He wrote Allen that he didn't really like sex with men. He suggested they find a girl they could both fuck to cure their queerness.

Calling him a "double-crossing faithless bitch," Allen refused to accept Neal's turnabout.[36] He believed that if he went to Denver he could change Neal's mind. With money from a Columbia poetry prize he bought a bus ticket in early July, and arrived to find Neal living with Carolyn. Neal hadn't told her of his gambols with Allen in New York, but she sensed a fresh tension in the air.

Allen played odd man out most of the summer. The Denver Columbians shunned him because of his eccentric clothes (he would wear a dress shirt and swim trunks downtown) and his closeness to Neal, whom they distrusted. It was a variant of the old Wolfean/non-Wolfean schism.

Meanwhile, Jack was aiming to join Allen and Neal in July. He spent much of the spring writing his novel; in his free time he boned up on Western history at the public library. He wrote Hal Chase in Denver: "My subject as a writer is of course America, and simply, I must know everything about it."[37]

Laying aside his half-done manuscript on July 17, 1947, he took the IRT subway to 242nd Street, where he planned to start hitchhiking west via Route 6. When he arrived at the end of the line, he realized he'd gone forty miles north, not west. He took a train back to Manhattan and caught a bus to Chicago. From there he began hitching to Denver via Route 66; it was the first leg of a journey that, several years and several cross-country trips later, he would chronicle in *On the Road*.

He did not forget to send his mother a postcard: "Dear Ma, I've been eating apple pie & ice cream all over Iowa & Nebraska, where the food is so good. . . . Love, Jacky XXX." In his novel, the hero eats apple pie à la mode exclusively because it "was nutritious and delicious of course."[38] Soon he reached Denver, "the dividing line between the East of my youth and the West of my future."[39] He spent "mad days with the whole gang," moving back and forth between Neal's seedy world and the college crowd's Denver. He met Carolyn at a dance and fell in love with her but considered her Neal's girl.

One day the gang traveled to Central City, a former mining town outside Denver where empty hotels and saloons had been refurbished to host visitors to the annual arts festival. Attending a performance of Beethoven's *Fidelio* by the Central City Opera Company, Jack interpreted Florestan's release from the dungeon as a metaphor for the artistic and sexual freedom his generation was seeking. Neal and Allen, he wrote in *On the Road,* "were like the man with the dungeon stone and the gloom rising from the underground, the sordid hipsters of America, a new beat generation that I was slowly joining."[40]

In reality, the revolutionary love of Neal and Allen was mired in complications. Neal was still sneaking trysts with LuAnne yet hot to marry Carolyn, who represented middle-class stability. For Carolyn, whose strict, cold father was a professor at Vanderbilt Medical School, in Nashville, Neal represented a walk on the wild side—all the way.

Finally, Allen talked Neal into letting him join him hitchhiking to New Waverly, Texas, to visit Bill Burroughs and Joan. Now married with a child, they were living squalidly on a remote farm, growing marijuana for their livelihood. They planned to sell their crop in New York in the fall; Neal was to drive it there in a jeep, accompanied by Burroughs and Herbert Huncke.

Allen's visit turned into a farce. Huncke tried to fix up a honeymoon bed for him and Neal, but it collapsed on their first night, reflecting the state of Neal's feeling for Allen, which had reached the point where he was disgusted by his touch. Allen was reduced to begging for charity sex. Thus it was demonstrated once again how sex can kill a friendship.

Neal was writing letters to Carolyn steeped in longing. Rejected and hurt, Allen decided to leave. Neal drove him to Houston, where he signed onto a merchant ship bound for Africa. Neal had promised farewell sex in their hotel, but he picked up a woman and passed out from booze and reds.

Meanwhile, Jack continued on the next leg of his journey—to San Francisco, to hook up with a friend who had promised to get him a berth on a cruise ship. The friend failed to deliver, but did find Jack a job as a guard at a camp for construction workers headed overseas. There he toted a gun, sent his pay to his mother, and made out with local girls. He was mistakenly jealous of Allen's hapless trip with Neal, telling him it was "obnoxious." Neal discouraged him from coming to Texas and driving back to New York with them—no room.

So Jack made his own way home. His Greyhound bus journey was pleasantly interrupted by a dalliance with a Chicana farm worker named Bea. He joined her family picking grapes in the San Joaquin Valley for a couple of weeks. Then he boarded a transcontinental bus that deposited him in Times Square, the cold concrete heart of the city. His mother told him that Neal had passed through, on his way back to Carolyn.

Allen arrived from Dakar to commit his mother to an asylum; she had deteriorated alarmingly. In November he signed a paper authorizing a prefrontal lobotomy. He was swept up in the agonizing life maelstrom that would be the subject of his great poem *Kaddish*.

He returned to Columbia in an agitated state. At four A.M. on January 11, 1948, he appeared at Jack's door and announced that he was going mad. Jack calmed him and read him parts of his novel in progress. Allen called it "greater than Melville, in a sense—the great American novel." As usual, Jack didn't believe a word of it; he wondered, "How can I help a man who wants to be a monster one minute and a god the next. . . ."[41]

In April, Allen invited Jack to a seder at his father's house in Paterson. Afterward, walking him to the bus station, he kept jabbing Jack with demands to be part of his life. Kerouac brushed him off, and Allen screamed wild-eyed, "Hit me, hit me!" The outburst shook Jack; he wrote in his journal: "Ginsberg went mad and begged me to hit him—which spells the end as far as I'm concerned."[42] He almost slugged Allen but was glad he hadn't. He closes: "I want to live and work, and raise a family."[43]

While Allen was flipping out, Jack was working "in a state of exalted absorption" on his novel.[44] He had typed 280,000 words of a projected Wolfean 330,000. In April he told Allen he would finish in May and asked him to send the manuscript to his mentor Mark Van Doren for an initial read. He had worked on it for two and a half years, interrupted by "poverty, disease, and bereavement and madness." Yet the novel hung together. "If that isn't the pertinacity or tenacity or something of genius I don't know what is."[45]

Allen read all of the bulky manuscript called "The Town and the City" and told Jack it was "big and profound." Privately, Jack's achievement depressed him, driving home his own failure to produce major work. But his praise elevated Jack, who noted that "the madness has left Allen now and I like him as much as ever."[46]

Acting as unofficial agent, Allen circulated among his hip New York friends a holographic manuscript of "The Town and the City" in a battered physician's bag. It garnered an underground reputation, recalled the novelist John Clellon Holmes. He met Kerouac at a big

Fourth of July party, looking like a T-shirted "John Garfield back in the neighborhood after college." Jack gazed agitatedly at the jabbering drinkers waving cigarettes in Holmes's crammed flat: "What am I doing here? Is this the way I'm supposed to feel?"[47] On the sidelines of another blast, they started comparing their postwar cohort to the Lost Generation, and Jack burst out, "You know this is really a beat generation." Holmes credited him with being the first to apply the adjective to their cohort.

Holmes also met Ginsberg that day and was impressed by the way he would puff Jack as a great novelist while Jack would talk him up as a future great poet.

Allen was trying to complete his academic requirements at Columbia while working as a file clerk. He lived alone in an apartment in Spanish Harlem. One Sunday, reading William Blake and masturbating, he heard a sonorous voice intone the words of Blake's poem "Ah, Sun-Flower!" Allen knew it was the voice of God, telling him "*this* existence was *it*!"[48] He crawled out onto the fire escape and cried to his next-door neighbors, "I've seen God!" The two frightened young women slammed their window.

In September, Kerouac started collecting rejection slips. Hearing negatively from one house, he wrote in his journal, "I'm getting more confident and angrier each time something like this happens because I *know* 'The Town and the City' is a great book in its own awkward way."[49]

Then it was the turn of Scribners, Thomas Wolfe's old house, where he hoped to find a father-editor like Max Perkins, who had died the previous year, one who could carve form out of his huge block of manuscript as Perkins had done for Wolfe's *Look Homeward, Angel.* Instead, he was anonymously told to cut drastically. When another house rejected the book as "too long," he wrote Neal, "I refuse to go on banking on the fantasy that I will make a living writing." He spoke of their working for Standard Oil or going to sea and using the money they saved up to buy a ranch or a farm in California.[50]

He was taking courses at the New School in Manhattan and living off the G.I. Bill. He wrote a paper on Whitman and the sexual revolution and launched a new novel. One night after class he joined Lucien, Allen, and others on a wild carouse. "At dawn I carried Allen and Lucien over each shoulder, for a block in my stocking feet . . . it was one of those Lucien-Daemonic nights . . . fights, dances, pukings from balconies, fallings-down-stairs, shouts and final half-expirings from alcoholic surfeit . . . in gutters, gutters the same old Rimbaud gutters." Lucien, he decided, was a combination of Rimbaud, Don Birman (the alcoholic in *The Lost Weekend*), and "an angel of death."[51]

M eanwhile, Neal Cassady, in California, heard from Jack that he couldn't come west. Neal resolved to bring him back. Now married to Carolyn, he took their life savings and brought a sharp '49 maroon-and-silver Hudson Hornet, then called Jack to say he was coming. Gabrielle answered and told him to pick them up in Rocky Mount, North Carolina, where they were spending Christmas with her daughter, Nin, her husband, Paul, and little Paul junior. Neal conned a friend, Al Hinkle, into coming along. All he had to do was marry his girlfriend, Helen, earlier than they planned; she would then turn over all her money to buy gas and food. This scheme was carried out, but Neal and Al jettisoned her in Tucson because she was holding them up. Neal roared to Denver to collect the lost LuAnne and floored it all the way east. Carolyn, with a baby and no money, spent a lonely Christmas on welfare.

Just before Christmas Day, a dirty, dented Hudson, its windshield slimed with mud, rolled up at Paul's house, and a dirty, disheveled Neal staggered out looking like the Creature from the Black Lagoon, to the consternation of watching neighbors. After a short rest he drove Lu-Anne and Al to New York and returned to haul Jack and Gabrielle and her furniture to her new apartment in Queens.

Neal and LuAnne sponged off Allen, who was working at a straight job and had a tenement apartment on York Avenue. When their fed-up host began proclaiming in a sepulchral voice, "The days of Wrath are yet to come," they realized it was time to split.[52] Neal, Jack, LuAnne, Al, and a girl named Rhoda piled into the Hudson and, with bop blaring on the radio, roared south. LuAnne was squeezed between Neal and Jack (who, let it be noted, hated driving), while Al made out with Rhoda in the back seat. In his journal, as edited by Douglas Brinkley, Jack immortalized the moment: "We in the car jubilant beating on the dashboard of the '49 Melvillean Hudson coupe . . . headed West . . . Neal and I and LuAnne talking of the value of life as we speed along, in such thoughts as 'whither goest thou America in thy shiny car at night?' And Neal drove with the music, huzzaing."[53]

On a bitter cold morning they arrived in Washington. It was Inauguration Day, and they observed the war equipment massed for the occasion. Later that day the newly elected Harry Truman denounced Communism from the Capitol steps. The Cold War was under way, and Jack approved; he believed America would have to fight the Soviets sooner or later.

Speeding away from history, they went on to their first destination, William Burroughs's farm at Algiers, across the river from New Orleans. He ordered the chattering Jack and Neal to calm down: "I want you to sit quiet for a minute and tell me what you're doing crossing the country like this?" Neither could explain. They had no purpose, no goal. The object was just to *go*.[54] The Road led west or south, anywhere and everywhere. The journey was improvised like a jazz solo.

. . .

In March 1950, Harcourt at last published Kerouac's first novel, *The Town and the City*. It had been accepted in March 1949 on the recommendation of Mark Van Doren, who was an adviser to the publisher. Jack felt so prosperous that he no longer considered himself Beat, he told the novelist Alan Harrington. With his $1,000 advance, he moved his mother to Denver and bought a Western dream house in a raw dirt suburban development. Carless, that dream died in the sagebrush and mud after a few months and they came back east.

The novel he had fantasized as his ticket to a steady income as a writer turned out to be another shattered dream. Reviews were positive but sales disappointing. Jack blamed this partly on the heavy cutting done by his editor, Robert Giroux, who reduced an unpublishable eleven-hundred page Wolfean manuscript to a manageable four hundred pages. Jack grew to hate his book; he insisted it had lost its guts. When he reread it, the style seemed dreary.

Seeing his writing mangled was a salutary shock; it bludgeoned Kerouac into abandoning the pseudo–Thomas Wolfe style. He would renounce that young author named "John Kerouac" who was portrayed in the jacket photo in a neat haircut, dark suit and tie. He wanted a style that expressed his radically new vision. He experimented with several versions of a new book, "On the Road," including one told by a modern Negro Huck Finn, but nothing worked. Discouraged, he cast about for guidance.

In March 1951 a revelation pierced his inner gloom. He read the manuscript of John Clellon Holmes's "Go!" It was the first Beat novel, drawing on the lives of their group, including Allen and Neal. Jack would call it a ripoff—he'd already thought of that title. But Holmes's story was far different from his road tale, and its existence prodded him to get on with his book. Holmes, who read the manuscript, advised him to go back and completely start over with a fresh slant. Jack agreed.

He'd read a lot of Herman Melville for Alfred Kazin's American Lit class at the New School. *Moby-Dick* was always on his mind. He envisioned Neal as a "mad Ahab at the wheel" relentlessly pursuing deeper truth. He was impressed by Melville's symbolism, most obviously in the White Whale, and sought what he called "deep form," a use of symbols to sound metaphysical depths. He told another New School teacher, Elbert Lenro: "Meanwhile I'm making *On the Road* a kind of Melvillean thing, in spite of myself."[55]

Melville's novel *Pierre,* a maimed, bitter, psychologically profound tale of an impoverished young author and his two loves, provided another epiphany. He underlined a sentence in the introduction, according to biographer Tom Clark: "Melville was not writing autobiography in the usual sense . . . he was writing the autobiography of his self-image."[56] This statement helped Jack conquer private inhibitions about the narrator. He made *On the Road* both a biography of the mythical Neal as Dean Moriarty and an autobiography of Kerouac's self-image. Thus, he created an alter-ego narrator, Sal Paradise. As biographer Ann Charters writes, he recast the book "as a confessional picaresque memoir about his adventures with Cassady."[57] The name "Sal Paradise" was itself suggested by Allen in a phrase from his Denver poems, "sad paradise." Sal is an onlooker, a follower of "the mad ones" who "burn, burn, burn, like fabulous yellow roman candles."

Back in 1948, Jack had written in his journal that he must "rediscover my *real* voice," which is "so often drowned by criticism and fear."[58] In December 1950, Cassady showed him the way. He sent Jack a fourteen-thousand-word letter describing Neal's teenage love for Joan Anderson. Jack read and reread it and wrote Neal that "it ranked among the best things ever written in America" and was "the exact stuff upon which American Literature is still to be founded. . . . You and I will be the two most important writers in America in 20 years at the least."[59] He showed the letter to Allen, who sent Neal exorbitant praise. Neal replied in his self-putdown style, "We still know I'm a whiff and a dream."[60]

Jack was sufficiently stirred to write a series of equally long letters to Neal relating the story of his early life in minute detail, imitating Neal's free-associative autobiographical style and uninhibited spontaneity. He had found the "method" he had sought since the Columbia New Vision days. It was a kind of improvisatory writing; you started not knowing where you were going or where you would end up. Like being on the road . . .

Ginsberg's letters also exerted an influence. In 1956 Kerouac told him, "It was not only from Neal's letters but from your wild racing crazy jumping don't care letters that all that sketching came out, it broke me off from American formalism a la Wolfe."[61] ("Sketching" refers to a technique that he developed around this time for writing descriptions.)

He discovered one last refinement; this had more to do with mechanics—his technique of typing on a continuous roll of paper. This discovery came about in a serendipitous way: In the fall of 1950, Jack was occupying a Manhattan loft that had belonged to Bill Cannastra, a wild law student who had been killed in a drunken subway escapade. He also inherited Cannastra's resident girlfriend, Joan Haverty. As he describes their courtship in his diary: they met on November 7; ten days later, a judge tied the knot.[62]

While working on his novel at Cannastra's, Jack decided that inserting new sheets of paper into the typewriter interrupted the spontaneous confessional flow he was seeking. Spotting some long sheets of architect's tracing paper, he taped them together to form a roll that eventually stretched to 120 feet. He scrolled the leading end into his typewriter and, fueled by strong coffee, began blowing. From April 2 through April 22, 1951, he averaged six thousand words a day in long stints at his rolltop desk sweating so hard he had to keep changing T-shirts.

In midstream Jack was interrupted by Joan's announcement that she was pregnant; he told her to get an abortion and resumed typing.

She kicked him out. He moved in with Carr—desk, typewriter, and paper roll. He finished the book in mid-May and wrote to Neal: "Book makes complete departure from *Town & City* and in fact from previous American Lit. . . . I've telled all the road now. Went fast because road is fast."[63]

He dramatically unfurled the manuscript in Robert Giroux's office. The editor gasped, "But Jack, how can you make corrections on a manuscript like that?"[64] Shouting that *this* was the final book and there would be *no* corrections, Jack stormed out.

His stubbornness about revisions partly explains why it would be more than five years before the book was published. Even Jack's Beat friends were negative at first. Carr (who hated being written about) called it "shit"; Allen found it formless, though on a later reading he assured Jack it was truly "beat." Neal pronounced the central theme "too trivial." Showing the impossible demands he placed on himself, he suggested that Jack "enlarge it into a mighty thing that merely uses what he's written as a Book I . . . he should create another and another work (like Proust) and then we'll have the great American novel."[65]

Later, Allen informed Cassady that Jack was having trouble with the ending because he could not imagine the fate of the Dean Moriarty character. He advised Neal (who was the model for it, after all) to write Jack "a serious self-prophetic letter foretelling your fortune in fate. . . . He needs help to understand last true longings of your soul."[66] Neal prophesied he would become an "ulcerated old color-blind RR conductor who never writes anything good and dies a painful lingering death from prostate gland trouble (cancer from excessive masturbation) at 45."[67]

In the spring of '52 Jack wrote much of "Visions of Neal," the "vertical" (in-depth) version of *On the Road,* while staying with Neal and Carolyn in San Francisco. (Ginsberg had preceded him in residence but was expelled when Carolyn caught him fellating Neal.) This visit had turned into a pleasant ménage à trois with Neal's tacit permission. But jealousy slithered in and Jack was pushed out. He took off for Mexico City and ran out of money. He wrote Carolyn, "I really am getting fucked again by the publishing business."[68]

Allen had wangled Jack an advance of $250 from Ace Books, which produced comic books and tough-guy novels with lurid covers. They were going to publish Bill Burroughs's first novel, *Junkie,* a downbeat slice-of-life story about addicts, under a pseudonym. Kerouac's contract was for three novels, including "Visions of Neal."

A novel about the drug scene was one thing; this was a hot genre on the paperback racks. Kerouac's novels were a different matter. They did not fit into *any* category—and were scatological to boot. When he read "Visions of Neal," Ginsberg squawked like a church lady. The book had too much sex, too many "insider references"; it was "crazy in a bad way."[69] He doubted that even an avant-garde publisher would touch it, let alone a mass-market house like Ace. And Ace duly rejected it and the other manuscripts Jack submitted.

Jack told the Ace editors that they were like all the narrow-minded hacks who had dismissed great writers of the past as incoherent—Joyce, Hemingway, Dreiser. His "Visions" would some day be published by people without today's blinders.[70] He hoped to have the pleasure of belting Allen's friends at Ace "on the kisser." As for Allen, he is "a disbeliever, a hater."[71]

Jack fired Ginsberg as his unofficial agent, and switched to Holmes's agent at MCA. Allen ran into Jack in New York at the end of 1952—"drunk & high in cab at dawn on way home. . . . I keep thinking he has no adult society and marriage world to write about and keeps repeating lament for Mother."[72] Like Burroughs, Allen condemned Jack's dependence on his mother as unhealthy and harmful to his work.

Later Allen rescued their friendship by praising Jack's latest manuscript, "Dr. Sax," a part-fantasy novel close to Jack's heart, who gratefully wrote Ginsberg that he was "like a little Russian brother."[73] The difference between them was that Allen was too academic, using words like "verbal" and "images," but Jack was grateful that he "REALLY did comprehend the book" and called him "my good boy." He remembered quarrels with Neal and how their deeper friendship pulled them back from a split. Once, after a quarrel, Neal had awakened him from a nap on the job, tenderly saying, *"There* you are buddy! Come on, now, come on, now, no words, come on now. . . ."[74]

Allen would keep a candle burning for the best in Jack. He had an almost infinite tolerance for the madness of others. Biographer Barry Miles plausibly suggests that for Allen, rejecting the mad ones would mean rejecting his mother. Jack had a similar reading: "I'd say you were always trying to justify your ma's madness as against the logical, sober but hateful sanity of the straight world."[75] In the future, Allen would need deep reservoirs of tolerance for Jack and Neal.

Five years after Kerouac unrolled the manuscript of "On the Road" in Robert Giroux's office, it at last found a publisher. This was largely through the heroic efforts of the critic and literary man of all work Malcolm Cowley, an advisory editor for Viking, who had first read the manuscript back in 1953. Initially, Kerouac rejected Cowley's suggestions for revisions, but he eventually came around to his idea of conflating several real journeys into a single fictional one. He also acquired a supportive new agent, Sterling Lord. In September 1956 he reported to Lord that he had heard Viking would publish the novel. Viking indeed came through with an advance of $1,000, payable in ten monthly installments, which for Kerouac was a living wage. The publisher worried that the thinly disguised real people in the novel might sue, and demanded that Jack get signed releases from them. (Cowley commented that these were not the kind of people who sued to defend their good names.)

In the ensuing months, Jack collected the releases, edited, revised, got drunk, smoked kif with Burroughs in Tangier. Then on an impulse he moved his mother to California, another of the many moves in her life, and an ill-advised one. They tried to live in a small apartment on Jack's monthly $100 advances from Viking and her Social Security check. She thought California was a "silly place for old people" and he said he could no longer live there "with a dissatisfied mother in poverty and shame." They decided to return to New Jersey.[76] Just before they caught a bus, Jack received advance copies of his novel in Berkeley. He presented one to Cassady, who had come to say goodbye. Neal leafed through and said nothing; he averted his eyes when they parted.

The next thing the Cassadys heard was a wild letter from Jack saying, "Everything exploded."[77]

September 5, 1957, was publication day for *On the Road*. Jack was staying in Manhattan with his new girlfriend, Joyce Glassman. They went out at midnight to buy *The New York Times*, ducked into a neighborhood bar, and turned to the book review by Gilbert Millstein, who was substituting for Orville Prescott, the regular daily reviewer. Prescott was a literary mossback, but Millstein dug the Beats and had commissioned John Clellon Holmes to write a 1952 article on them for the *Times*. He proclaimed *On the Road* to be an "authentic work of art," its publication "an historic occasion." It was "the most beautifully executed, the clearest and most important utterance yet made by the generation Kerouac himself named years ago as 'beat,' and whose principal avatar he is."[78]

Biographer Ellis Amburn, who was Kerouac's editor later in his career, contends that much of the review "echoed" the copy on Viking's dust jacket, written by none other than Malcolm Cowley. This was "one of the most graphic displays on record of an editor's power to engineer an author's critical reception," says ex-editor Amburn, though it may have been a case of Cowley and Millstein converging on the same road from different starting points. Millstein said that *On the Road* "caught the spirit of the postwar generation as no other novel had."[79] He nominated it as the 1950s *The Sun Also Rises.*

"After the war everybody was waiting for the next Hemingway-Fitzgerald generation to appear," Jack's contemporary Gore Vidal recalled. Thus, every new novel by members of the postwar generation was greeted with great expectations and hailed as the voice of a new sensibility.[80]

Glassman's phone rang steadily during the next weeks. Jack was swept up in a frenetic swirl of parties, interviews, signings. "I don't know who I am any more," he wailed to her at one point. There were new women—two, three at a time, he boasted to Neal. Visions of movie sales boogied in his head. A studio offered $150,000, but Lord thought he could get more from Marlon Brando, who wanted to play Dean Moriarty. There were interviews with skeptical reporters demanding to know who were these alien beings called Beats.

His novel enjoyed a brief stay on the *Times* best-seller list but was sucked off by a backdraft of outrage from the middlebrow magazines. *Time*'s critic warned that Kerouac was attempting to "create a rationale for the fevered young who twitch around the nation's juke boxes and brawl endlessly in the midnight streets." *Newsweek* called Dean Moriarty "a frantic animal-like delinquent . . . a kind of T-shirt Ahab of the automobile." The *Times Book Review* primly warned that Kerouac's characters were on "a road . . . that leads nowhere."[81]

Disdaining any literary or sociological assessment of Kerouac's achievement and contemporary voice, critics leveled ad hominem attacks reflecting the McCarthyite Cold War mind-set, always on the *qui vive* for subversive ideas. One front of this fight was the face-off between the squares and the hipsters. Kerouac's characters represented the latter; they were pop-culture successors to Brando's gang of bikers in the 1954 movie *The Wild One.* Someone asks Brando's character, "What are you rebelling against?" "Whaddya got?" he mumbles. Brando was personally denounced for this character, as was James Dean for his role in *Rebel Without a Cause*. Jack went on the defensive, insisting to a TV interviewer that they were a religious generation, "waiting for God to show his face."

Yet for young writers like Thomas Pynchon, Kerouac's book was "exciting, liberating, strongly positive." In the literary community, the hip-square fight shaped up, Pynchon said, as "traditional vs. Beat Fiction."[82]

On the Road was not a conventional novel with interpretations of character and narrative line; it was an impressionistic, picaresque tale of freedom with a subtext of postwar children fleeing an atom-doomed Cold War world. When the mainstream media critics countered, "Freedom for what?" they thought they had scored a devastating hit. But freedom was what the generation coming of age in the late forties craved in their secret souls, and *On the Road* whispered the word to them like a siren song. Freedom was the necessary precondition for self-discovery.

To *Time* and its ilk, the novel was, rather, a siren song of irresponsibility. When John Updike parodied *On the Road* in *The New Yorker* as "On the Sidewalk," he infantilized the Beats, caricaturing Jack as a little boy riding a tricycle whose mommy won't let him cross the street. He won't grow up! As Morris Dickstein writes in his history of postwar literature, *Leopards in the Temple*: " 'Maturity' was the albatross of the postwar generation; [J. D.] Salinger and the Beats helped their readers see beyond it, to find the sensitive child, the thwarted adolescent in themselves. This in turn connected them to the newly emerging values of personal fulfillment, individuality, and unlimited consumption." The emblematic characters of its fiction, like Holden Caulfield, Augie March, Sal Paradise, and even Updike's Rabbit Angstrom, were all seeking to escape the "maturity trap," which restrained them from realizing these values.[83]

The novel's impact on Jack's friends who were characters in it was mixed. Allen wrote from Paris that he had read Millstein's review and "almost cried so fine and true."[84] But Neal was wounded by reviewers' comparisons of Dean Moriarty to a criminal psychopath. He was the father of three kids now, with a steady job as a brakeman on the Southern Pacific. Carolyn was shaken by the cruelty of critics like Art Cohn, the *San Francisco Chronicle* gossip columnist, who called the Beats "pathetic, self-pitying, degenerate bums."[85]

Bill Burroughs, the canny ex-junkie, blamed Neal's later drug bust on the notoriety he acquired from the novel. But Cassady's biographer William Plummer writes that Neal admitted that he had become arrogant and careless. When two strangers gave him a ride, he rewarded them with several joints. They turned out to be narcs. He was convicted of trafficking and sentenced to five years in San Quentin.

Jack giddily rode the wave and inevitably crashed. Naturally shy, withdrawn, and diffident when sober, he was not made for the adulation of strangers or for manufactured media controversy. He was thin-skinned; harsh reviews hurt. He was also miscast. People (women) assumed that *he* was the cocksman Dean Moriarty when actually he was the passive follower Sal Paradise.

His publisher urged him to type up a quick sequel to keep his name in the public eye. He had a pile of worthy rejected manuscripts in his trunk, including brilliant avant-garde work like "Dr. Sax," but Malcolm Cowley advised him to write a more commercial novel of boyhood. Instead, Jack put a new roll in his typewriter and unreeled *The Dharma Bums,* another road-buddies story celebrating his poet friend Gary Snyder and Buddhism. After reading it, Allen warned him, "Viking and Lord are neglecting your good books and trying to get you to write 'potboilers.' " That was too harsh, although *The Dharma Bums* did run out of steam at the end. As though he realized it, Allen wrote a review of it, praising Jack's "Spontaneous Bop Prosody," which he linked to the "struggle for the development of an American prosody to match our own speech and thinking rhythms."[86] It was one of the few favorable reviews the novel received; another was from *The American Buddhist.*

Jack's plan was to heed Cassady's advice and write a great Proustian cycle based on his life, "The Duluoz Legend," over the next ten or fifteen years. His editors at Viking, who were contemptuous of "Dr. Sax" and "Visions of Gerard," were unsympathetic with Kerouac's "self-fingering explorations of his childhood," as one put it in a memo.[87]

The reviewers piled on his next novel, *The Subterraneans.* It was a very hip and "now" story of an interracial love affair (autobiographical), but conservative critics were discomfited by the miscegenation theme and called it immoral.

The critical posse continued to string up each new offspring of Jack's typewriter. Kerouac hid behind his "liquid suit of armor." Scotch with beer chasers became his favored tope from morning till the wee hours when the long-distance cries for help leaped across America. Carolyn Cassady, whom he phoned frequently, attributed his compulsive drinking to his "extreme shyness," chronic guilt, rebelliousness against polite society, and constant battle for acceptance of his voice and vision.[88] He once told her, "I just *can't* stop [drinking]. Thinking of those critics and the rubbish I've gone through with publishers starts filling my mind and I reach for the bottle."[89] He wrote Ginsberg that he'd go on the wagon and feel better for about a week "but slowly become bored and wondering what to do now."[90] Writing left him emptied, agitated, and feeling unworthy.

He was obviously having trouble coping with celebrity, at a time when the tabloid version of the Beat "movement" was magnetizing young converts. People were always accosting him on the street, telephoning him at three A.M., besieging his house, challenging him to bar fights. He warned Gary Snyder: "If you only knew how horrible it is to be 'famous' you wouldn't want it."[91] He was so ill at ease in public appearances that he had to load up with alcohol, which transformed him into a buffoon. He complained to Sterling Lord about "vast nervous parties where everybody is staring at me and fulfilling their preconceptions of me as a drunken fool." His fans had a "frightening intensity."[92]

In his last years, Jack withdrew from the world and retreated to a safe place inside himself. "Drinking heavily," he told Amburn, "you abandon people, and they abandon you—and you abandon yourself— It's a form of self murder."[93] But self-murder was the name of the game. Carolyn Cassady said he told a friend he intended to drink himself to death.

In 1966 he married Sammy Sampas's sister, Stella, who had carried a torch for him since they were growing up in Lowell. She was older, and homely, but he needed someone to help take care of his mother, who had been incapacitated by a stroke.

As others drifted out of Jack's life, Allen tried periodically to reach him, but Gabrielle, echoing Leo's hatred of "the Cockroach," threatened to summon the FBI if he ever came to their door. She opened his letters to Jack and wrote obscene replies. Later, Jack blamed her stroke on Allen's surprise appearance at their house.

She and Allen seemed almost rivals for him. He scorned Allen's idea that it was "abnormal" for a grown man "to take care of his old widowed mother." In a letter to John Holmes, he said people who said this were "a bunch of libertine cads shaking their hairy asses in the Sodom capitals of the West"—like Allen Ginsberg.[94]

As his books sank out of print, he spewed venom at the Jewish writers who came into vogue in the early sixties like Philip Roth, Herbert Gold, Saul Bellow, and Bernard Malamud, and the critics who touted them "with their jew talk." His only audience now is the "kids who steal my books in bookstores."[95]

It was as if Leo Kerouac's raging spirit now possessed Jack. He was anti-fag, anti-Red, anti-beatnik, and anti-Semitic. Public nudity, beards, drugs revolted him. He half-truthfully told the novelist Alan

Harrington in 1949: "I was never a 'rebel,' only a happy, sheepish imbecile."[96] John Clellon Holmes said Kerouac's was "a deeply traditional nature thrown out of kilter."[97]

Jack wanted no more public identification with the Beats. He refused to earn $3,000, which he badly needed, by appearing in a film because Allen was also in it. He took his name off a Beat anthology, writing to the Italian editor Fernanda Pivano that the Beats, including Ginsberg, were a bunch of "frustrated hysterical provocateurs and attention-seekers with nothing on their mind but rancor towards 'America' and the life of ordinary people."[98] This was Jack the patriotic proletarian writer talking; but he was now becoming the booze-bloated, red-faced, foul-mouthed Archie Bunker so cruelly eviscerated in an *Esquire* article.

His political views were late McCarthyite. He told Allen that the peaceniks behind the demonstrations at the 1968 Democratic convention in Chicago were "dirty Jew Communists." Allen decided to stop turning the other cheek and told Jack he was talking like his foul-mouthed old bitch of a mother. Rather than getting angry, Jack laughed. Allen concluded from this experiment that Kerouac's talk about dirty Jews, dirty whoevers, was his way of baiting him. Amburn, who listened to plenty of late-night phone tirades, thought the anecdote really revealed how far Ginsberg bent over backward to excuse Jack.

Allen coped with fame better than Jack did. Around the time Jack was racing west with Neal in 1949, Allen's life had sunk to a state beater than beat. He had allowed the homeless Huncke and his addict cronies to move in with him at his York Avenue apartment. They stashed stolen goods there, and when the cops caught them, Ginsberg was arrested as an accessory. He avoided jail by agreeing to sign himself into the Psychiatric Institute at Columbia Presbyterian Hospital for treatment; there he met Carl Solomon, a fellow patient. On the advice of his psychiatrists, he embraced the straight life, sleeping with women, working at marketing research jobs in suit and tie. But it was all a mask. Poetry brought him back to who he was. Living in San Francisco, he fell in love with a pretty young faun named Peter Orlovsky, started experimenting with Jack's "Spontaneous Bop Prosody," and began writing *Howl,* drawing on his experiences at the Psychiatric Institute, making heroes of angel-headed hipsters like Carl Solomon, Huncke, Jack, Neal, and others. He told Jack that writing *Howl* "was the first time I sat down to blow, it came out in your method, sounding like you, an imitation practically."[99]

Howl made its debut in 1955 at a poetry reading at San Francisco's Six Gallery. Cassady attended in his brakeman's uniform. He knew hardly anyone and asked Orlovsky to stand next to him. Kerouac circulated among the crowd cadging coins to buy jugs of wine, which he passed around. When Ginsberg began reading, Jack roused the audience by chanting "Go!" after each line—faster, faster, until they were shouting, crying, aware they were present at a moment of heart-nakedness never before exhibited by an American poet.

The fifties were Jack's era, when he reigned as King of the Beats. The sixties would be Allen's heyday. While Jack withdrew into himself, Allen turned outward, searching the world for the Blakean visions he experienced in Spanish Harlem. He immersed himself in the ancient cultures of Mexico, Japan, India. When he returned he became a leader of the hippie-rock-psychedelic-drugs-peace movement. He joined forces with Dr. Timothy Leary to turn America on to LSD. (Kerouac considered hallucinogens a Communist plot to undermine American youth.)

Political issues—civil rights, the war, drugs, sexual freedom, free speech—jostled to the forefront of Ginsberg's life, but he continued to write. He was more comfortable with politics than Jack was. Activism was part of the Jewish socialist tradition in which he was raised. Though at first he was so nervous he threw up before public readings, he adjusted to being a public figure, the rare poet who had an audience—to the point where he would strip naked and call on the audience to join him.

He became a guru of the world youth culture. Prague students crowned him King of the May. In Havana he sided with young poets against the literary commissars. He issued manifestos and agitated for artistic freedom (the publisher of *Howl* was prosecuted for violation of obscenity laws but was cleared in 1957). He called for the legalization of drugs and demonstrated against the war in Vietnam. He chanted "Om" for seven hours at the riotous 1968 Chicago Democratic convention.

And Neal? After serving his prison sentence and trying to settle down with Carolyn and their children, Cassady was drawn into the early-sixties West Coast psychedelic drug scene. He became the star of novelist Ken Kesey's Merry Pranksters, a living link between Beatitude and Hippiedom. In 1965, high-wired on speed, he drove Kesey's Day-Glo-painted bus named Further to New York City. Jack came to the hotel where the Pranksters were staying, and they talked. He was reportedly offended by the disrespectful way the Pranksters draped the American flag on a sofa and invited him to sit on it for pictures. It was the last time the two friends saw each other. Neal sometimes referred to himself as "Keroassady," i.e., a fictional invention of Jack's. In late 1967 he walked out on Carolyn and the kids for the last time.

In February 1968, high on reds and pulque at a wedding party in Mexico, Cassady started walking along a railroad track. He told friends that he intended to count the number of ties to the next town. At some point he collapsed; his body was found the next day.

Jack predicted to Carolyn that he'd soon be with Neal. In the end he was virtually alone, save for Gabrielle, Stella and her brothers, and some drinking buddies in St. Petersburg. On the morning of October 20, 1969, his overtaxed liver massively hemorrhaged. He was forty-seven. Reporters swarmed to the hospital, where a distraught Stella told them, "He was a very lonely guy."[100]

The body was taken to Lowell for burial. The undertakers dressed the corpse in a sharp checked sport coat and snappy bow tie. Gabrielle thought her Jacky was beautiful. Ginsberg came to the funeral parlor and laid his hand on the body in farewell. He wrote Carolyn that Kerouac appeared "mid-aged heavy, looked like his father had become from earlier dream decades."[101]

For the Road leads back to where we came from.

NOTES

Chapter 1

1 Walter Mosley, *Morning Edition,* National Public Radio, August 3, 2004.
2 Matthew J. Bruccoli, *Fitzgerald and Hemingway: A Dangerous Friendship,* 3.
3 Hemingway to Fitzgerald, in Carlos Baker, ed., *Ernest Hemingway: Selected Letters,* c. October 24 or 31, 1929, 310.
4 Sherwood Anderson, *Memoirs,* 463.
5 Carla Kaplan, ed., *Zora Neale Hurston: A Life in Letters,* 41.
6 Emily Bernard, ed., *Remember Me to Harlem,* LH to CVV, June 4, 1925, 19.
7 Kaplan, *Zora Neale Hurston,* ZNH to LH, September 20, 1928, 126.
8 Ibid., 163.
9 Mark Edmundson, "The Risk of Reading," *The New York Times Magazine,* August 1, 2004, 12.
10 Mosley, *Morning Edition.*
11 Joyce Johnson, *Minor Characters,* 169.
12 Simon Karlinsky, *Dear Bunny, Dear Volodya,* 29.
13 Quoted in Carol Brightman, ed., *Between Friends,* xxix–xxx.
14 Karlinsky, 16.
15 Fred Hobson, *Mencken,* 165.
16 Quoted in ibid., 279.

17 Grant Richards to Dreiser, March 24, 1912 (University of Illinois).

18 SOJ to WC in Fields, ed., *Letters of Sara Orne Jewett*, 259.

19 Quoted in Mark Schorer, *Sinclair Lewis*, 804.

Chapter 2

1 Herman Melville to Nathaniel Hawthorne, November 17[?], 1851, quoted in James C. Wilson, *The Hawthorne and Melville Friendship*, 436.

2 Newton Arvin, ed., *The Heart of Hawthorne's Journals*, 230.

3 Quoted in Hershel Parker, *Herman Melville*, Vol. I, 757.

4 Cornelius Mathews, "Several Days in Berkshire," *Literary World*, August 31, 1850, quoted in Wilson, 166.

5 Jay Leyda, ed., *The Melville Log*, Vol. I, 383.

6 *National Intelligencer*, August 31, 1850, Log I, 390.

7   Quoted in Wilson, 175.

8 NH to Longfellow, quoted in Wilson, 176.

9 Quoted in Wilson, fn. 1, 253.

10 Quoted in Parker, I, 745.

11 Quoted in Wilson, 173.

12 Quoted in Brenda Wineapple, *Nathaniel Hawthorne*, 224.

13   Quoted in Arvin, *Melville*, 5–6.

14 Sarah Morewood to George Duyckinck, December 28, 1851, Log I, 441.

15 Quoted in Log I, 417.

16 Quotes from "Hawthorne and His Mosses" in Wilson, 218–25.

17 Martin and Person, *Emerson Society Quarterly*, Vol. 46, 2004, 103.

18 Newton Arvin, *Melville*, 139.

19 Log I, 391.

20 Ibid., 392.

21 Ibid., 391.

22 Ibid., 393–94.

23 Arvin, 139.

24 Quoted in Parker, I, 725.

25 Ibid., 730.

26 Quoted in Wineapple, "Hawthorne and Melville; or, The Ambiguities," *Emerson Society Quarterly*, Vol. 46, 2000, 90.

27 Ibid.

28 M to H, June 1851, quoted in Wilson, 234.

29 Log I, 423.

30 Quoted in Parker, I, 813.

31 H to M, March 27, 1851, quoted in Wilson, 255.

32 Log I, 419.

33 Parker, I, 834.

34 Log I, 408.

35 Ibid., 416.

36 HM to ED, February 12, 1851, Log I, 406.

37 Quoted in Parker, I, 835.

38 M to H, April[?], 16[?], 1851, quoted in Wilson, 231.

39 M to H, June[?], 1851, Wilson, 235–37.

40 M to H, June 29, 1851, Wilson, 239.

41 Parker, I, 847.

42 Log I, 419.

43 NH to William Pike, July 29, 1851, quoted in Wineapple, *Hawthorne*, 241.

44 Log I, 443.

45 M to H, November 17[?], 1851, quoted in Wilson, 240–41.

46 Wineapple, *Hawthorne*, 227.

47 Log I, 430–31.

48 Ibid., 437.

49 Ibid., 438.

50 Sarah Morewood to George Duyckinck, December 28, 1851, Log I, 441.

51 M to H, July 17, 1852, quoted in Wilson, 245.

52 Ibid.

53 Wineapple, 270.

54 Milder, *Emerson Society Quarterly*, Vol. 46, 2000, 25. Wilson, 53.

55 Maria Melville to Peter Gansevoort, April 20, 1853, Log I, 469.

56 Newton Arvin, ed., *The Heart of Hawthorne's Journals*, 230.

57 Arvin, ed., *Journals*, 230–31.

58 Ibid., 231.

59 Quoted in Wilson, 181.

60 Arvin, ed., *Journals*, 231–32.

61 Quoted in Parker, I, 835.

62 Ibid., 343.

63 Quoted in Parker, II, 731.

64 Quoted in Wilson, 180.

Chapter 3

1 Samuel Clemens to William Dean Howells, July 21, 1885, quoted in Frederick Anderson, William M. Gibson, and Henry Nash Smith, eds., *Selected Mark Twain–Howells Letters, 1872–1910,* 249. (Note: All letter citations are to this volume unless otherwise noted.)

2 H to C, August 2, 1898, 320.

3 Quoted in Kenneth S. Lynn, *William Dean Howells,* 106.

4 Quoted in J. C. Wilson, 172.

5 Lynn, 157.

6 Quoted in *Letters,* 4.

7 Quoted in Justin Kaplan, *Mr. Clemens and Mark Twain,* 108.

8 Howells, *My Mark Twain,* 4.

9 Quoted in Kaplan, 144.

10 Ibid., 6.

11 Quoted in Lynn, 168.

12 Quoted in Lynn, 157.

13 C to H, [Hartford? June 1872], 9.

14 C to H, October 19, 1875, 58.

15 C to H, June 25, [1872], 10.

16 H to C, November 30, 1876, 83–84.

17 Ibid.

18 Quoted in Ellery Sedgwick, *A History of the Atlantic Monthly,* 142.

19 C to H, [October 24, 1874], 26.

20 H to C, November 23, 1874, 32.

21 H to C, December 3, 1874, 33.

22 H to C, December 11, 1874, 35.

23 C to H, [December 14, 1874], 36–37.

24 C to H, February 10, [1875], 43.

25 Quoted in Sedgwick, 143.

26 C to H, [October 4, 1907], 394.

27 C to H, December 8, [1874], 34.

28 Kaplan, 181.

29 Ibid., 144–45.

30 Lynn, 169.

31 Ibid.

32 Ibid., 170.

33 Quoted in Henry Nash Smith, *Mark Twain: The Development of a Writer,* 96.

34 Quoted in Lynn, 172.

35 Howells, *My Mark Twain,* 61.

36 Ibid., 60.

37 Quoted in Lynn, 173.

38 C to H, December 23, 1877, 102–3.

39 Ibid.

40 Quoted in Henry Nash Smith, 99.

41 Quoted in Lynn, 173.

42 Ibid., 174.

43 Quoted in Smith, 102.

44 Kaplan, 296.

45 Quoted in Lynn, 176.

46 Ibid., 177.

47 C to H, January 3, [1879], 120.

48 H to C, February 4, 1880, 143.

49 C to H., September 19, [1877], 161.

50 H to C, July 3, 1875, 47.

51 H to C, November 21, 1875, 61.

52 C to H, January 19, 1876, 68.

53 Ibid.

54 H to C, January 18, 1886, 260.

55 C to H, August 9, [1876], 75.

56 C to H, March 23, 1878, 108.

57 C to H, July 21, 1885, 249.

58 C to H, November 4, 1882, 204.

59 C to H, February 2, [1879], 123.

60 C to H, September 15, [1879], 134.

61 H to C, September 17, 1879, 135.

62 C to H, May 13, 1886, 264.

63 Ibid., 265.

64 C to H, August 22, 1887, 276.

65 Quoted in Lynn, 8.

66 Quoted in *Letters,* 275.

67 Quoted in Lynn, 8.

68 C to H, August 5, 1889, 283.

69 H to C, October 22, 1889, 290.

70 Quoted in *Letters,* fn 1, 292.

71 H to C, October 17, 1889, 287.

72 C to H, October 21, 1889, 288.

73 C to H, September 22, 1889, 287.

74 Quoted in Kaplan, 350.

75 Ibid., 335.

76 C to H, February 23, 1897, 313.

77 H to C, May 21, 1889, 281.

78 H to C, September 13, 1896, 310.

79 C to H, September 24, 1896, 312.

80 H to C, January 9, 1898, 315.

81 C to H, January 2, 1898, 318.

82 C to H, June 6, 1904, 375.

83 Quoted in *Letters,* 350.

84 C to H, May 12, 1899, 335–36.

85 H to C, December 20, 1903, 369.

86 H to C, February 28, 1906, 385.

87 C to H, March 12, 1909, 399.

88 Quoted in *Letters,* 400.

89 Howells, *My Mark Twain,* 99.

90 Ibid., 5.

91 Quoted in Lynn, 324.

Chapter 4

1 Quoted in Fred Kaplan, *Henry James,* 508.

2 Quoted in R.W.B. Lewis, *Edith Wharton,* 272.

3 Quoted in Millicent Bell, *Edith Wharton and Henry James,* 80.

4 Edith Wharton, *A Backward Glance,* 69.

5 Quoted in Lewis, 131.

6 Quoted in Leon Edel, *Henry James: The Master,* 202.

7 Quoted in Bell, 223.

8 Ibid., 217.

9 Quoted in Lewis, 131–32.

10 Quoted in Edel, 201.

11 Ibid., 202.

12 Lyall H. Powers, ed., *Henry James and Edith Wharton: Letters, 1900–1915,* James

to Wharton, October 26, 1900, 32. (All letter citations are to this volume unless otherwise noted.)

13 Quoted in Lewis, 126.

14 Ibid., 125.

15 Wharton, *A Backward Glance*, 246.

16 J to W, August 17, 1902, 34.

17 Quoted in Lewis, 127.

18 Bell, 243.

19 Quoted in Bell, 228.

20 Quoted in Edel, 204.

21 Quoted in Kaplan, 482.

22 Quoted in Lewis, 128.

23 Ibid., 166.

24 Wharton, *A Backward Glance*, 244.

25 Wharton, *A Motor-Flight Through France*, 1.

26 Quoted in Bell, 93.

27 Wharton, *A Backward Glance*, 248–49.

28 Ibid., 242–43.

29 Ibid., 189.

30 Quoted in Lewis, 136.

31 Quoted in Edel, 343.

32 Quoted in Kaplan, 507.

33 Ibid., 508.

34 Quoted in Bell, 122.

35 Quoted in Powers, ed., 14.

36 Quoted in Bell, 122.

37 Quoted in Kaplan, 536.

38 Quoted in Lewis, 166.

39 Edel, 207.

40 Bell, 149.

41 Quoted in Bell, 187.

42 Kaplan, 407.

43 Quoted in Kaplan, 409.

44 Ibid., 507.

45 Ibid., 508.

46 Ibid., 511.

47 Quoted in Lewis, 224, 232.

48 Lewis, 222.

49 Quoted in Lewis, 220.

50 Ibid., 226.

51 Ibid., 238.

52 Quoted in Edel, 410.

53 J to W, October 13, 1908, 101.

54 Quoted in Kaplan, 512.

55 Quoted in Lewis, 247.

56 Quoted in Edel, 410.

57 J to W, April 19, 1909, 111.

58 Kaplan, 513.

59 Quoted in Lewis, 264.

60 Quoted in Bell, 135–36.

61 J to W, May 9, 1909, 112.

62 Quoted in Bell, 272.

63 Ibid., 272.

64 Powers, 17.

65 J to W, April 19, 1909, 110.

66 Quoted in Lewis, 262.

67 J to W, Christmas Eve, 1909, 130–31.

68 Quoted in Lewis, 276.

69 J to W, April 19, 1909, 111.

70 Quoted in Kaplan, 524.

71 J to W, February 8, 1910, 146.

72 J to W, February 16, 1910, 148.

73 J to W, February 8, 1910, 147.

74 Quoted in Lewis, 317. James, Lewis says, was "exploiting his own fiction for an appraisal of actual life."

75 Quoted in Bell, 177.

76 Quoted in Lewis, 320.

77 Ibid., 323.

78 Quoted in Edel, 477.

79 Ibid., 503.

80 Henry James, *The Black Tower,* Notes, 217.

81 Ibid., 221.

82 J to W, November 9, 1914, 316; see Powers, ed., 291.

83 J to W, June 11, 1913, 257.

84 Quoted in Kaplan, 553.

85 Ibid., 552.

86 Quoted in Wharton, *A Backward Glance,* 367.

87 Wharton to Miss Bosanquet, March 1, [1916], 391.

Chapter 5

1 Willa Cather, *Not Under Forty,* 94–95.

2 Jewett to Cather, December 19, 1908, in Annie Fields, ed., *Letters of Sarah Orne Jewett,* 250.

3 Cather, *Not Under Forty,* 62–63.

4 Lillian Faderman, *Surpassing the Love of Men,* 204.

5 Quoted in Faderman, 205–6.

6 Joan Acocella, *Willa Cather and the Politics of Criticism,* 50. Because of legal restrictions, Cather's letters can only be paraphrased. I am adopting Joan Acocella's paraphrase, which strikes me (having read the original) as more accurate than Sharon O'Brien's in her Cather biography, *The Emerging Voice,* p. 131. O'Brien's runs as follows: "It was so unfair that feminine friendship should be unnatural, but she agreed with Miss De Pue [a classmate] that it was."

7 Phyllis C. Robinson, *Willa: The Life of Willa Cather,* 60–61.

8 Quoted in Robinson, 61.

9 Ibid., 106.

10 Cather, *Not Under Forty,* v.

11 Quoted in Brenda Wineapple, *Hawthorne: A Life,* 354.

12 Mark De Wolfe Howe, *Memories of a Hostess,* 281.

13 Fields, *Letters,* October 5, 1882, 16.

14 Quoted in Robinson, 155.

15 Quoted in Peter Lyon, *Success Story: The Life and Times of S. S. McClure,* 390.

16 Quoted in Robinson, 156.

17 Fields, *Letters,* 235.

18 Cather, *Not Under Forty,* 85.

19 Ibid., 91.

20 Quoted in Margaret Roman, *Sarah Orne Jewett: Reconstructing Gender,* 339.

21 Quoted in O'Brien, 337.

22 J to C, November 27, 1908, Fields, *Letters,* 246.

23 C to J, December 19, [1908], Houghton Library.

24　J to Fields, Fields, *Letters,* 47.

25　Fields, *Letters,* 247–48.

26　Ibid., 248.

27　Ibid., 249.

28　Ibid.

29　Ibid., 259.

30　C to J, December 19, 1908, Houghton Library.

31　C to Fields, July 17, 1908, Houghton Library.

32　Quoted in O'Brien, 346.

33　Cather, *Not Under Forty,* 81.

34　Ibid., 88.

35　Quoted in O'Brien, 345.

36　Cather, *Not Under Forty,* 83.

37　Ibid., 83–84.

38　Ibid., 80, 78.

39　Quoted in O'Brien, 346.

40　Ibid., 423.

41　Ibid., 301.

42　Cather, *Not Under Forty,* 82.

43　C to Witter Bynner, June 7, 1905, Houghton Library.

44　C to J, October 24, 1908, Houghton Library.

Chapter 6

1　Dreiser to Mencken, March 27, 1943, in Thomas J. Riggio, ed., *Dreiser-Mencken Letters,* Vol. II, 690. (All letter citations are to Vol. I or Vol. II of this work, unless otherwise indicated.)

2　H. L. Mencken, "Theodore Dreiser," 786, 787.

3　Mencken, *The Days of H. L. Mencken,* viii.

4　Quoted in Isaac Goldberg, *The Man Mencken,* 379.

5　M to D, April 1, 1945, II, 693.

6　Quoted in Goldberg, 379.

7　D to M, December 29, 1909, I, 36.

8　M to D, March 7, 1909, I, 22.

9　Quoted in Elias, *Letters of Theodore Dreiser,* Vol. I, 97.

10　M to D, November 3, [1909], I, 38.

11　D to M, February 24, 1911, I, 63.

12 M to D, March 3, [1911], I, 64.

13 M to D, April 23, [1911], I, 68.

14 M to Earnest Boyd, August 20, 1925, Guy Forgue, ed., *Letters of H. L. Mencken,* 281.

15 D to M, April 28, [1911], I, 71.

16 Grant Richards to D, March 24, 1912, University of Illinois.

17 D to M, [ca. November 1, 1910], I, 80.

18 M to D, January 11, 1914, I, 130.

19 M to Harry Leon Wilson, December 10, [1912], Forgue, ed., 28.

20 Quoted in William Manchester, *H. L. Mencken: Disturber of the Peace,* 111.

21 M to D, December 8, [1915], I, 211.

22 Thomas Riggio, ed., *Theodore Dreiser: The American Diaries,* June 6, 1917, 165.

23 Quoted in Riggio, ed., *Letters,* I, 184.

24 D to M, April 20, 1915, I, 194.

25 M to D, April 22, [1915], I, 196.

26 D to M, April 26, 1915, I, 197.

27 M to D, August 4, 1916, I, 251.

28 M to D, December 20, 1916, I, 285.

29 M to D, [December 26, 1916], I, 281–82.

30 D to M, December 21, 1916, I, 287.

31 Quoted in Riggio, ed., *Letters,* II, 786.

32 Riggio, ed., *Diaries,* 181.

33 M to Boyd, [1917], New York Public Library Special Collections.

34 M to B. W. Huebsch, August 16, 1918, Carl Bode, ed., *New Mencken Letters,* 84–85.

35 Quoted in Fred Hobson, *Mencken: A Life,* 165.

36 D to B. W. Huebsch, March 10, 1918, Elias, ed., *Letters,* I, 250.

37 M to Kubitz, January 23, 1918, and October 19, 1918, New York Public Library Special Collections.

38 M to Burton Rascoe, [Summer 1920?], Forgue, 185.

39 D to M, September 7, 1920, II, 388; M to D, September 13, [1920], II, 388.

40 M to D, November 29, [1919], II, 364.

41 D to M, April 2, 1921, II, 438.

42 M to D, November 15, [1921], II, 452–53.

43 Quoted in Riggio, ed., *Letters,* II, 323.

44 Quoted in Ibid., 793.

45 M to D, March 27, 1921, II, 437.

46 M to Helen Richardson, January 30, 1946, II, 727.

47 M to D, February 5, [1926], II, 552–54.

48 D to M, February 8, 1926, II, 554.

49 Quoted in Charles Angoff, *H. L. Mencken: A Portrait from Memory*, 101.

50 D to M, December 24, 1934, II, 565.

51 M to Helen Dreiser, December 30, 1945, II, 724–25.

52 *Diary of H. L. Mencken*, 401.

53 D to M, March 27, 1943, II, 690.

54 Helen Dreiser to M, December 29, 1945, II, 560.

Chapter 7

1 F. Scott Fitzgerald to Zelda Fitzgerald, Summer? 1930, Matthew J. Bruccoli, ed., *F. Scott Fitzgerald: A Life in Letters*, 18.

2 Ernest Hemingway to F, March 31, 1927, Carlos Baker, ed., *Ernest Hemingway: Selected Letters*, 250.

3 Bruccoli, *Fitzgerald and Hemingway*, 1.

4 Quoted in Bruccoli, *Some Sort of Epic Grandeur*, 229.

5 Quoted in Kenneth S. Lynn, *Hemingway*, 278.

6 Bruccoli, *F&H*, 4.

7 F to Edmund Wilson, ca. February 1933, Bruccoli, *Letters*, 227.

8 Ibid., May 1925, 110.

9 F to Maxwell Perkins, October 10, 1924, ibid., 82.

10 F to T. R. Smith, late May 1925, ibid., 114.

11 Quoted in Lynn, 280.

12 A. Scott Berg, *Max Perkins*, 112.

13 Ibid., 229.

14 Bruccoli, *Epic Grandeur*, 218.

15 Wharton to F, June 8, 1925, quoted in *The Crack-Up*, 309.

16 Quoted in Bruccoli, *F&H*, 60.

17 Bruccoli, *F&H*, 110.

18 Quoted in Lynn, 282.

19 Quoted in Bruccoli, *F&H*, 24.

20 Ibid., 228.

21 F to Zelda, Summer 1930, Bruccoli, *Letters*, 187.

22 Quoted in Bruccoli, *F&H*, 60.

23 Quoted in Bruccoli, *Epic Grandeur,* 228.

24 Quoted in Bruccoli, *F&H,* 26.

25 Quoted in Lynn, 286.

26 Quoted in Scott Donaldson, *Hemingway vs. Fitzgerald,* 100.

27 Lynn, 286.

28 Lynn, 277; Bruccoli, *Epic Grandeur,* 226.

29 Quoted in Lynn, 277.

30 Ibid., 278.

31 Quoted in Bruccoli, *F&H,* 82.

32 Ibid., 182.

33 Quoted in Donaldson, *H vs. F,* 73.

34 F to H, November 30, 1925, Bruccoli, *Letters,* 130. Actually, according to his logbook, he was getting $2,250 in 1925. Bruccoli, *Epic Grandeur,* 530.

35 Donaldson, 72.

36 H to Horace Liveright, December 7, 1925, Baker, *Letters,* 173.

37 Quoted in Walker Gilmer, *Horace Liveright,* 124.

38 H to Liveright, January 19, 1926, Baker, *Letters,* 191.

39 Quoted in Donaldson, 74–75.

40 Ibid., 76.

41 F to Perkins, before March 1, 1926, Bruccoli, *Letters,* 138.

42 Perkins to F, March 4, 1926, quoted in Donaldson, 77.

43 Quoted in Donaldson, 95.

44 Quoted in Berg, 95.

45 F to Perkins, c. June 25, 1926, Bruccoli, *Letters,* 144.

46 Quoted in Bruccoli, *F&H,* 59.

47 Quoted in Donaldson, 79.

48 F to John O'Hara, July 25, 1936, Bruccoli, *Letters,* 303.

49 F to H, December 1926, Bruccoli, *Letters,* 148.

50 F to H, March 18, 1927, quoted in Bruccoli, *F&H,* 82.

51 H to F, March 31, 1927, quoted in Bruccoli, *F&H,* 83.

52 H to F, December 21, 1935, Baker, *Letters,* 428.

53 Quoted in Bruccoli, *F&H,* 111.

54 Bruccoli, *F&H,* 108–9.

55 Lynn, 284–85.

56 Quoted in Bruccoli, *F&H,* 286.

57 Ibid., 146.

58 "[In the 1920s] people's interpretation of physical contact became

extraordinarily 'privatized and sexualized,' so that all types of touching, kissing, and holding were seen as sexual foreplay rather than accepted as ordinary means of communication that carried different meanings in different contexts. . . . It is not that homosexuality was acceptable before; but now a wider range of behavior opened a person up to being branded as a homosexual. . . . Increasingly, either genital sex between men or careful physical and emotional distancing 'crowded out more sublimated erotic relations' and replaced more nuanced male friendships." Stephanie Coontz, *The Way We Never Were*, 195.

59 F to H, June 1, 1934, Bruccoli, *Letters*, 264.

60 Bruccoli, *F&H*, 149–51.

61 F to H, June 1929, Bruccoli, *Letters*, 164–67.

62 Ibid., 167.

63 H to F, September 4, 1929, Baker, *Letters*, 305.

64 F to H, September 9, 1929, Bruccoli, *Letters*, 69.

65 H to F, September 13, 1929, Baker, *Letters*, 306–7.

66 Quoted in Bruccoli, *Epic Grandeur*, 362.

67 Quoted in Donaldson, 152.

68 Quoted in Bruccoli, *F&H*, 161.

69 H to Max Perkins, July 27, 1932, Baker, *Letters*, 364–65.

70 Quoted in Bruccoli, *F&H*, 59.

71 F to H, May 10, 1934, Bruccoli, *Letters*, 259.

72 H to F, May 28, 1934, Baker, *Letters*, 407–8.

73 F to H, June 1, 1934, Bruccoli, *Letters*, 262–63.

74 H to Perkins, March 25, 1939, Baker, *Letters*, 483.

75 Quoted in Bruccoli, *F&H*, 184.

76 H to Perkins, March 25, 1939, Baker, *Letters*, 483.

77 Quoted in Donaldson, 193.

78 Quoted in Lynn, 438.

79 F to H, July 16, 1936, Bruccoli, *Letters*, 302.

80 Quoted in Bruccoli, *F&H*, 172.

81 Ibid., 165.

82 Ibid., 205.

83 Ibid., 165.

84 Ibid., 205.

85 Ibid., 203.

86 Quoted in Donaldson, 162.

87 F to Perkins, May 20, 1940, Bruccoli, *Letters,* 445, 446.

88 Quoted in Bruccoli, *F&H,* 218,

Chapter 8

1 Jack Kerouac to Allen Ginsberg, December 26, 1956, Ann Charters, ed., *Jack Kerouac: Selected Letters, 1940–1956* [hereinafter *Letters I*], 595.

2 Quoted in *Letters I,* 120.

3 Neal Cassady to K, December 1947, ibid., 136.

4 Quoted in Ellis Amburn, *Subterranean Kerouac,* 363.

5 Quoted in Tom Clark, *Jack Kerouac,* 61.

6 Quoted in Barry Miles, *Ginsberg: A Biography,* 45.

7 Quoted in *Letters I,* 80.

8 Ibid., 63.

9 Quoted in Clark, 61.

10 K to G, August 23, 1945, *Letters I,* 92.

11 Quoted in Michael Schumacher, *Dharma Lion,* 31–32.

12 Quoted in Miles, 65.

13 K to G, September 6, [1945], *Letters I,* 98.

14 Quoted in Miles, 65.

15 Quoted in Clark, 71.

16 Quoted in William Plummer, *The Holy Goof,* 46.

17 Joyce Johnson, *Minor Characters,* 26.

18 Quoted in Gerald Nicosia, *Memory Babe,* 159.

19 Quoted in Miles, 61.

20 Ibid., 72.

21 Amburn, 95; Miles, 66.

22 Quoted in Amburn, 95.

23 Quoted in Clark, 72–73.

24 Ibid., 87.

25 Quoted in Plummer, 135.

26 Plummer, 54.

27 Quoted in Clark, 177.

28 Amburn, 102.

29 Quoted in Amburn, 107.

30 K to C, May 7, 1948, *Letters I,* 148–49.

31 Ibid., 10.

32 Ibid., 7.

33 Ibid.

34 Jack Kerouac, *On the Road,* 10.

35 *Letters I,* 84.

36 Quoted in Amburn, 114.

37 K to Chase, April 19, 1947, *Letters I,* 107.

38 K to Gabrielle Kerouac, July 24, 1947, *Letters I,* 110.

39 K, *Road,* 17.

40 Ibid., 117.

41 Douglas Brinkley, ed., *Windblown World: The Journals of Jack Kerouac,*
     1947–1954, January 11, 1948, 43.

42 Ibid., April 17, 1948, 67.

43 Ibid., April 17, 1948, 69.

44 Ibid., January 13, 1948, 44.

45   K to G, [April?] 1948, *Letters I,* 147.

46 Brinkley, June 2, 1948, 88.

47 Quoted in Nicosia, 557.

48 Quoted in Miles, 100.

49 Brinkley, September 9, 1948, 129.

50 K to C, December 8, 1948, *Letters I,* 172.

51 Brinkley, November 23, 1948, 173.

52 Quoted in Clark, 81.

53 Brinkley, [January 1949], 285.

54 Quoted in Clark, 82.

55 K to Elbert Lenro, June 28, 1949, *Letters I,* 205.

56 Quoted in Clark, 95.

57 *Letters I,* 310.

58 Brinkley, November 1, 1948, 159.

59 K to C, December 27, 1950, *Letters I,* 242–43.

60 Quoted in *Letters I,* fn 3, 244.

61 K to G, December 26, 1956, *Letters I,* 595.

62 Brinkley, November 7, 1950 (typescript), 231. (My thanks to Professor
     Brinkley for allowing me to read the original manuscript of his edition
     of Kerouac's journals.)

63 K to C, May 22, 1951, *Letters I,* 315–16.

64 Quoted in Amburn, 166.

65 Quoted in Carolyn Cassady, *Off the Road,* 145.

66 Ibid., 144.

67 Ibid., 145.

68 Quoted in *Letters I*, 375.

69 G to K, June 11, 1952, *Letters I*, 172–73.

70 K to Carl, Mr. Wyn, Miss James, August 5, 1952, *Letters I*, 377.

71 K to G, October 8, 1952, *Letters I*, 378–79.

72 Quoted in Clark, 119.

73 K to G, November 8, 1952, *Letters I*, 383–84.

74 Ibid., 384.

75 K to G, June 20, 1949, *Letters I*, 191.

76 Quoted in Clark, 157.

77 Douglas Brinkley, "In the Kerouac Archive," *The Atlantic*, November 1998, 51.

78 Quoted in Gerald Nicosia, *Memory Babe*, 556.

79 Amburn, 275.

80 Ibid., 141–42.

81 Quoted in Nicosia, 556.

82 Ann Charters, ed., *Jack Kerouac: Selected Letters, 1957–1969* [hereinafter *Letters II*], xxvii.

83 Morris Dickstein, *Leopards in the Temple*, 103. See also Ross Posnock, "Letting Go," *Raritan*, Spring 2004, Vol. 23, No. 4, 10.

84 Quoted in *Letters II*, 73.

85 Quoted in Cassady, 290.

86 Quoted in *Letters II*, 196–97.

87 Ibid., fn 82, 196.

88 Carolyn Cassady, Foreword to Clark, xv, xvi.

89 Cassady, 347.

90 K to G, [early May 1954], *Letters I*, 410.

91 K to Gary Snyder, December 1, 1958, *Letters II*, 192.

92 K to Sterling Lord, February 3, 1959, ibid., 207.

93 Amburn, 200.

94 K to John Clellon Holmes, September 22, 1966, *Letters II*, 483.

95 K to Carolyn Cassady, October 21, 1962, quoted in *Letters II*, 395.

96 K to Alan Harrington, August 23, 1949, *Letters I*, 188.

97 Quoted in Plummer, 62.

98 K to Fernanda Pivano, [early 1964], *Letters II*, 429.

99 G to K, August 25, 1955, quoted in *Letters I*, fn 1, 508.

100 Quoted in Clark, 216.

101 Quoted in Cassady, 424.

INDEX

abstract expressionism, 194
Ace Books, 213
Adams, Henry, 98
alcohol, 19
Aldrich, Thomas Bailey, 55
Allart, Hortense, 94, 98
Amburn, Ellis, 215, 220
American Mercury, The, 155, 156, 157, 170
American Publishing Company, 54, 58
American Renaissance, 21
Anderson, Sherwood, 5
  Dark Laughter, 171
  Hemingway and, 163, 171–73
  Winesburg, Ohio, 163
Angoff, Charles, 156
anti-Semitism, 117, 157, 196–97, 220, 221
Arendt, Hannah, 14
Arlen, Michael, 168
  The Green Hat, 168
Arnold, Matthew, 112
  Tristram and Iseult, 112
Arvin, Newton, 32, 34
Atlantic Monthly, 9, 10, 52, 53, 54, 83, 118, 174
  Howells as editor of, 52, 54–69
  search for Western literature, 56–57
  Twain's contributions to, 60–69
Authors League, 148

Baker, Ray Stannard, 120
Baltimore, 134, 136, 145, 155
Baltimore Herald, 134
Baltimore Sun, 134
  Mencken's column in, 148, 150

Balzac, Honoré de, 117, 135
Barney, Natalie, 169
Beach, Sylvia, 163, 165
Beats, 12, 190, 194
  development of aesthetic, 194–96, 206
  effect of fame on, 12–13, 216–23
  life of, 195–208
Bell, Millicent, 85, 95
Bellow, Saul, 220
Bentley, Richard, 28, 34
Berkman, Alexander, 117
Berkshires, 81
  Hawthorne-Melville friendship in, 21–26, 33–43
  Wharton-James friendship in, 90–91, 97, 106–7
Berry, Walter Van Rensselaer, 87, 99, 100, 104
black culture, 5–6
Blake, William, 206
blank-page anxiety, 18
Bloom, Marion, 143, 151
Bohemian, The, 137, 139
Bolshevik revolution, 13
Boni & Liveright, 165–66, 171–74
Bookman, The, 170, 184
Booth, Edwin, 112
bop, 194
Boston, 7, 31, 37n., 53, 55, 112, 119, 120, 156
  Brahmin caste, 25, 53, 57, 63, 112–14
  Twain's Whittier dinner speech in, 63–67

"Boston marriage," 114–15, 116, 118–20,
    132
Boston Post, 43
Boston *Transcript,* 23, 66
Bourget, Paul, 82, 91
Bowdoin College, 23, 24
Boyesen, H. H., 58
Bradstreet, Anne, 124
Brandeis, Louis D., 112
Brando, Marlon, 216–17
Bridge, Horace, 24
Brightman, Carol, 14
Brinkley, Douglas, 208
Brooke, Sir Charles, 96
Brooke, Margaret, Ranee of Sarawak, 96
Brownell, William Crary, 81–82, 83, 85
Bruccoli, Matthew J., 161, 164, 170, 179,
    184
    *Fitzgerald and Hemingway: A Dangerous
       Friendship,* 4
Bryant, William Cullen, 25
Burroughs, William, 193, 194, 196, 197,
    203, 208, 215, 218
    Junkie, 213
Butterick Publications, 135–36, 140, 152
Bynner, Witter, 132
Byron, Lord, 57

Callaghan, Morley, 181
Cannastra, Bill, 211
Carlyle, Thomas, 34
Carr, Lucien, 190–91, 193–94, 196, 197,
    207, 212
Cassady, Carolyn, 199, 202–4, 207, 212,
    213, 218, 219, 220, 223, 224
Cassady, Neal, 190, 198–224
    as Beat muse, 190, 200–201, 209–11,
       212
    boyhood of, 198–99
    death of, 223
    drug bust and prison sentence, 218,
       223
    fame of, 218
    at *Howl* debut, 222
    physical appearance of, 199
    sexuality of, 199–204, 212
Cassady-Kerouac-Ginsberg friendship,
    see Kerouac-Ginsberg-Cassady
    friendship

Cather, Willa, 7, 112–33
    Alexander's Bridge, 130
    "Alexandra," 130
    "The Bohemian Girl," 130
    "Coming, Aphrodite!," 132
    death of, 133
    early stories, 116–17, 120, 125, 127,
       129–30
    identity crisis, 115–18, 123, 125, 128
    lesbianism of, 115–18, 123, 125–27,
       132–33
    Edith Lewis and, 132–33
    A Lost Lady, 123, 132
    as *McClure's* editor, 117, 120–22,
       127–28, 130
    My Ántonia, 132
    Nebraska childhood and subject
       matter, 115, 123, 126, 129, 130,
       131–32
    Not Under Forty, 118
    "On the Gull's Road," 125
    O Pioneers!, 131–32
    "Paul's Case," 120
    physical appearance of, 122
    The Professor's House, 117
    "The Sculptor's Funeral," 120, 127,
       129
    The Song of the Lark, 123
    The Troll Garden, 120
    "The Wagner Matinee," 120, 129–30
Cather-Jewett friendship, 7, 9–10, 17,
    112–33
    correspondence, 122, 124–27, 131,
       132–33
    death of Jewett, 128, 129
    first meeting at Annie Fields's home,
       112–14, 122
    Jewett on Cather's work, 125–27,
       129–32
    Jewett as mother figure in, 124–25
Catholicism, 139, 158
Cedar Tavern, New York, 194
censorship, 142, 144–48, 156
Chaplin, Duncan, 160
Charters, Ann, 210
Chase, Hal, 197, 198, 202
Chicago, 135, 162
Christian Science, 120, 138, 143
Cicero, 3, 9, 11–12

Civil War, 50, 110
Clark, Tom, 210
Clay, Bertha M., 151
Clemens, Clara, 78
Clemens, Olivia (Livy), 58, 59, 61–62, 65, 69, 72, 74, 75–76, 79
 death of, 77
Clemens, Samuel, *see* Twain, Mark
Clemens, Susy, 75–76, 77
Closerie des Lilas, Paris, 166, 168
Cold War, 208, 216, 217
collaboration, 7, 18
Colom, Mary, 186
Columbia University, 190–91, 196–98, 204, 211
Columbus, Ohio, 52, 53
Communism, 13, 157–58, 192, 208, 221, 222
Comstock, Anthony, 142, 144
Concord, Massachusetts, 37n., 44, 45, 53
Conrad, Joseph, 154, 169
Cook, Charles, 89
Cooper, James Fenimore, 21
Cowley, Malcolm, 214, 215, 218
Crane, Stephen, 10, 140, 162
criticism, 7–10
Cudlipp, Thelma, 140
cultural differences, 13–14
cummings, e. e., *The Enormous Room*, 166

Damned Human Race Club, 78
Dana, Richard Henry, 34
 Two Years Before the Mast, 34
Darwinism, 139
Dean, James, 217
DeForest, John W., 58
Delineator, The, 136–37, 138
Dell, Floyd, 145, 146
de Maupassant, Guy, 93
Denver, 198, 199, 201, 202, 203, 209
Depression, 157, 184
Dial, The, 37n., 165
Dickens, Charles, 112, 113
Dickstein, Morris, *Leopards in the Temple*, 217
Dingo American Bar, Paris, 160, 188
Donaldson, Scott, 161
Dos Passos, John, 164, 184
Dostoevsky, Fyodor, 191

Dreiser, Sara White, 152
Dreiser, Theodore, 7, 10, 17, 19, 85, 134–59, 213
 An American Tragedy, 153, 154–56
 The Blue Sphere, 144
 bohemian lifestyle of, 142, 143–49, 158
 censorship of, 145–48, 150–51, 152, 156, 159
 death of, 158
 depressive tendencies, 138, 140, 142, 144, 155
 editorial work, 135–38, 157
 The Financier, 142
 The "Genius," 8, 144–48, 151, 152, 156
 German heritage and sympathies, 138, 142–43, 146, 149, 153, 156–57
 in Greenwich Village, 142–49
 The Hand of the Potter, 147
 Hey, Rub-a-Dub-Dub!, 154
 in Hollywood, 152–54, 157
 A Hoosier Holiday, 142
 Indiana boyhood of, 135, 142, 158
 Jennie Gerhardt, 17, 135, 138, 140–42, 146, 150
 "The Lost Phoebe," 144
 National Academy of Arts and Letters Award of Merit, 158
 physical appearance of, 137
 political views of, 157–58
 realism of, 135, 141, 142, 145, 150
 religious views of, 138–39, 157–58
 sexuality of, 143, 144, 145–48, 151, 152, 158
 Sister Carrie, 10, 135, 138, 150
 The Titan, 142
 wartime exile, 150–51
Dreiser-Mencken friendship, 7, 8, 15–16, 17, 134–59
 author-critic collaboration, 7, 8, 140–42, 148–56, 159
 censorship issues, 145–48, 150–51, 152, 156, 159
 correspondence, 143, 148, 151, 152, 156, 157, 159
 first meeting, 136–37
 German heritage and sympathies, 138, 142–43, 146, 149–50, 153, 155, 156–57

Dreiser-Mencken friendship (*cont'd*)
  Mencken on Dreiser's work, 135,
    140–42, 144–56
  Mencken's disapproval of Dreiser's
    bohemian lifestyle, 143–49, 158
  mutual Anglophobia, 142–43
  political disagreements, 157–58
  religious quarrels, 139, 157–58
  World War I and, 142–43, 150–51, 157
Dumas *fils,* 93
Dunne, Finley Peter, 78
Duyckinck, Evert, 17, 21, 22–23, 25, 28,
    32–33, 37, 43–44, 47
Dwight, Reverend Timothy, *Travels in
    New England and New York,* 29

Eastman, Max, 145, 146
Ebb, Fred, 18
Eddy, Mary Baker, 120, 121–22
Edel, Leon, 94
Edinburgh Review, 21
Edison, Thomas A., 72
Edmundson, Mark, 10
Edwards, Jonathan, 24, 29, 33
Eggleston, Edward, *The Hoosier
    Schoolmaster,* 57
Eliot, George, 70
Eliot, T. S., 167
Elmira, New York, 58
Emerson, Ralph Waldo, 10–11, 53, 112
  Mark Twain and, 63, 64, 65, 66
  Walt Whitman and, 10–11
Emerson Society Quarterly, 32
envy, 11–12
Esquire, 7, 187, 221

Faderman, Lillian, 114
fame, 12–13
faulty communication, 14–17
Field, David Dudley, 22, 25
Fielding, Henry, 172
Fields, Annie, 53, 65, 112–14, 118–20,
    126, 128
  "Boston marriage" with Sarah Orne
    Jewett, 114, 118–20, 128, 132
  The Letters of Sarah Orne Jewett, 131
Fields, James T., 24, 53, 54, 55, 56, 57, 112,
    113, 118–19
  death of, 119

Fitzgerald, F. Scott, 4–5, 160–89
  The Beautiful and Damned, 161
  "Berenice Bobs Her Hair," 176
  boyhood of, 162
  death of, 188
  decline and crackup of, 182–88
  drinking and feverish lifestyle,
    161–62, 164, 167, 169–70, 174,
    177–78, 179, 183, 189
  financial problems, 162, 164, 167, 178,
    184, 187
  The Great Gatsby, 164, 167, 168, 169,
    170, 176, 183
  as Hollywood scriptwriter, 177, 188
  The Last Tycoon, 188
  marriage of, 161–62, 164, 167,
    169–70, 178, 179, 183–85
  Max Perkins and, 166, 173, 174, 180,
    182, 184–85, 187, 188
  physical appearance of, 161, 179
  posthumous revival of, 188–89
  Post stories, 163, 164, 166–67, 176, 178,
    183
  at Princeton, 162–63, 164
  "The Rich Boy," 169, 186
  sexual problems, 179
  Tender Is the Night, 171, 185–86
  This Side of Paradise, 161, 166
Fitzgerald, Scottie, 164
Fitzgerald, Zelda, 160, 161–62, 164, 167,
    169–70, 174, 176, 178, 179
  mental instability of, 169, 183–84, 185
  rivalry with Hemingway, 169–70,
    179–80, 184
  Save Me the Waltz, 184
Fitzgerald-Hemingway friendship, 4–5,
    12, 160–89, 216
  Callaghan boxing match, 181
  censorship issues, 175–76, 182
  competitive nature of, 161, 164, 174,
    181–82, 184–85, 188–89
  effect of fame on, 12, 177, 181, 184,
    186, 187–88
  first meeting, 160–61, 165, 188
  Fitzgerald on Hemingway's work,
    170, 173–74, 175–77, 181–82, 185,
    187
  Fitzgerald's decline and crackup,
    182–88

in France, 160–61, 164–77, 178, 188
Hemingway on Fitzgerald's work, 168,
182–83, 185–87, 189
Hemingway's domination in, 170, 177,
179, 184–88
homosexuality rumors, 179–81
Lyon motor trip, 168–69
Max Perkins and, 165–66, 173–74,
175–76, 184–87
posterity sweepstakes, 188–89
summer of 1928, 179–82
Zelda's role in, 169–79, 176, 179–80,
184, 185
Flaubert, Gustave, 93, 117
Florence, 77
France, 90, 91, 117, 164
Fitzgerald-Hemingway friendship in,
160–61, 164–74, 178, 188
Wharton-James friendship in, 91–93,
95, 97–98, 107
World War I, 110, 142
Fremstad, Olive, 123
Frick, Henry, 117
friendship, pitfalls of, 3–19
Frohman, Daniel, 72
Fullerton, Morton, 95–104

Garber, Lyra, 123
Garber, Silas, 123
Germany, 16
Nazi, 157
World War I, 110, 142–43
Gingrich, Arnold, 187
Ginsberg, Allen, 12–13, 190–224
boyhood of, 192, 193
at Columbia, 190–91, 193, 196, 204,
206
connection with Kerouac, 191–98,
205, 213–14, 220, 221, 222, 224
drug and alcohol use, 195, 197, 213,
222
effect of fame on, 221–23
Howl, 190, 222, 223
as a Jew, 196–97, 221
Kaddish, 195, 204
"Laughing Gas," 195
love affair with Cassady, 198–99,
201–4, 212
physical appearance of, 192

political activism of, 222–23
in psychiatric hospital, 221–22
relationship with his mother, 192,
204
sexuality of, 191, 197–98, 212, 222
Ginsberg, Eugene, 192
Ginsberg, Louis, 192
Ginsberg, Naomi, 192, 204
Ginsberg-Kerouac-Cassady friendship,
see Kerouac-Ginsberg-Cassady
friendship
Giroux, Robert, 209, 212, 214
Glassman, Joyce, 215, 216
Gold, Herbert, 220
Gosse, Edmund, 107
Grant, Ulysses S., 75
Great Britain, 17, 21, 46
American literature dominated by, 21,
29, 30
Wharton-James friendship in, 87–91,
99–100, 107
Oscar Wilde sex scandal, 116
World War I, 110, 142
Great Cities series, 101
Greenwich Village, 142–48, 171
Guthrie, Pat, 160

Hammett, Dashiell, 197
Hannibal, Missouri, 52, 53, 69–70
Harcourt, Brace, 173, 174, 209
Hardwick, Elizabeth, 14
Harlem Renaissance, 5–6
Harper's Monthly, 10, 54, 73, 77
"Editor's Study" column, 73, 74
Harrington, Alan, 209, 220–21
Harte, Bret, 56, 59, 70
The Luck of Roaring Camp and Other
Stories, 56
Hartford, Connecticut, 58, 63, 76
Harvard University, 80, 193
Harvey, George, 78
Haverty, Joan, 211, 212
Hawthorne, Julian, 23, 35–36, 49
Hawthorne, Nathaniel, 16, 20–51, 53,
70, 112, 118, 140
background of, 23, 26
in Berkshires, 21–26, 33–43
The Blithedale Romance, 44–45
consulship in Great Britain, 46–47

Hawthorne, Nathaniel (cont'd)
  death of, 49, 50
  financial insecurity, 28, 35
  The House of the Seven Gables, 24, 28, 35,
    38, 39
  Mosses from an Old Manse, 28–32, 37
  posthumous reputation, 49–50
  Puritanism and, 23, 24
  The Scarlet Letter, 20, 21, 23, 28, 35, 123
  Twice-Told Tales, 24, 37
Hawthorne, Sophia, 23, 24, 33, 35, 36, 37,
    40, 41, 49, 118
Hawthorne, Una, 23, 36, 37
Hawthorne-Melville friendship, 16,
    20–51
  Berkshires period, 21–26, 33–43
  in Concord, 45
  correspondence, 38, 40–41
  first meeting, 21, 24–26
  Hawthorne on Melville's work, 27, 33,
    40–41, 43–44
  last meeting, 49, 50
  in Liverpool, 47–49, 50
  Melville on Hawthorne's work,
    28–32, 33, 37, 38, 39, 45
  Moby-Dick and, 34–37, 38–44, 46
  Mosses review, 28–32, 33
  possible homosexual attraction, 20,
    32, 41–43, 46, 50–51
Hay, John, 59
Hayes, Rutherford B., 56, 63
Headley, J. T., 23
Hearth & Home, 59
Hemingway, Ernest, 4–5, 160–89, 213
  Sherwood Anderson and, 163, 171–73
  boyhood of, 162
  censorship issues, 175–76, 182
  "A Day's Wait," 168
  death of, 189
  effect of fame on, 12, 177, 181, 184,
    186, 187–88
  A Farewell to Arms, 178, 181–82, 184
  father figures killed by, 5, 171–73
  "Fifty Grand," 174, 176
  For Whom the Bell Tolls, 187
  in France, 160–61, 163, 165–77, 178,
    188
  Green Hills of Africa, 186
  homosexuality rumors, 179–81

In Our Time, 165, 166, 170, 171, 173
  Liveright contract, 165–66, 171–74
  macho nature of, 170, 180, 186, 188
  Mencken on, 170
  A Moveable Feast, 160–61, 168, 176, 179
  newspaper work, 162, 163
  Max Perkins and, 165, 173–74,
    175–76, 182, 184–87
  physical appearance of, 162
  "The Snows of Kilimanjaro," 186, 187
  The Sun Also Rises, 160, 169, 170,
    174–77, 181, 182, 216
  Three Stories and Twelve Poems, 165
  To Have and Have Not, 187
  The Torrents of Spring, 171–74
  "Up in Michigan," 171
  in World War I, 162, 163, 164, 170
  as World War II correspondent, 188
Hemingway, John (Bumby), 163, 174,
    178
Hemingway, Patrick, 177, 178
Hemingway-Fitzgerald friendship, see
    Fitzgerald-Hemingway friendship
Henderson, LuAnne, 199, 201, 203, 207,
    208
Hesperian, The, 116
Hirshberg, Dr. Leonard, 136
Hitler, Adolf, 157
Hobson, Fred, 15
Hollywood:
  Dreiser in, 152–54, 157
  Fitzgerald in, 177, 188
Holmes, John Clellon, 205–6, 213, 215,
    220, 221
  "Go!," 209
Holmes, Oliver Wendell, 23, 25, 53, 55,
    59, 63, 64, 65, 113
Homer, Winslow, 112
homosexual attraction, 20, 32, 96, 116,
    170, 180
  Fitzgerald-Hemingway rumors,
    179–81
  Kerouac-Ginsberg-Cassady, 191,
    197–204, 212
  of Melville to Hawthorne, 20, 32,
    41–43, 46, 50–51
  seafaring, 42
  Oscar Wilde scandal, 116
  see also same-sex relations

honesty, 8–10
Howe, Mark De Wolfe, 118, 120
Howells, Elinor, 54, 59, 61, 62, 73, 76
Howells, John, 78
Howells, William Dean, 7, 10, 52–79,
    118, 140
  as *Atlantic Monthly* editor, 52, 54–69
  background of, 53
  A Boy's Town, 70
  Colonel Sellers as Scientist, 70–73
  consulship in Venice, 54
  A Counterfeit Presentment, 71
  death of, 79
  death of daughter Winnie, 76
  Harper's Monthly column, 73, 74
  A Hazard of New Fortunes, 74
  Indian Summer, 70
  Henry James and, 57–58, 98, 107
  multicultural vision of, 57–58
  newspaper career, 52, 53
  old age, 78–79
  physical appearance of, 60
  political views of, 73–74, 77, 79
  theatrical work, 70–73
Howells, Winnie, 76
Howells-Twain friendship, *see* Twain-
    Howells friendship
Hughes, Langston, 5–6
  Zora Neale Hurston and, 5–6
  Mule Bone, 6
Huncke, Herbert, 195, 203, 221, 222
Hurd and Houghton, 60
Hurston, Zora Neale, 5–6
  Langston Hughes and, 5–6
  Mule Bone, 6
Huxley, Thomas, 139

Ibsen, Henrik, 135, 137
Illinois, 162
Indiana, 57, 135
Irving, Washington, 21, 30–31, 37
Italy, 19

James, G.P.R., 23
James, Henry, 7, 10, 57, 70, 73, 80–111,
    119, 123, 130, 131, 167, 175
  The Ambassadors, 57, 82, 99
  The American, 57
  The American Scene, 92
  Daisy Miller, 82
  death of, 111
  Morton Fullerton and, 95–104
  The Golden Bowl, 82, 88, 108
  William Dean Howells and, 57–58,
    98, 107
  ill health, 105–6, 108, 109, 111
  lack of a world reputation, 107
  at Lamb House, 87–88, 89, 97, 110
  last work, 108–10
  late-life awards and honors, 107–8
  later novels, 82–83, 84, 88, 101, 103,
    111
  New York Edition, 102–3, 108
  The Portrait of a Lady, 9, 57, 82, 105
  The Sacred Fount, 82, 83, 84
  sexuality of, 93, 95, 96–97
  "The Velvet Glove," 101–2
  views on wealth, 88, 92, 94, 105, 106,
    107, 109
  The Wings of the Dove, 82, 84, 101
James, William, 106, 107
James-Wharton friendship, *see*
    Wharton-James friendship
jazz, 194
Jazz Age, 163, 167
  end of, 184
Jefferson, Joseph, 112
Jefferson, Ohio, 52
Jewett, Sarah Orne, 7, 17, 58, 112–33
  "Boston marriage" with Annie Fields,
    114, 118–20, 128, 132
  childhood of, 119, 123
  The Country of the Pointed Firs, 123,
    124
  death of, 128, 131
  female role models of, 124
  "Martha's Lady," 125–26
  stroke of, 128
Jewett-Cather friendship, *see* Cather-
    Jewett friendship
Johnson, Joyce, 12, 195–96
Jones, Mary Cadwalader, 82
Joyce, James, 163, 169, 213
Jozan, Edouard, 164

Kammerer, David, 191
Kander, John, 18
Kansas City Star, 162

Kaplan, Carla, *Zora Neale Hurston: A Life in Letters,* 5
Kaplan, Fred, 96, 100
Kaplan, Justin, *Mr. Clemens and Mark Twain,* 63, 66
Karlinsky, Simon, 14
Kazin, Alfred, 209
Kerouac, Gabrielle, 192–93, 197, 203, 209, 213, 215, 220, 221, 224
Kerouac, Gerard, 192, 201
Kerouac, Jack, 12–13, 19, 190–224
  boyhood of, 192, 193, 219
  Cassady as muse of, 190, 200–201, 209–12
  at Columbia, 191, 196–97, 211
  cross-country trips, 202–8, 212–13
  decline of, 219–21, 223–24
  The Dharma Bums, 218
  "Dr. Sax," 213, 218, 219
  drug and alcohol use, 194–95, 197, 200, 215, 219–20, 222, 224
  effect of fame on, 12–13, 215–21
  at *Howl* debut, 222
  in merchant marine, 191
  Moby-Dick influence, 209–10
  On the Road, 12, 190, 201, 202, 203, 209–18
  physical appearance of, 191, 192
  relationship with his mother, 192–93, 197, 203, 209, 213, 215, 217, 220, 221, 224
  sexuality of, 197–98, 199–200, 212–13
  stubbornness about revisions, 212, 214
  The Subterraneans, 219
  The Town and the City, 205, 206, 209, 212
  Visions of Cody, 199
  writing techniques and habits, 210–12
Kerouac, Leo, 192–93, 196, 200, 220
Kerouac, Nin, 192
Kerouac, Stella, 220, 224
Kerouac-Ginsberg-Cassady friendship, 12–13, 190–224
  Beat life, 195–208
  Cassady as muse in, 190, 200–201, 209–11, 212

cross-country trips, 202–8, 212–13
development of Beat aesthetic, 194–96, 206
drug and alcohol use, 194–95, 197, 200, 213, 218, 219
effect of fame on, 12–13, 215–23
first meeting of Kerouac and Ginsberg, 191–92
Ginsberg-Cassady connection, 198–99, 201–4, 212
Ginsberg on Kerouac's work, 212–14, 218–19
Howl debut, 222
Kerouac-Cassady connection, 199–201, 209–11, 215
Kerouac-Ginsberg connection, 191–98, 205, 213–14, 220, 221, 222, 224
Night of the Wolfeans, 197
On the Road and, 209–18
pre-Beat period, 191–94
sexuality of, 191, 197–204, 212–13
Kesey, Ken, 200, 223
Key West, 177, 178, 182
Kipling, Rudyard, 115, 119
Knopf, Alfred A., 157
Kubitz, Estelle, 151

Lardner, Ring, 164
Leary, Dr. Timothy, 222
Lenro, Elbert, 210
lesbianism, 116, 169
  of Willa Cather, 115–18, 123, 125–27, 132–33
  in Paris, 169
  see also same-sex relations
Lewis, Edith, 121, 132–33
Lewis, R.W.B., 85, 101
Lewis, Sinclair, 10, 12, 19
Leyda, Jay, *Melville Log,* 44
Library of American Books, 21, 22
Lincoln, Abraham, 54
Literary World, 21, 22, 32, 33, 43–44
Liveright, Horace, 152, 165–66, 171–73, 174
Liverpool, 46, 47, 49
Locke, John, 99
London, 56, 82, 86, 96, 99, 100

London, Jack, 162
London *Athenaeum*, 43
loneliness, 18, 19
Longfellow, Henry Wadsworth, 24, 32,
    63, 113
    Mark Twain and, 63, 64, 65, 66
Lord, Sterling, 214, 216, 220
Lorimer, George Horace, 151, 166–67
Lowell, James Russell, 53, 54, 63, 113
Lynn, Kenneth S., 54, 63, 170, 179
Lyon, 168

Macmillan, 101
Maeterlinck, Maurice, 107
Mailer, Norman, 7
Maine, 119, 122, 123, 124, 130, 131, 132
Malamud, Bernard, 220
Mann, Horace, 40
Martin, Robert K., 32
Martin, Violet, 115
Marxism, 13
Masses, The, 145
Mathews, Cornelius, 22–23, 25, 28
Maugham, Somerset, 18
McAlmon, Robert, 165, 180
McCarthy, Mary, 14
McCarthyism, 216, 221
McClung, Isabelle, 117–18, 123, 133
McClure, Phillips, 120, 121
McClure, S. S., 120–21, 128
McClure's Magazine, 117, 120–22
    Cather as editor of, 117, 120–22,
        127–28, 130
Melvill, Robert, 22, 23
Melville, Elizabeth (Lizzie), 22
Melville, Herman, 16–17, 20–51, 140
    background of, 23, 26
    in Berkshires, 21–26, 33–43
    career difficulties and decline, 16–17,
        27–28, 46–51
    Clarel, 50, 51
    The Confidence-Man, 39, 50
    fall into obscurity, 16–17, 47–51
    financial insecurity, 27–28, 35, 38,
        46–47, 50
    influence on Kerouac, 209–10
    irreverence and passion of, 22, 42,
        43–44, 47, 50
    Mardi, 28, 33

Moby-Dick, 16, 17, 20, 21, 34–37,
    38–44, 46, 47, 209–10
    "Monody," 49, 50–51
    Mosses review, 28–32, 33
    Omoo, 28
    Pierre, or The Ambiguities, 44, 45, 46–47,
        210
    possible homosexuality, 20, 32, 41–43,
        46, 50–51
    religious views of, 27, 29, 39, 47
    short stories and poems, 47, 49,
        50–51
    Typee, 22, 27
Melville, Malcolm, 22
Melville, Maria Gansevoort, 22
Melville-Hawthorne friendship, *see*
    Hawthorne-Melville friendship
Mencken, H. L., 7, 15–16, 134–59, 170
    as *American Mercury* editor, 155, 156,
        157
    Book of Prefaces, 148–49
    death of his mother, 155
    German heritage and sympathies, 138,
        142–43, 149–50, 153, 156–57
    on Hemingway, 170
    newspaper career, 134, 148, 150
    The Philosophy of Friedrich Nietzsche, 138
    physical appearance of, 136–37
    political views of, 157–58
    religious views of, 138–39, 143
    sexuality of, 143, 151
    as *Smart Set* editor, 140–45, 156
Mencken-Dreiser friendship, *see*
    Dreiser-Mencken friendship
mentor-protégé relationship, 9, 10–11
Merry Pranksters, 223
Milder, Robert, 46
Miles, Barry, 214
Miller, Edwin, 32
Millstein, Gilbert, 215, 216, 218
Mississippi River, 61
Missouri, 52, 53
Mizener, Arthur, 189
Monk, Thelonious, 194
Morewood, Robert and Sarah, 23, 27, 44
Mosley, Walter, 3–4, 8, 11
Munson, Gorham, 184
Murphy, Gerald, 174, 185
Murphy, Sara, 174, 185

Nabokov, Vladimir, 13–14
  Bend Sinister, 15
  Lolita, 13
  Edmund Wilson and, 13–14, 15
Nantucket, 44, 45
Nathan, George Jean, 143, 144, 145, 149, 156
Nation, The, 54
National Academy of Arts and Letters, 158
National Intelligencer, 23
Nazism, 157
Nebraska, 115, 116, 117, 121, 122, 123, 124, 130, 131–32
Newport, Rhode Island, 56, 82
Newsweek, 216
New York, 54, 73, 77, 78, 120–21, 135, 136, 142, 156
  Beats in, 194–96
  Dreiser's bohemian life in, 142, 143–49
  Greenwich Village, 142–48, 171
  society, 80, 82, 85
New Yorker, The, 13, 217
New York Herald Tribune, The, 181
New York Review of Books, The, 13
New York Society for the Suppression of Vice, 144
New York Times, The, 62, 215, 216
New York World, 154
Nietzsche, Friedrich, 135, 137, 138, 198
nineteenth-century friendships, 16–17
  American Renaissance and, 21
  Hawthorne-Melville, 20–51
Norris, Frank, 10, 140
North American Review, 37n., 54, 63
Norton, Charles Eliot, 63, 81, 92, 99
Norton, Sara, 99

Oak Park, Illinois, 162
Ober, Harold, 170
O'Brien, Sharon, 115, 126
O'Hara, John, 19, 164, 176
Ohio, 52, 53, 56
O'Neill, Eugene, 156
Orlovsky, Peter, 222

Paine, Albert Bigelow, 79
Paris, 5, 12, 13, 96, 142

Fitzgerald-Hemingway friendship in, 160–61, 164–77, 178, 188
  Wharton-James friendship in, 91–93, 97–98, 107
Parisienne, La, 144
Parker, Charlie, 194
Parker, Edie, 191, 194, 197, 198
Parker, Hershel, 40, 46, 47
Parton, James, 54
Perkins, Max, 165, 180, 206
  Fitzgerald-Hemingway friendship and, 165–66, 173–76, 182–88
Person, Leland S., 32
Pfeiffer, Pauline, 174, 177, 178, 179
Phillips, John, 121
Pierce, Franklin, 24, 46, 47
pitfalls of friendship, 3–19
Pittsburgh, 117
Pittsfield, Massachusetts, 22
Pivano, Fernanda, 221
Plummer, William, 200, 218
Poe, Edgar Allan, 37n.
Pollock, Jackson, 194
Pound, Louise, 116, 125
Pound, Roscoe, 116
Powers, Lyman H., 103, 110
Prescott, Orville, 215
Prince, Nan, The Country Doctor, 119
Princeton University, 162, 163, 164, 165
Proust, Marcel, 91
Puritanism, 16, 23, 24
Pynchon, Thomas, 217

Rascoe, Burton, 151
Raymond, John T., 70–71
realism, 10, 162
  of Dreiser, 135, 141, 142, 145, 150
Rebel Without a Cause (movie), 217
Red Cloud, Nebraska, 115, 122, 128
Richards, Grant, 17
Richardson, Hadley, 162, 163, 172, 174, 177, 178
Richardson, Helen, 152, 154, 155, 157, 158, 159
Richardson, Samuel, Pamela, 172
Riggio, Thomas, 143
Rilke, Rainer Maria, 3
Rimbaud, Arthur, 193, 194, 207
rivalry, 4–6

Robinson, Phyllis C., 116
Rogers, Henry H., 75
Roth, Philip, 220
Russell, Vickie, 194

St. Louis, 135
Salem, Massachusetts, 23, 26
Salem *Advertiser,* 27
Salinger, J. D., 217
same-sex relations, 20, 32, 42, 96, 169,
  170, 180
  "Boston marriages," 114–15, 116,
    118–20, 132
  Kerouac-Ginsberg-Cassady, 191,
    197–204, 212
  Oscar Wilde scandal, 116
  see also homosexual attraction;
    lesbianism
Sampas, Sammy, 198, 220, 224
Sand, George, 92–93, 94, 98
San Francisco, 204
  Howl debut in, 222
San Francisco Chronicle, 218
Sargent, John Singer, 108, 112
Saturday Evening Post, The, 144, 150, 163,
  164, 166–67, 176, 183
Schumacher, Michael, 193
Scipio, 3, 11
screenwriting, 18, 177
Scribner, Charles, 103, 108, 166, 189
Scribner's (Charles) Sons, 81, 102–3,
  166–67, 171, 174, 175, 177, 184, 206
Scribner's Magazine, 81, 83, 174, 182
seafaring, 26, 37
  homosexuality, 42
Sedgwick, Catharine, 23
Sedgwick, Ellery, 57
Seldes, Gilbert, 167, 176, 183
Sergeant, Elizabeth, 129, 130, 131, 133
sex, 5–6, 10, 19, 204
  friendship killed by, 4, 204
  in Victorian America, 22, 114, 180
  see also homosexual attraction;
    lesbianism; same-sex relations
Shakespeare, William, 30, 34
Shakespeare & Co. bookshop, Paris, 165
Shaw, George Bernard, 135
Shaw, Lemuel, 47
Sherman, Stuart P., 155

slavery, 60
Smart Set, The, 140–45, 156
Smith, Henry Nash, 65, 68
Smith, Reverend Sydney, 20–21
Smith, T. R., 165, 166
Snyder, Gary, 218, 219
sociability, 17–18
solitude, 17, 18
Solomon, Carl, 221
Somerville, Edith, 115
South Berwick, Maine, 119, 122, 124, 130
Spencer, Herbert, 139
Stalin, Joseph, 157
Steffens, Lincoln, 120
Stein, Gertrude, 163, 165, 169, 171
Stockbridge, Massachusetts, 21, 22, 23,
  25
stock market crash (1929), 184
Stowe, Harriet Beecher, 57, 124
  The Pearl of Orr's Island, 124, 126–27
Sturgis, Howard, 89, 100, 105, 107
subscription publishing houses, 54–55
Sumner, John, 144, 145, 148, 152
Sutherland, Ronald, 96
Sweden, 107

Tarbell, Ida, 120–21
Teagarden, Jack, 194
Terre Haute, Indiana, 135
Thackeray, William Makepeace, 112
  Henry Esmond, 112
Thoreau, Henry David, 53
  Walden, 21
Ticknor & Fields, 53, 55, 118
Times Book Review, 216
Times of London, 95, 96
Toklas, Alice B., 169
Tolstoy, Leo, 73, 117
Toronto Star, 163
Transcendentalism, 44
Trilling, Lionel, 196–97
Truman, Harry, 208
Turgenev, Ivan, 117
Twain, Mark, 7, 52–79, 140
  Adventures of Huckleberry Finn, 9, 53, 60,
    69–70, 123, 141, 163
  The Adventures of Tom Sawyer, 67–69
  Atlantic contributions, 60–69
  Colonel Sellers as Scientist, 70–73

Twain, Mark (cont'd)
  A Connecticut Yankee in King Arthur's
    Court, 69, 73, 74
  death of, 79
  death of daughter Susy, 75–77
  in Europe, 75–77
  The Gilded Age, 70–71
  guilt complex of, 65–67
  Hannibal boyhood of, 52, 53, 69–70
  Bert Harte and, 56
  hatred of New England, 63
  humor of, 59, 61, 62, 64–67
  The Innocents Abroad, 54–55, 58–59, 63,
    67
  lavish lifestyle and financial troubles,
    58, 60, 70, 75
  Life on the Mississippi, 61–62, 69
  "A Literary Nightmare," 67
  The Mysterious Stranger, 77–78
  newspaper work, 52, 58
  "Old Times on the Mississippi," 61,
    68, 69
  Paige typesetter venture, 74, 75
  physical appearance of, 55, 60
  political views of, 74, 77, 79
  profanity and obscenity issues, 61–63,
    67–69, 74, 78
  religious views of, 74, 77–78
  Roughing It, 58
  theatrical work, 70–73
  "To the Person Sitting in Darkness,"
    77
  Whittier dinner speech debacle,
    63–67
Twain-Howells friendship, 7, 8–9,
    52–79
  of 1880s-90s, 73–77
  first meeting, 55–56
  Howells as editor of Twain's work,
    68–70
  Howells on Twain's work, 54–55,
    58–59, 63, 68–70, 74
  last meeting, 79
  literary collaborations, 70–73
  old age, 78–79
  profanity and obscenity issues, 61–63,
    67–69, 74, 78
  Twain on Howell's work, 70, 71
  Twain's Atlantic contributions, 60–69

  Whittier dinner speech debacle,
    63–67
Twysden, Lady Duff, 160

Updike, John, 217

Van Doren, Mark, 196, 205, 209
Van Vechten, Carl, 5
Venice, 54, 82
Victorian America, sex in, 22, 114, 180
Vidal, Gore, 216
Vienna, 77
Vietnam War, 223
Viking, 214, 215, 218, 219
Vollmer, Joan, 191, 194, 197, 203
von Kurowsky, Agnes, 162

Wallace, Alfred Russell, Man's Place in the
    Universe, 78
Watch and Ward Society, 156
Wells, H. G., 110
Wescott, Glenway, 170
Western literature, 56–57, 66
Wharton, Edith, 7, 80–111, 167
  A Backward Glance, 88, 90, 102
  Berkshires home of, 90–91, 97, 99,
    106–7
  The Custom of the Country, 97
  Ethan Frome, 103, 105
  "The Eyes," 103
  The Fruit of the Tree, 102–3
  Morris Fullerton and, 95, 97–104
  The Greater Inclination, 81
  growing fame of, 86–87
  The House of Mirth, 85–86, 91
  identity as a female writer, 83–86, 91,
    94
  "The Letters," 103
  marital troubles of, 80, 81, 85–87, 93,
    95, 97, 99, 100, 104–5, 107, 109
  A Motor-Flight Through France, 89
  The Reef, 103
  sexuality of, 93, 94, 95, 98–100,
    103–4
  Summer, 103
  The Valley of Decision, 84–85
  wealth of, 80–81, 92, 94, 104–5, 109
Wharton, Teddy, 80, 81, 85–87, 89, 92,
    93, 95, 97, 99, 100, 104–5, 107, 109

Wharton-James friendship, 7, 9, 80–111
  correspondence, 84, 105, 106, 109,
    110
  fascination with George Sand, 92–93
  first meeting, 86–87, 89
  in France, 91–93, 95, 97–98, 107
  Morton Fullerton and, 95–104
  in Great Britain, 87–91, 99–100, 107
  James on Wharton's work, 84, 85, 92,
    102
  mentor-protégé period, 82–86
  motor trips, 89–95, 98, 110
  at the Mount, 90–91, 97, 106–7
  sexual roles, 93–104
  Wharton on James's work, 82–83, 84,
    101, 103
  World War I and, 110
White, Ed, 198
Whitman, Walt, 10–11, 57, 110, 207
  Ralph Waldo Emerson and, 10–11
  Leaves of Grass, 11, 21, 90

Whittier, James Greenleaf, 63, 113, 119
Wilde, Oscar, 96, 97, 116
Wilder, George, 136, 137, 140
Wild One, The (movie), 216
Wiley & Putnam, 21
Wilson, Edmund (Bunny), 13–14, 165,
    169, 186
  Vladimir Nabokov and, 13–14, 15
Wilson, James C., 26
Wineapple, Brenda, 42, 46
Wolfe, Thomas, 206, 209, 211
  Look Homeward, Angel, 206
Wolff, Geoffrey, 19
Worcester *Gazette,* 66
World War I, 16, 110, 142–43, 150, 157,
    162, 163
World War II, 188, 192
Wright, Willard Huntington, 149–50

Yankee Doodle, 21, 22
Young America movement, 22, 29

ABOUT THE AUTHOR

RICHARD LINGEMAN is currently a senior editor at *The Nation*. He has written for numerous publications, including *The New York Times Magazine,* and has been an editor and reviewer for *The New York Times Book Review.* He is the author of *Small Town America* (an American Book Award nominee), a two-volume biography of Theodore Dreiser (*Chicago Sun-Times* Book of the Year), and a biography of Sinclair Lewis. He lives in Manhattan.

ABOUT THE TYPE

This book was set in Requiem, a typeface designed by the Hoefler Type Foundry. It is a modern typeface inspired by inscriptional capitals in Ludovico Vincentino degli Arrighi's 1523 writing manual, *Il modo de temperare le penne*. An original lowercase, a set of figures, and an italic in the "chancery" style that Arrighi helped popularize were created to make this adaptation of a classical design into a complete font family.